IMAGES
of America

LONG HILL TOWNSHIP

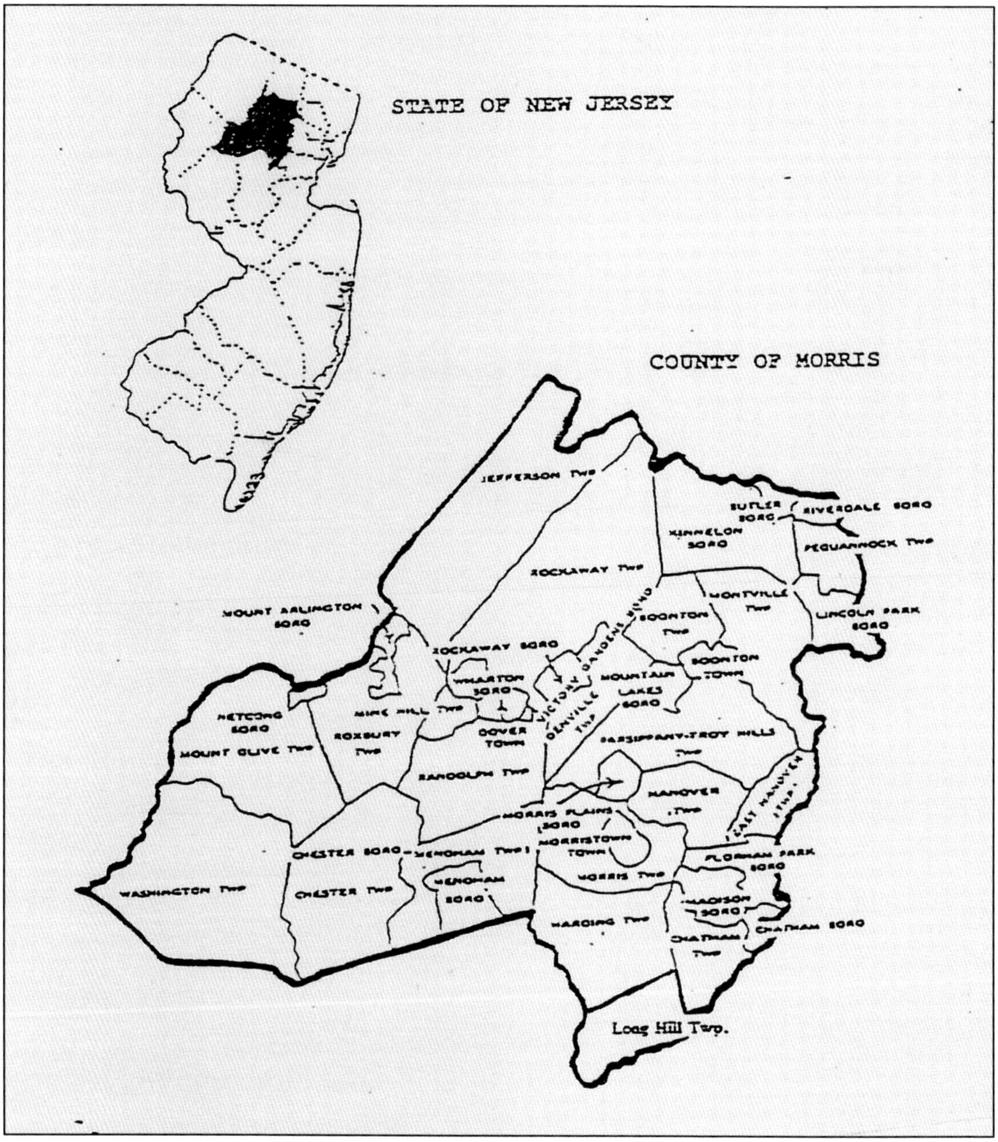

Morris County and Long Hill Township. The blackened area within the map of New Jersey illustrates the site and placement of Morris County in comparison to the state as a whole. The map of Morris County, drawn to a larger scale, displays the location of Long Hill Township. (Lynne Combs.)

COVER ILLUSTRATION: Charles Castle and family. From left to right are as follows: (seated) wife Annie, daughter Edwina, and Charles Sr.; (standing) George Wesley, Charles Hamilton, and John Charles.

IMAGES
of America

Long Hill Township

Mary Lou Weller

ARCADIA
PUBLISHING

ISBN 978-0-7385-9048-6

Published by Arcadia Publishing
Charleston, South Carolina

Printed in the United States of America

For all general information contact Arcadia Publishing at:
Telephone 843-853-2070
Fax 843-853-0044
E-mail sales@arcadiapublishing.com
For customer service and orders:
Toll-Free 1-888-313-2665

Visit us on the Internet at www.arcadiapublishing.com

This book is dedicated to my family:
my husband, Bill, and our children, Sally, Eileen, and Douglas,
who believed in me, and who shared in my happiness
with each new picture found.

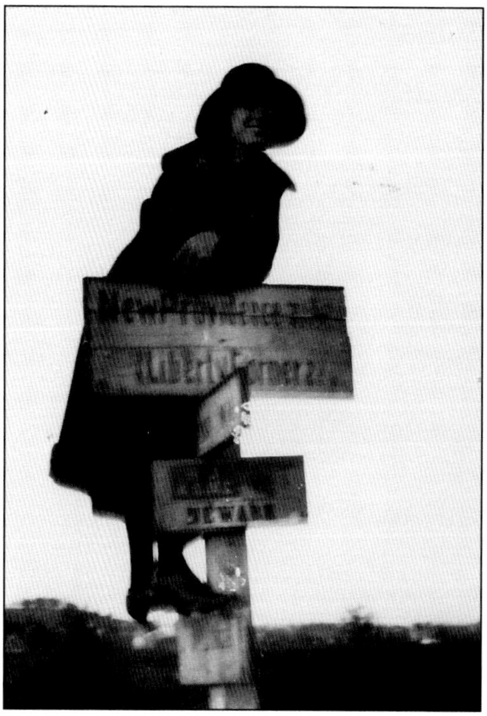

Mary Kocisko, *c.* 1919, atop a primitively made wooden sign directing newcomers to the area, whether visiting New Providence, Liberty Corner, the Acme Harrow Factory, or Newark. (Winifred Shimol.)

Contents

Acknowledgments

An antique suitcase filled with family pictures . . . that's how it started for me. Nothing is more gratifying than discovering the forgotten faces of loved ones and friends through vintage snapshots. It's as if they had been patiently waiting to be found again—wanting to be shared with the community at large. That's when I realized what was once a hobby had become a responsibility—a responsibility to formally organize, by researching and interviewing, along with the guidance of others, my suitcase of memories into one eternal photograph album. This endeavor would not have been possible if not for the unlimited contributions from the residents of Long Hill Township. I can't help but think that if everyone hadn't so graciously shared their suitcases and photograph albums with me, this project would not have been the rewarding experience it was. I would like to honor all those who took part:

The Long Hill Township Historical Society, Marion Armstrong, Betty Stapperfenne, Edward Meeker, Inge Lincoln, Emma & Archibald Stiles, Eleanor & Edward Kielblock, Rosemarie Cafaro, Irving H. Zander, Paul Becker, Pam Thievon, Lynne Spurrier, Dale Monetti, Carol Metzler, Mary Gehling, the Long Hill Woman's Club, Adele Fellows, Jean Falzarano, Stella & Robert Dorsi, the Karg Fuel Oil Company, Inc., Frank Cerulli, Carolyn & Ralph Malfatone, Winifred Shimol, Ann Manailovich, Mary Thoms, Barbara Corcoran, Patricia Cunningham, Eleanor Dolan, Ann Barta, Vincent Pepe, Jennie & Louis Delli Paoli, JoAnn Wall, Paula Ross, Barbara & Robert Hedden, Robert & Josphine Richter, Sister Genevieve Hartman, Dorothy Vincent, the Stirling Volunteer Fire Company #1, Leo Maren, Lilas & Charles Schmidt, Italo Quinto, Ruth Griffin, Joseph Jacenty, Eleanor Groves, Ann MacDougall, Hilda Kling, Mrs. J.B. Cornish, Charles Dropp, Cindi & Scott Heller, Joan Ogden, Craig Engesser, John C. Castle, Mildred Ledder, Lois Stortz, Harriet Holland, Evelyn Headley, Ruth McMane, the All Saints Episcopal Church, Mr. & Mrs. Donald Kuhn, the Millington Fire Company #1, Irma Mikulyak, Thomas Mecavon, Lynne Combs, William D. Oehley, Andy Burns, Betty Skrobacz, June Kennedy, Alma Eriksen, Mary Schmidt, Frank Reilly, Albert Chiappi, Carolyn Gegauff, Elizabeth Parker, Lorraine Hellyer, Adele Burke, Karin Stenhel, Eleanor Murphy, Virgil Hilbert, Paul Kielblock, Scott Hale, Salvadore Lo Presti, Arline Most, the Long Hill Township Public Library, Christina P. Dickson, Alan Siegel, Virginia Troeger, Carolyn Swenson, Jamie Carter, and ARCADIA Publishing.

Introduction

To this very day, residents of our enclave of towns that comprises what is known as Long Hill Township continue to have the great fortune of unearthing Indian arrowheads in their backyards—arrowheads that date as far back as 7,000 years in civilized history. The township's original inhabitants were the tribes of the Lenape Indians, who established themselves among the forested hills and winding valleys of the area, and who stayed there until 1759, when they began a western migration to escape from the influx of settlers. The vast expanse of land was then surveyed under the Lord Stirling Grant and the Elizabethtown Grant, which was comprised of 500,000 acres. In 1769, John Littell, a cartographer and resident of the region in the 1800s, designed a map of what he referred to as Long Hill and Passaic Valley, Passaic meaning "valley" in Indian. This map also included the towns of Logansville, Pleasantville, New Vernon, Green Village, White Bridge, Meyersville, Stirling Valley, and Millington. At that time the Great Swamp was known as Lake Passaic, with much of the surrounding land being primarily used for agricultural purposes, and sparsely populated. Our particular township was comprised of the high land of Long Hill, Millington, the valleys of Stirling and Gillette, the vast open farmland of Meyersville, and the Passaic River, along with a smattering of streams, which were primarily used for fishing.

In the late eighteenth century, a stagecoach route slowly began to develop from east to west across the land. By an act of the state legislature in 1866, what is now Long Hill Township was established as Passaic Township. Modest development continued in the area until after 1871, when the West Line Railroad burst on through from Summit to Bernardsville and began to change the face of the community as a whole. Each village began to take on an individual purpose: farming and agricultural continued to flourish in Meyersville, Stirling developed its industrial side, Gillette remained a small residential village, and Millington became known for its estates, mills, and hilly terrain. Yet with all this individuality came a cohesiveness, once the villages were linked together within one township.

In the 1920s New Vernon separated from Passaic Township to become Harding Township. At the same time, L. Preston Gates was in the process of developing a large subdivision within Passaic Township, an addition known as Homestead Park, which was to be a new summer housing community for vacationers, complete with a private lake. All this development brings us to the present day, with our cluster of the five towns of Stirling, Gillette, Homestead Park, Meyersville, and Millington now making up one township. In 1992 a majority of voters elected to change the name of Passaic Township to Long Hill Township.

Our community will continue to face many changes as we progress into the twenty-first century. Having lived here all of my life, I have witnessed firsthand our transformation from being small and rural into being the congruous metropolitan community we are today.

Mary Lou Weller

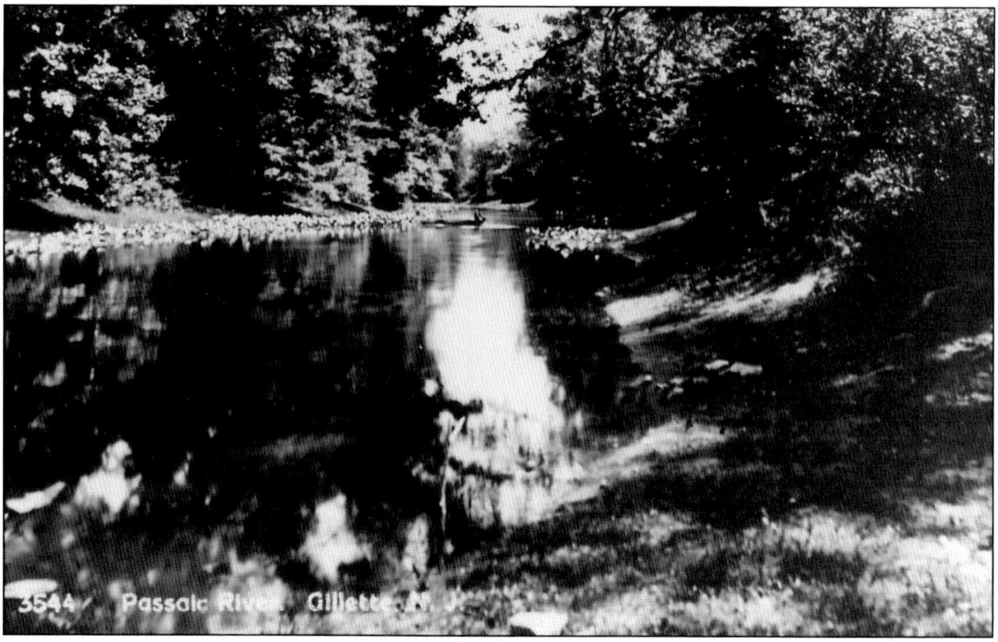

A scene of the Passaic River in Gillette, *c.* 1940. It is the second longest river in New Jersey and a remnant of ancient Lake Passaic. (Ruth Castle Griffen.)

References

History of Morris County. New Jersey-New York: W.W. Munsell & Co., 1882.

Littell, John L. *Family Records or Genealogies of the First Settlers of Passaic Valley*. N.p.: Littell, 1852.

Morris County Heritage Commission. Morris County Historic Sites Survey, Long Hill Township.

Passaic Township Historical Society. *Passaic Township-A Short History*. N.p., 1964.

Whitehead, John. *The Passaic Valley*. New Jersey: L.L.D., 1901.

One

Meyersville

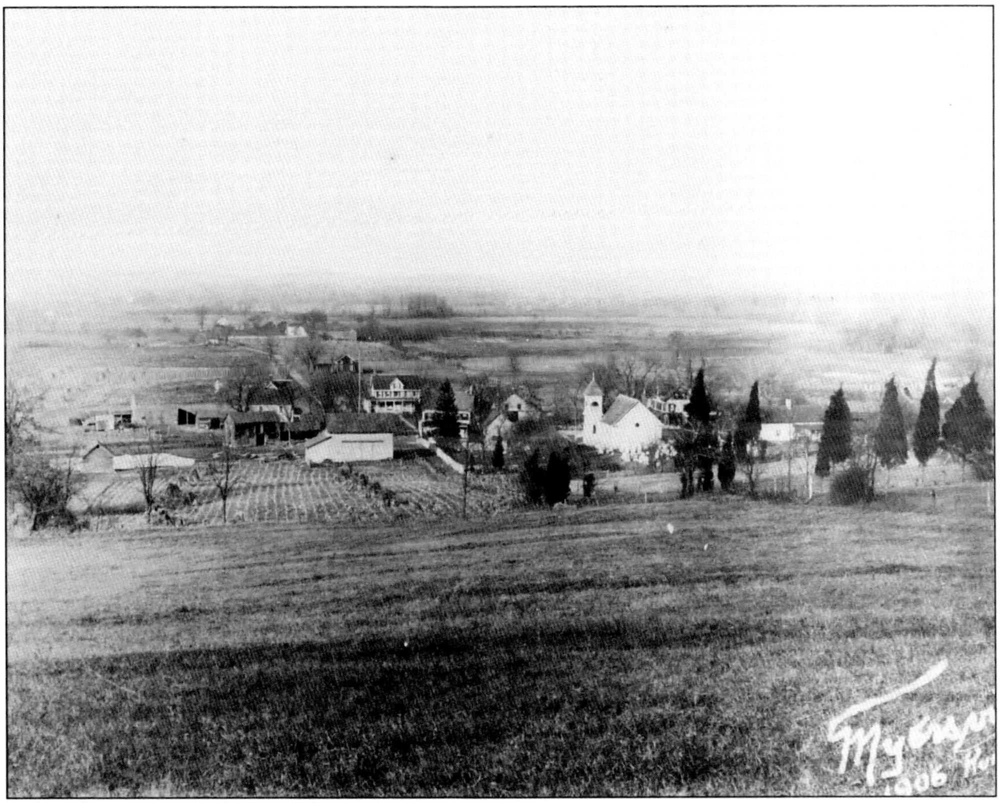

Meyersville, c. 1906. This settlement dates back to the early 1700s, and is the oldest settlement in Long Hill Township. Kasper W. Meyer, a well-to-do man of his day who owned much of the fertile woodland in Meyersville, donated land for a German church and cemetery. Note that Meyersville in its earliest times was spelled Myersville. (Marion McCollum Armstrong.)

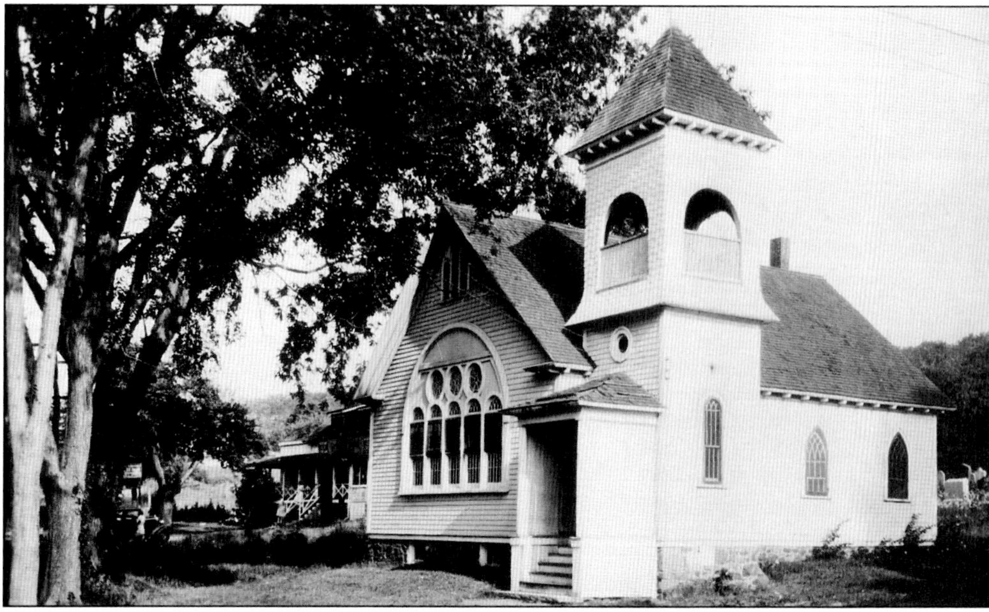

The Meyersville Presbyterian Church, *c.* 1930. This church started with a dedicated group of residents meeting in homes. In 1847 a cornerstone was laid and the land dedicated for what was to become the German Evangelical church. The small original church was moved to New Vernon Road for use as a private residence, and a new church was built in 1895. By 1949 it was enlarged to meet the needs of a growing congregation. The house pictured on the left of the church is two hundred years old, and was used as a post office and store at one time. (Betty & Robert Stapperfenne.)

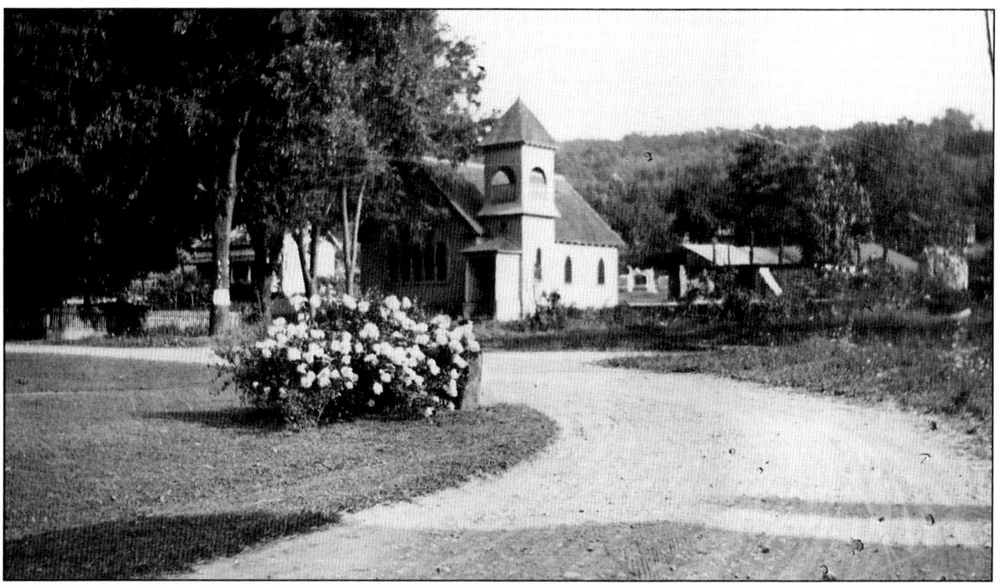

The Meyersville Circle as it appeared in the 1930s, coming south from the Great Swamp. The main industry in this area was farming, and families would travel to Plainfield and Newark to sell their season's harvest of fruits and vegetables. John Henry Ortman maintained a blacksmith shop at 618 Meyersville Road, in the center of town, for forty-three years. The building still stands today. (Marion McCollum Armstrong.)

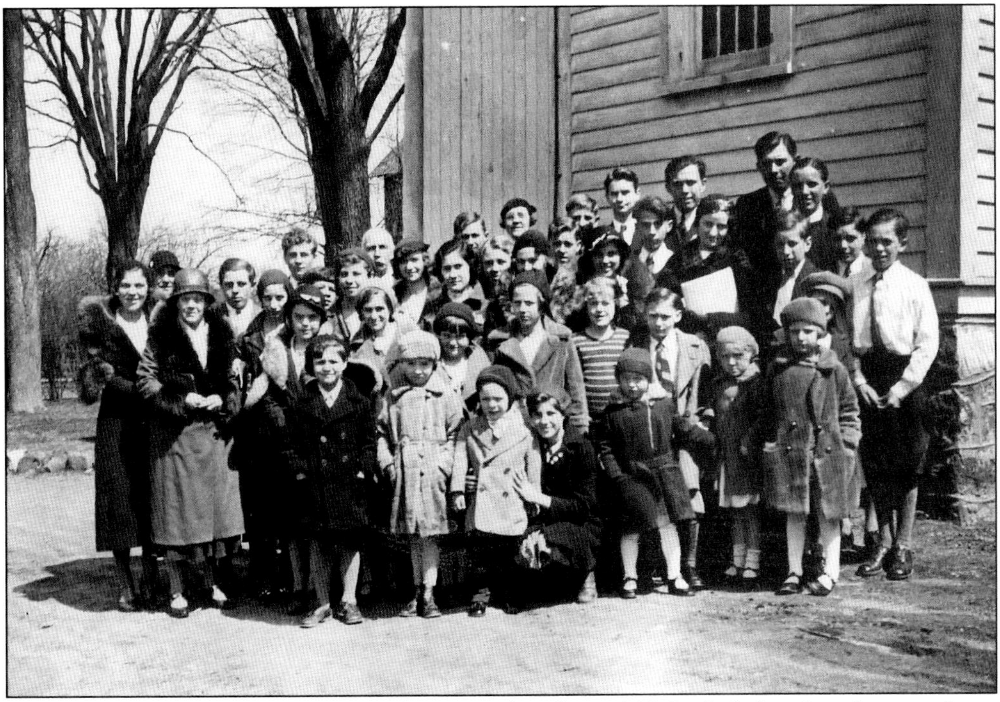

Sunday school at the Meyersville Presbyterian Church, *c.* 1933. Included in this photograph are Mary Schmidt, Mr. and Mrs. Baumann, Calvin Franklin, Rose Whally, August Schmidt, Mrs. Scharrer, Joseph Jacenty, Rose Paukow, Eleanor Jacenty, Elsie Meile, Ann Havriluk, Helen Jimison, Ruth Kielblock, Peggy Jimison, and Willie Ziegelmeier. (Edward Meeker.)

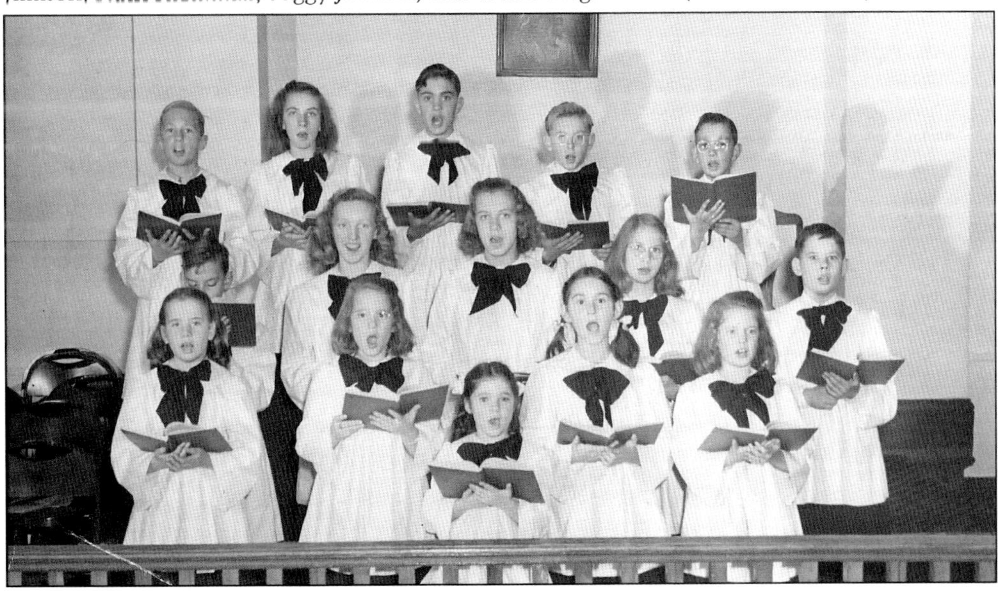

The Meyersville Presbyterian Church Junior Choir, *c.* 1947. From left to right are as follows: (front row) Hannah Dictrich, Barbara Ortman, Margaret Weller, Inge Rist, and Jean Ortman; (middle row) George Hoser, Addie Radder, Helga Gruendling, Kay Leppo, and Peter Deitrich; (back row) Dick Howell, Ruthe Gruendling, James Frey, Leon Radder, and Richard Frey. (Inge Rist Lincoln.)

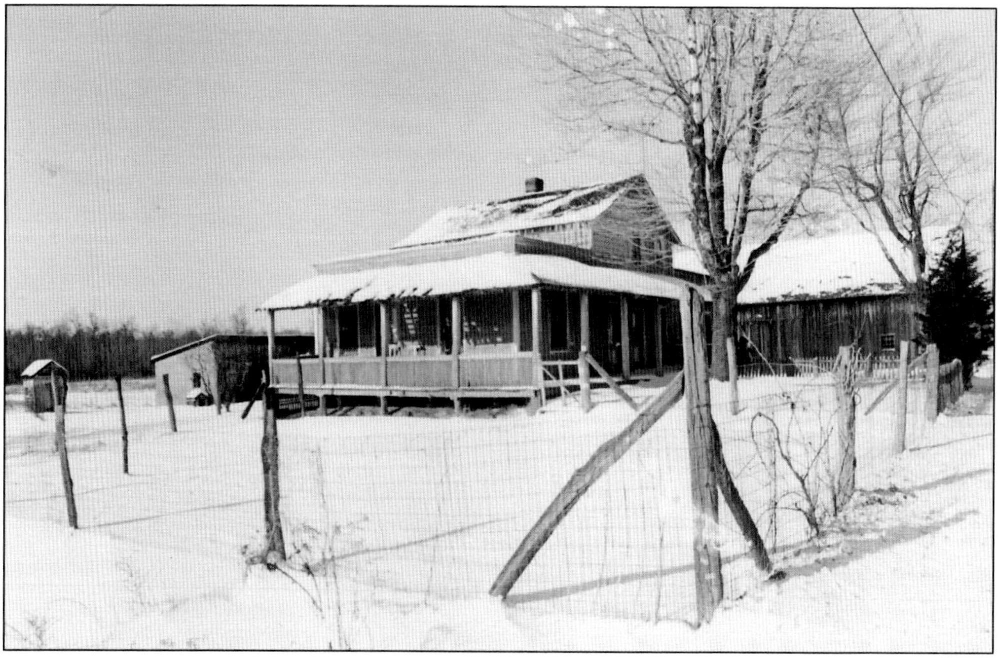

A *c.* 1960 photograph of a now-unoccupied farmhouse. The property that this farmhouse rests on was first developed by Lewis Meeker in 1868. Inge Rist Lincoln's great-uncle, Martin Zullhann, lived there for years. Later, Andrew Havriluk purchased it and had a dairy farm on the land, from which he sold milk and cream. The house is now unoccupied. (Emma & Archibald Stiles.)

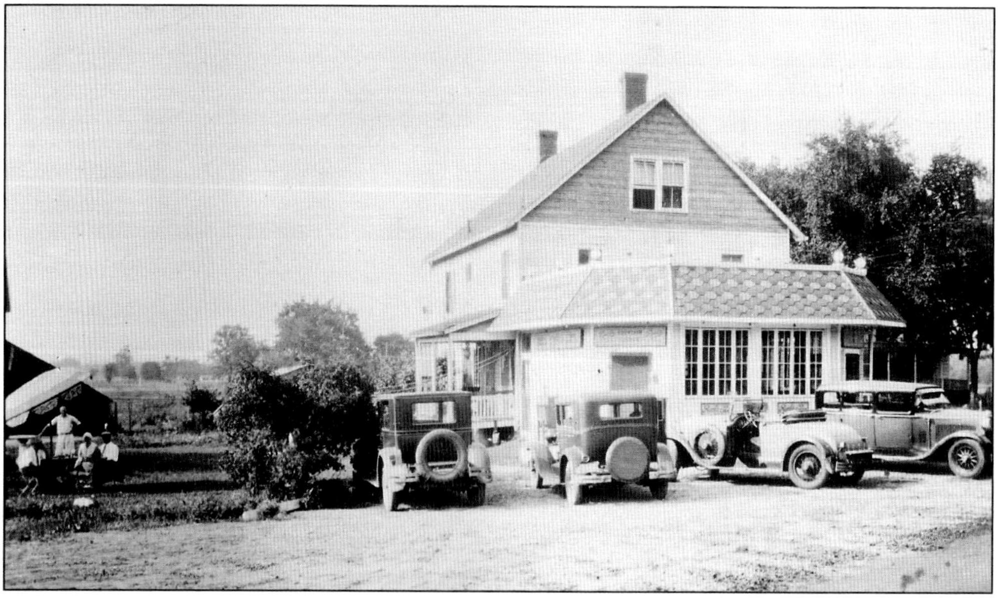

The Meyersville Inn, *c.* 1930. Established in 1900, it was used for various interests. John Henry Ortman had a general store here early on, as well as quite the prestigious gas station for visiting automobiles passing through. It became Donner & Clark's Bar and Restaurant in the 1930s. The building has long been a social landmark in Meyersville, and continues as a restaurant today. (Emma & Archibald Stiles.)

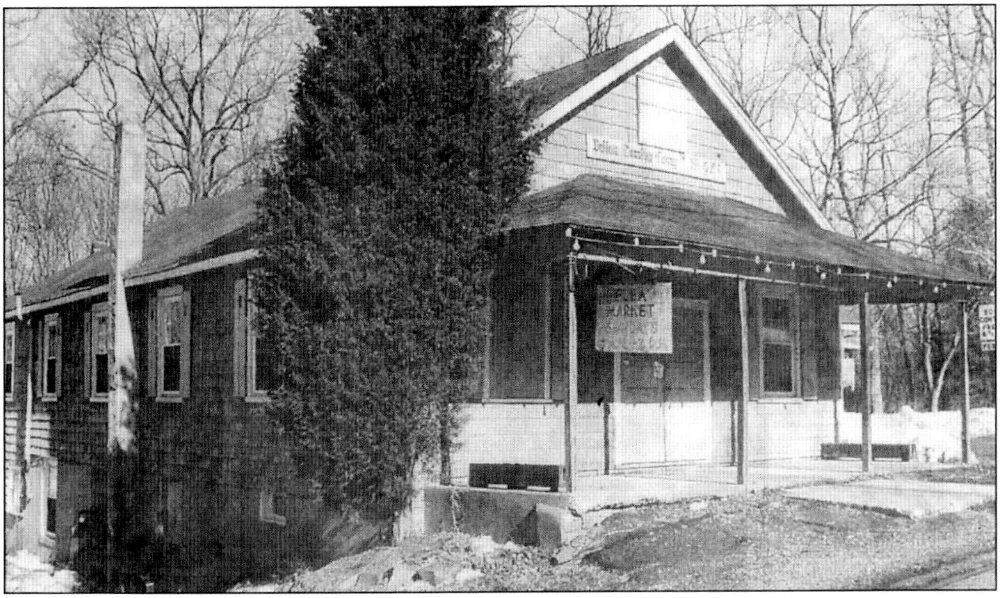

The Passaic Township Grange No. 188. The Grange started with a group of residents meeting in homes and in settings such as Henry Ortman's blacksmith shop in the center of town. They became charter members in 1909. The group became dormant during World War I, but was reactivated in 1922. The historic building in Meyersville was erected in 1926 to serve as the official meeting place for this organization. The Grange was formed for the benefit of the farmers, and for social and cultural affairs. (Long Hill Township Historical Society.)

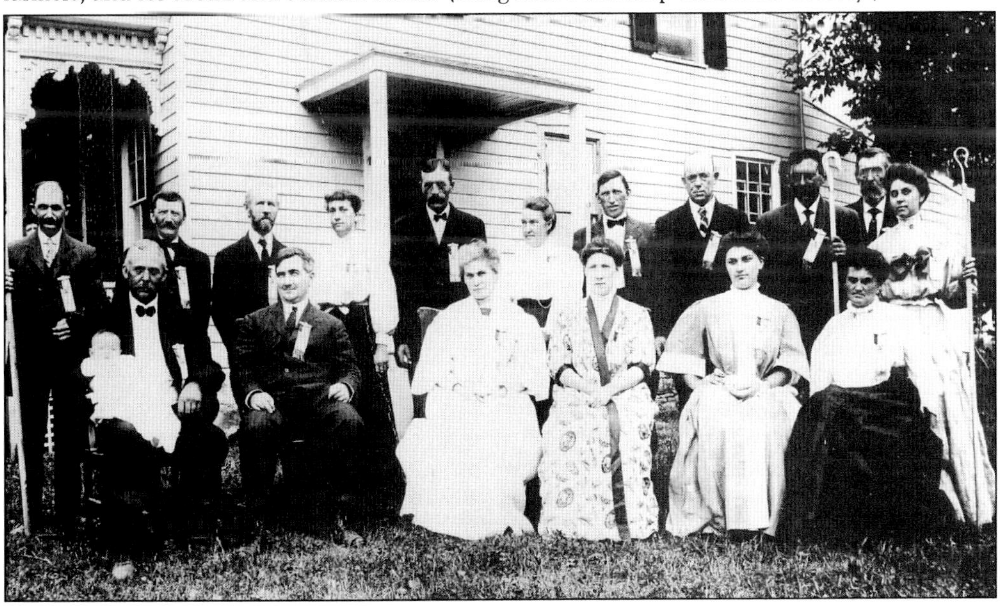

The charter members of the Passaic Township Grange, photographed at Sweeny's homestead, which stood in the center of town across from the Meyersville Inn during the early 1900s. From left to right are: (front row) August Fund, Mr. Sweeny, Mrs. Sweeny, LuLu Meile, Louise Knickle, and Mrs. Fund; (back row) Andrew Knickle, Fred Meile, J.H. Ortman, Mrs. Knickle, Edward Meeker, Mrs. Fred Meile, Willie Meile, John Scharrer, George Bauman, Lewis Meeker, and Bertha Ortman. (Long Hill Township Historical Society.)

SPECIAL ANNOUNCEMENT.

A Meeting will be held Under the Auspics of

Passaic Township Grange,

at which MISS JULIA R. LEVY, a Member of
the State Chamber Staff, will Speak
on the Subject of

"A RURAL STATE POLICE,"

ON

Monday, December 10th, 1917.

AT 8 P. M.

in Myersville Hall.

THE PUBLIC IS CORDIALLY INVITED.

ADMISSION FREE.

A notice posted of a meeting to be held at the Grange in Meyersville, c. 1917. (Eleanor and Edward Kielblock.)

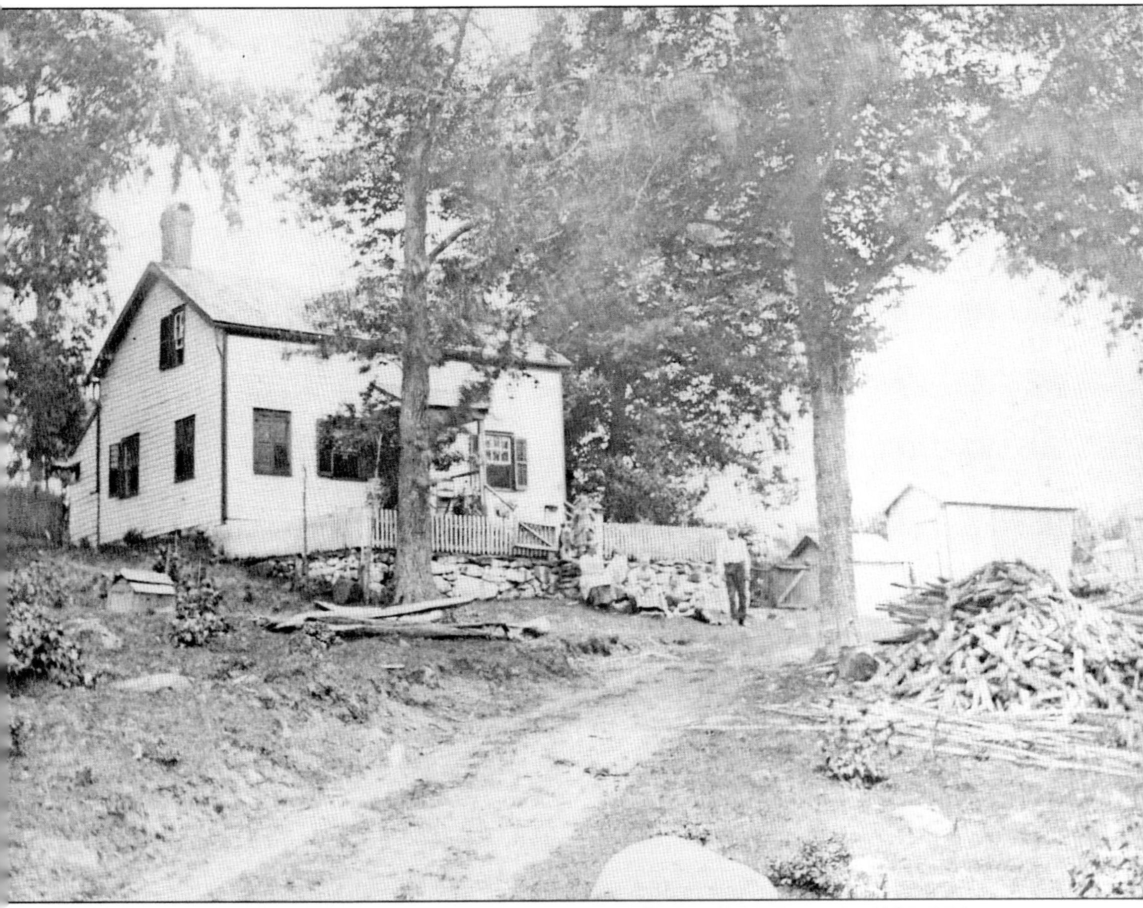

The scenic piece of land high on the hill at 223 Meyersville Road. In the early 1800s Valentine Knickle traveled from Germany to Meyersville to plant his future. His son Andrew (shown in the foreground) took over the farm in 1898. Six generations have farmed the homestead, harvesting the land for vegetables, pumpkins, apples, peaches, strawberries, and flowers. It has become an annual field-trip destination for schoolchildren, and serves as the location for many public social gatherings. The homestead is now called Hillview Farms, and presently Eleanor and Edward carry out the Knickle's tradition. (Eleanor and Edward Kielblock.)

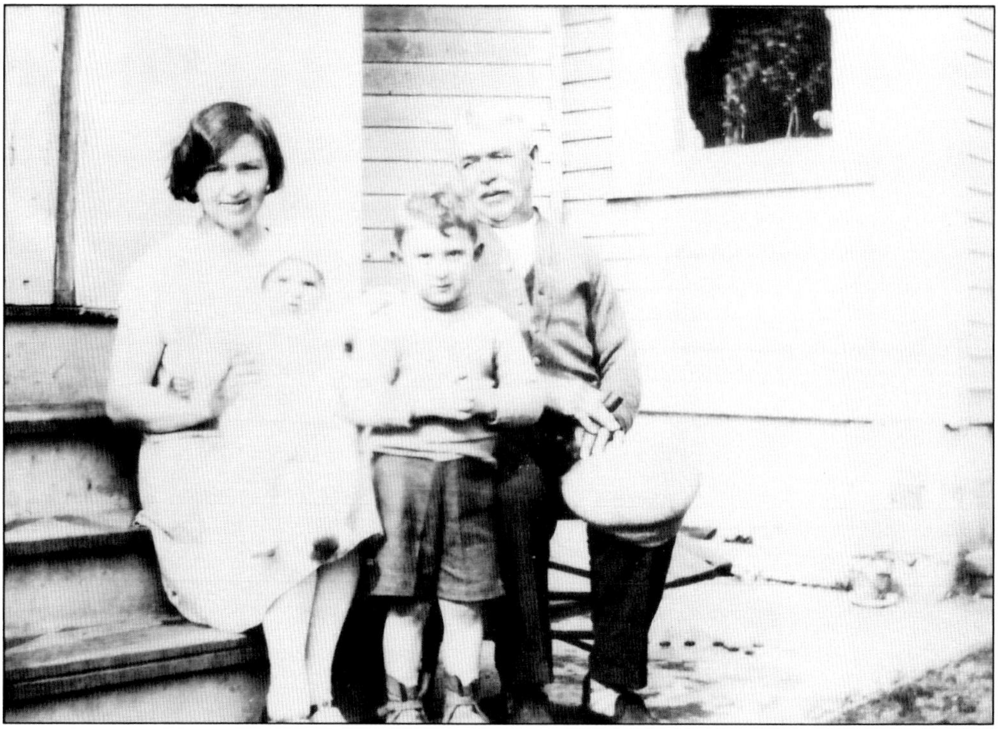

Posing on the back steps, *c.* 1930. From left to right are Margaret Zullhann Rist, Helen Rist (on lap), Reinhard Rist (standing), and their great-uncle, Martin Zullhann. (Inge Rist Lincoln.)

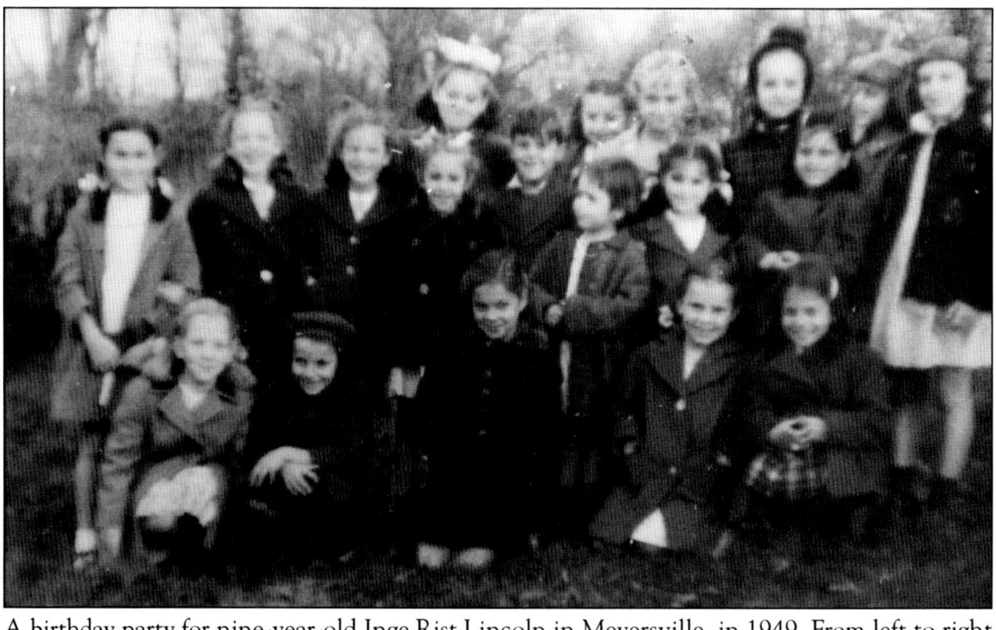

A birthday party for nine-year-old Inge Rist Lincoln in Meyersville, in 1949. From left to right are as follows: (front row) Elsa Rist, Hilda Mueller, Hannah Dietrich, and Marie Dupont; (middle row) Inge Rist, Barbara Ortman, Jean Ortman, Jiggie Williams, Karl Mueller, unknown, Margaret Weller, ? Dupont, and Joanie Williams; (back row) Linda Ward, Eleanor Greaf, Alice Wright, Regina Vande Sande, and Gladys Mains. (Inge Rist Lincoln.)

The Pleasant Plains Methodist Episcopal Church, *c.* 1919. This was actually a mission church built in 1871 on the southwest corner of Pleasant Plains and White Bridge Roads in Meyersville. Church suppers were always a highlight. Charles F. Oehley was the last preacher there, before the building burned to the ground in 1931, leaving the foundation as the only visible remains. (William D. Oehley.)

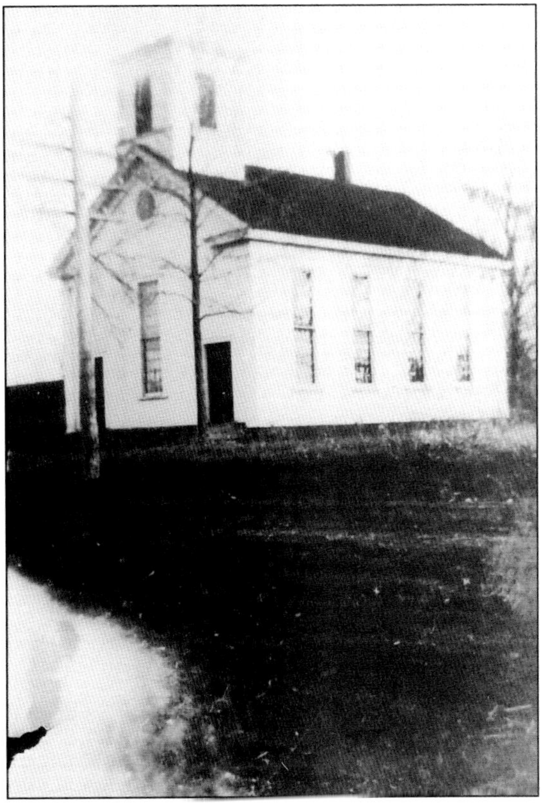

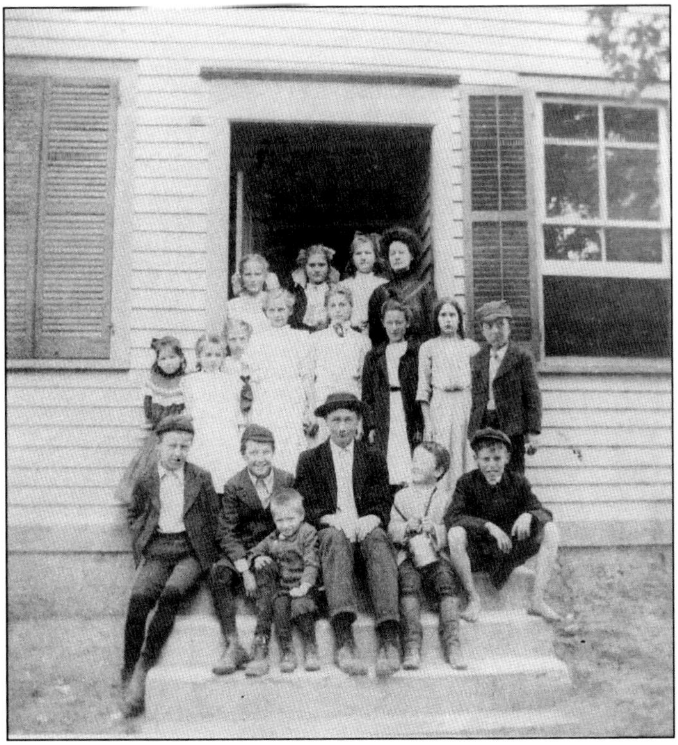

The Swamp School, as it was called in Meyersville, *c.* 1900. The school was located in the Great Swamp, on the corner of White Bridge and Meyersville Roads. A one-room schoolhouse, it served its basic purpose of teaching children of all ages. The property for the school was donated by William Kister in 1880 (Anna Kister Harman was William Kister's niece). The building is now a private residence. (Rosemarie Zander Cafaro.)

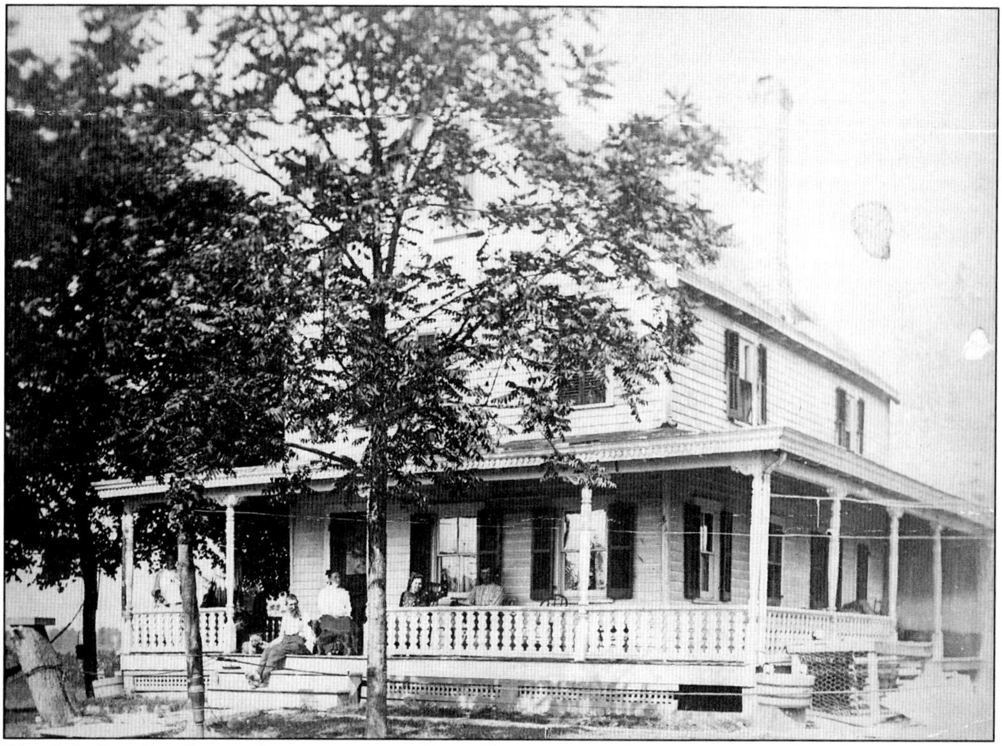

The Meeker family on their wraparound porch, *c.* 1900. The Meekers, who were among the first settlers of Meyersville, farmed the land on 508 White Bridge Road adjacent to the Great Swamp. Edward and Lewis Meeker were charter members of the Passaic Township Grange in Meyersville. (Edward Meeker.)

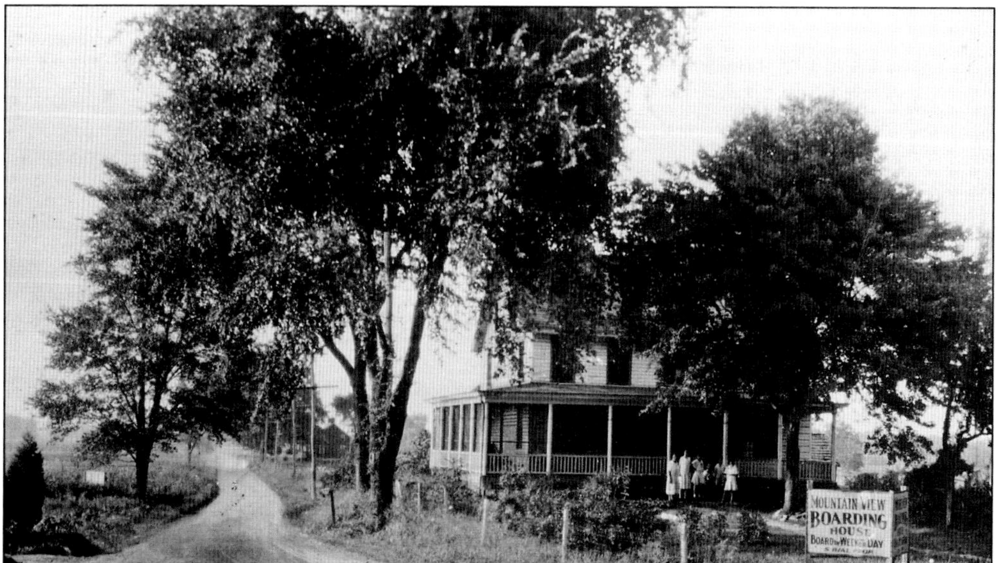

The northeast corner of the intersection in Meyersville, *c.* 1930. This building, now a private residence, was the Mountain View Boarding House at the turn of the century. (Betty & Robert Stapperfenne.)

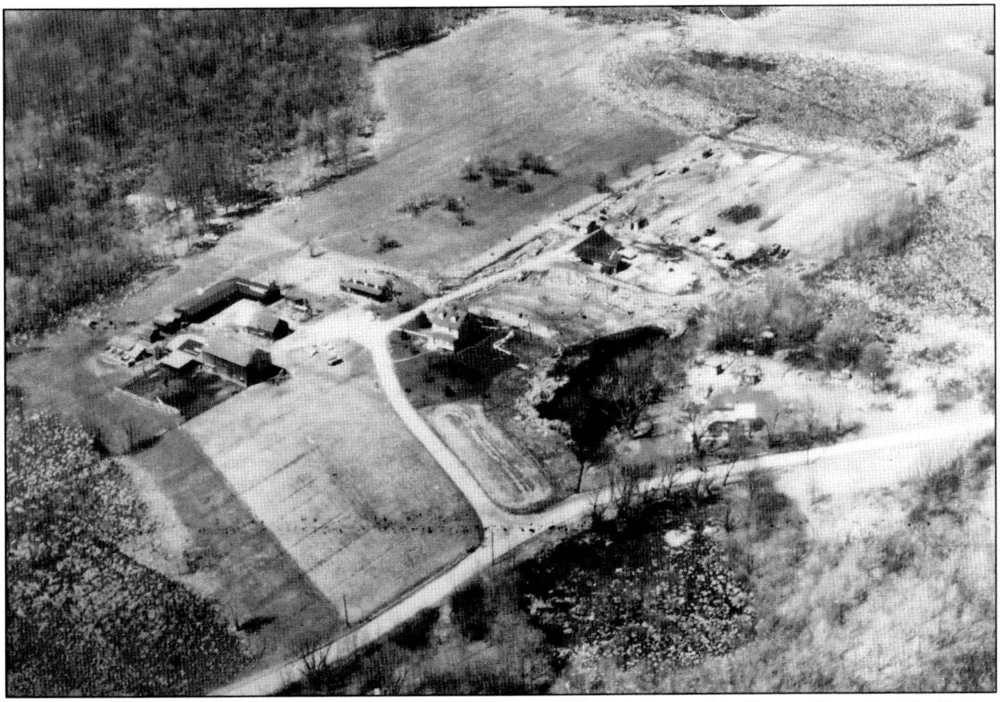

A 1960s aerial view of the Zander farm and homestead adjoining the Great Swamp. Christian Zander settled in Meyersville at the turn of the century, and his son Albert started a sawmill on White Bridge Road in 1919. Albert and Esther raised nine children on the land, and the Zander's operated their business through 1967. (Alberta & Irving H. Zander.)

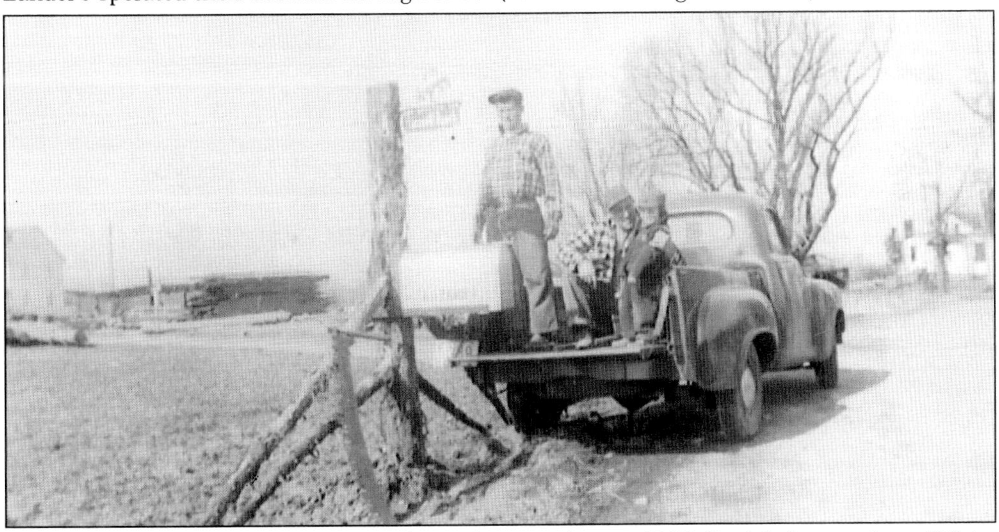

Ready to start the work day. Posing for a photograph in a 1953 Studebaker truck on White Bridge Road are, from left to right, Irving H. Zander, Donald Conger (Irving's brother-in-law), and Irving Jr. Up until the 1950s, living in the pristine wilderness of the Great Swamp brought the many bountiful rewards of nature, such as skating, hunting, trapping, and fishing, along with a bevy of wild berry bushes, nut trees, beaver, mink, otter, deer, pheasant, and rabbit. In 1959, the federal government purchased 3,000 acres of swamp and donated it to create a national wildlife refuge. (Alberta & Irving H. Zander.)

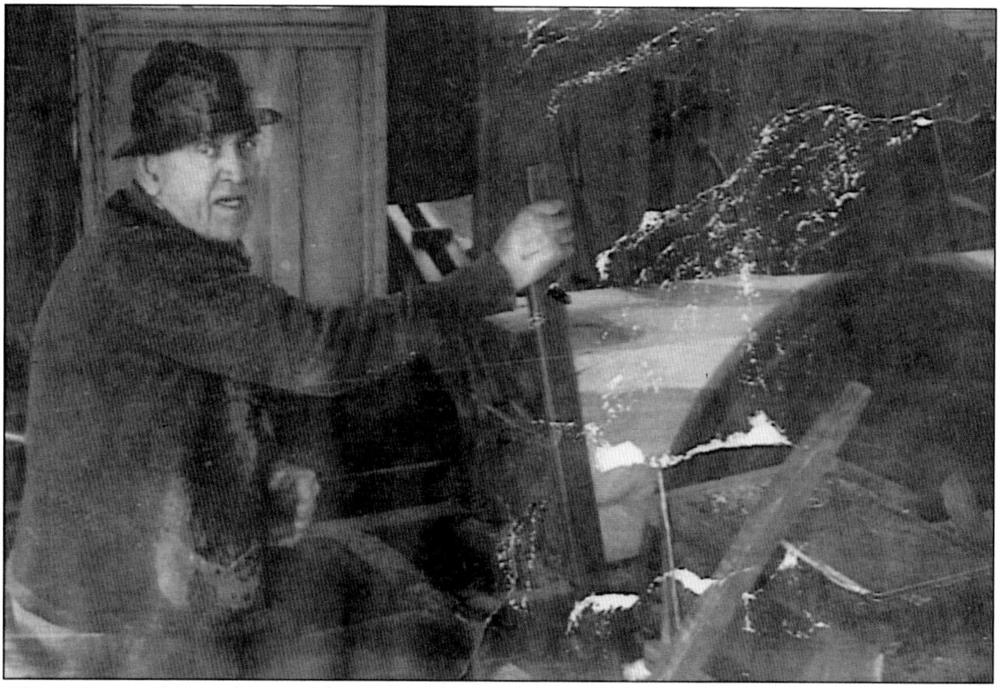

Albert G. Zander working at the sawmill on White Bridge Road, c. 1950. Townsfolk would deliver their lumber to the sawmill to be cut and then schedule it for pick-up. Albert would charge 7¢ a foot for each piece of lumber to be cut. (Alberta & Irving H. Zander.)

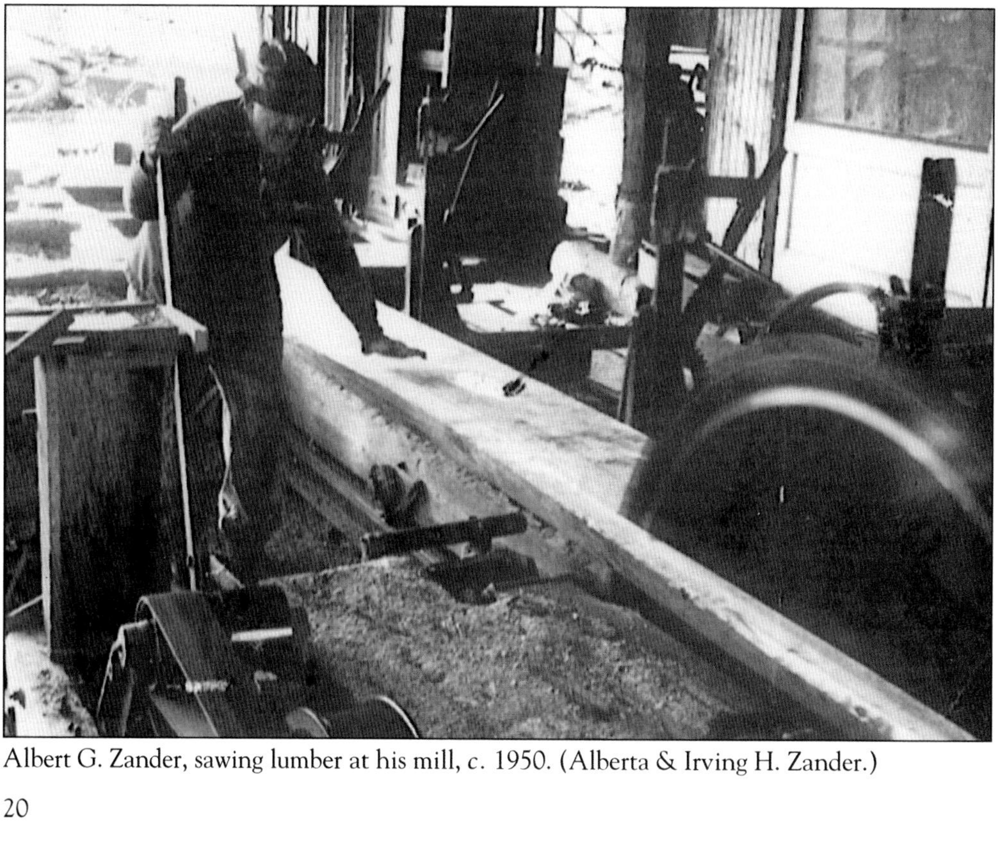

Albert G. Zander, sawing lumber at his mill, c. 1950. (Alberta & Irving H. Zander.)

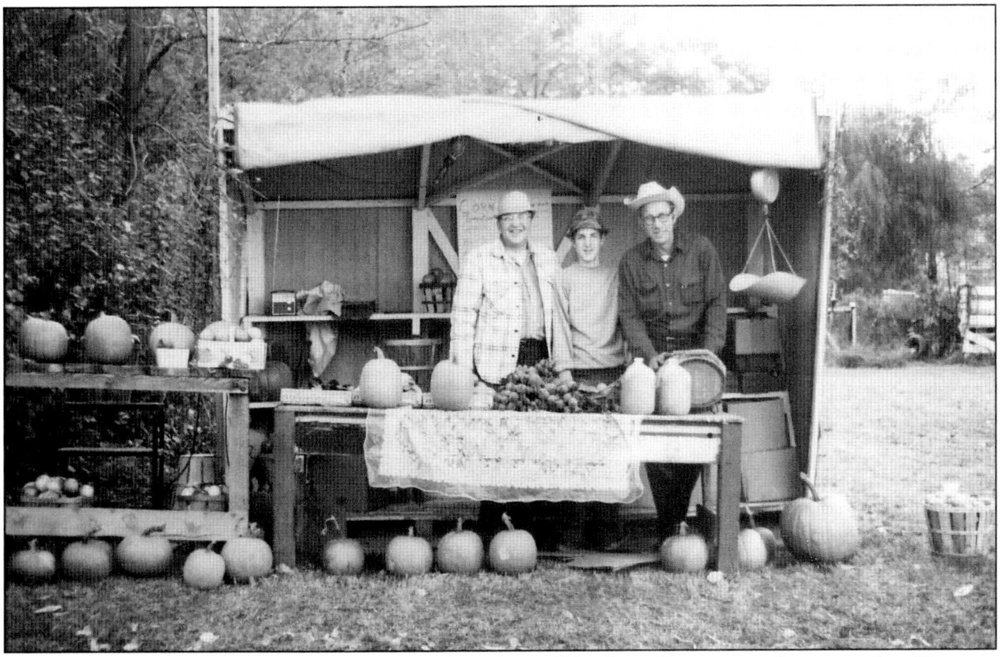

John Skrobacz, his son Steven, and Edward Kielblock selling pumpkins at the Harvest Bazaar, *c.* 1970. The bazaar is an annual event at the Meyersville Presbyterian Church. (Betty Skrobacz.)

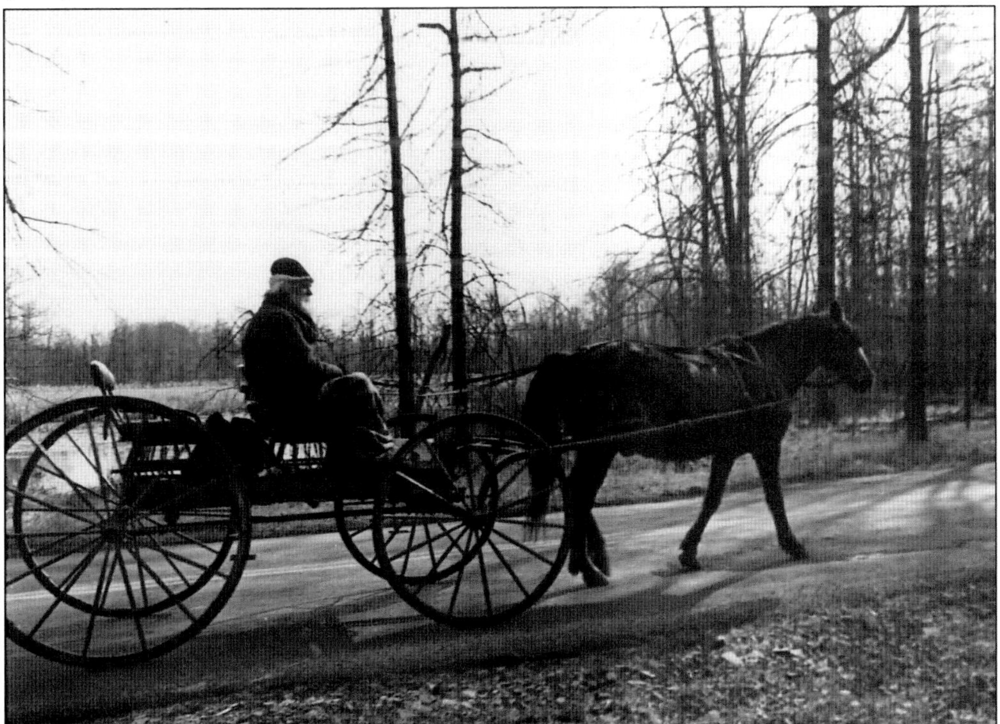

Archie Stiles in his horse-drawn wagon, enjoying a twilight ride through the Great Swamp, *c.* 1960. (Emma & Archibald Stiles.)

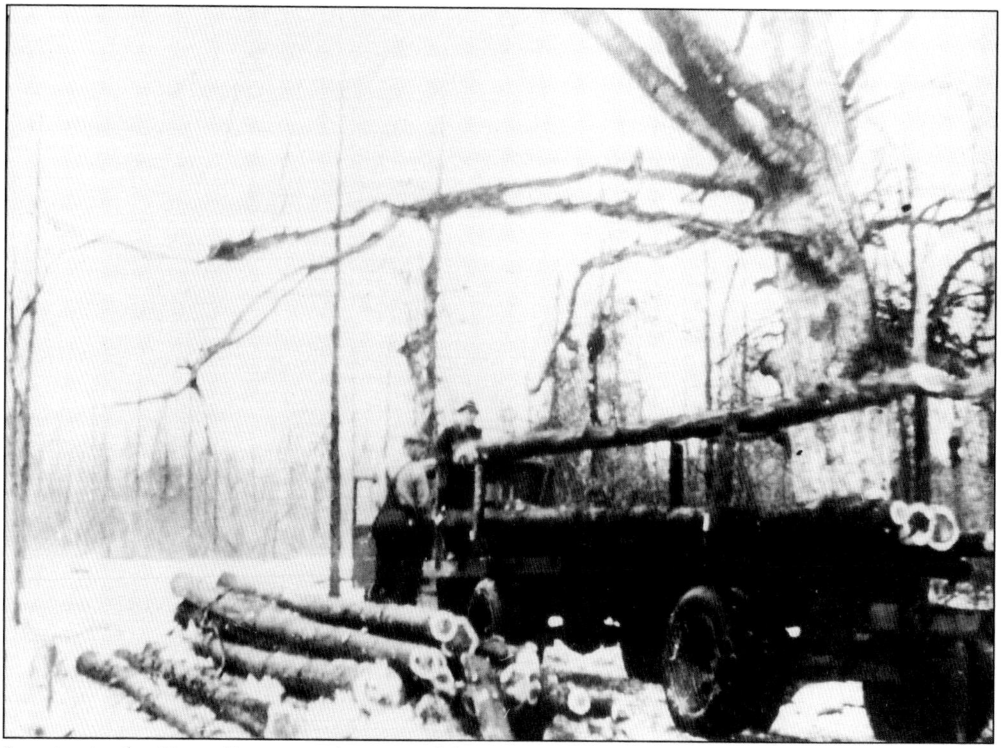

Logging in the Great Swamp at the turn of the century. This is believed to be known as Decker's Woods, on Pleasant Plains Road in Meyersville, on the west side before White Bridge Road. (Paul Becker—Somerset County Park Commission.)

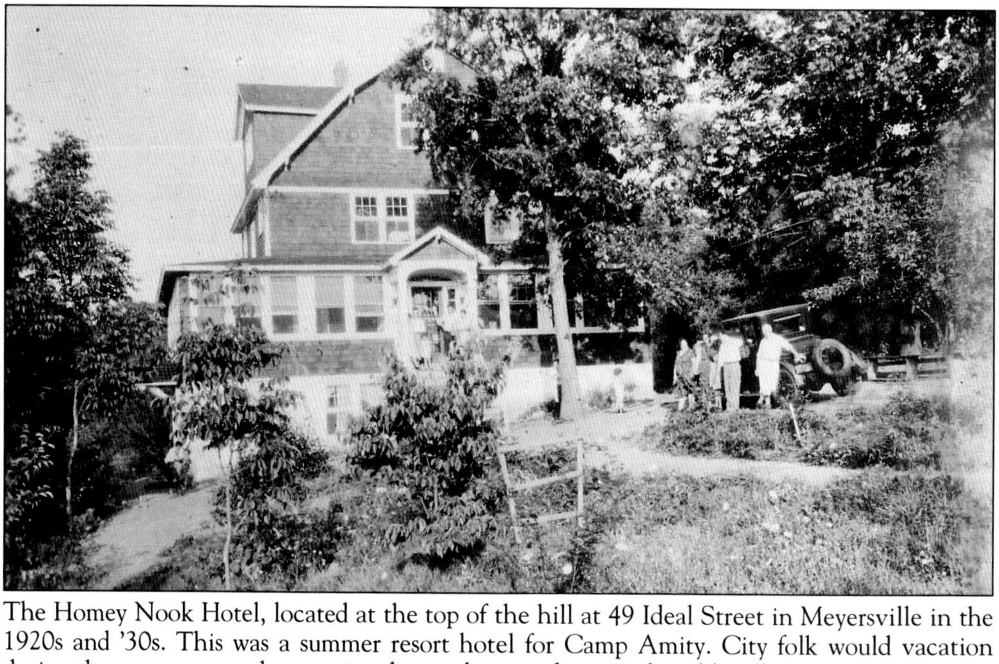

The Homey Nook Hotel, located at the top of the hill at 49 Ideal Street in Meyersville in the 1920s and '30s. This was a summer resort hotel for Camp Amity. City folk would vacation during the summer months to enjoy the rural atmosphere, and could walk down the hill to the center of town for food and enjoyment. (Betty & Robert Stapperfenne.)

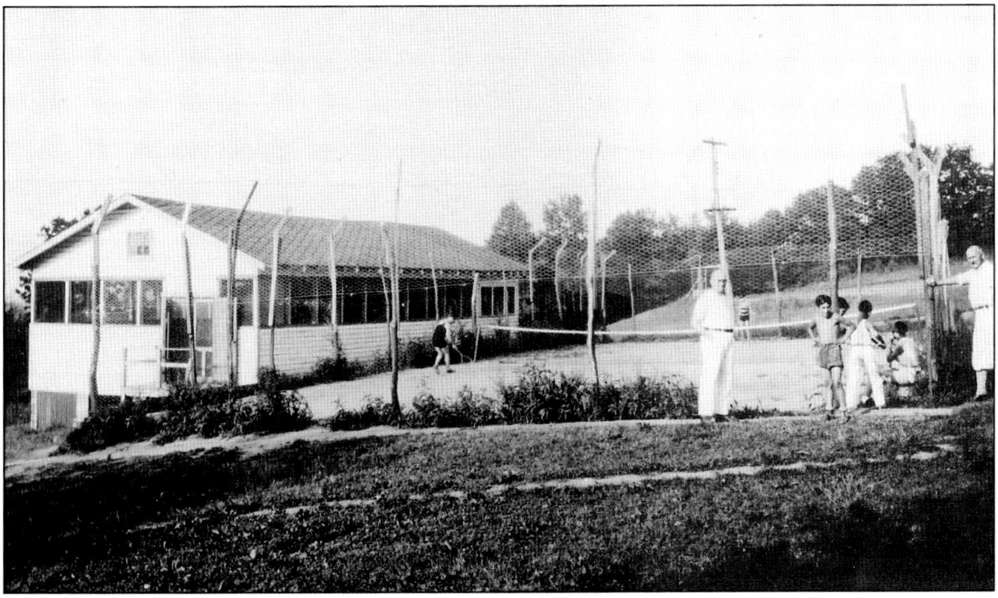

A leisurely game of tennis on the courts at Camp Amity, on the hill in Meyersville on Ideal Street, *c.* 1930. (Betty & Robert Stapperfenne.)

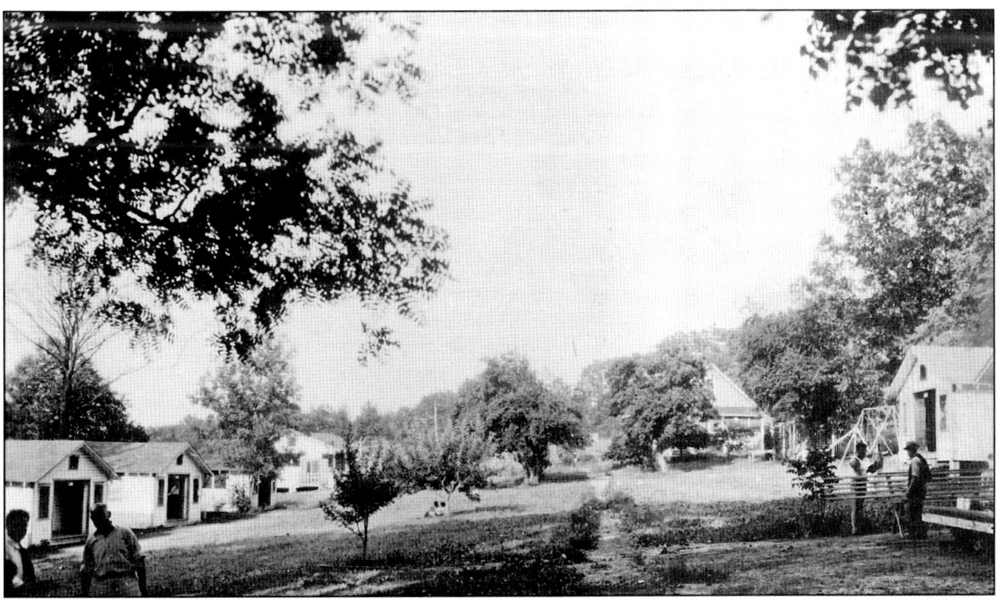

Summer cabins at Camp Amity, *c.* 1920. With its hotel, tennis courts, and cabins, Camp Amity made a pleasant summer stay for New Yorkers, and also provided employment opportunities for some Meyersville residents. (Betty & Robert Stapperfenne.)

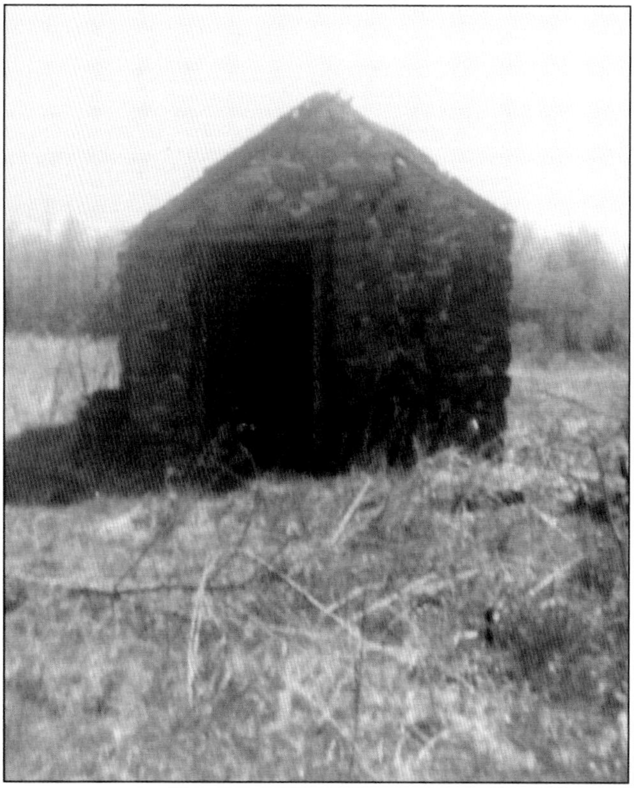

"The tramp house," *c*. 1960. This stone house was built in the 1800s on Joseph Hilbert's farm at 735 New Vernon Road, in Harding Township (which was part of Long Hill Township prior to the 1920s). The house was used as a stopover for the poor in need of shelter, food, and a night's stay while walking through the Great Swamp. It was taken down stone by stone and in 1988 reconstructed on the property of the Harding Township Historical Society. The dedication of the tramp house took place on October 2, 1988. (Mary Lou Landwehr Weller.)

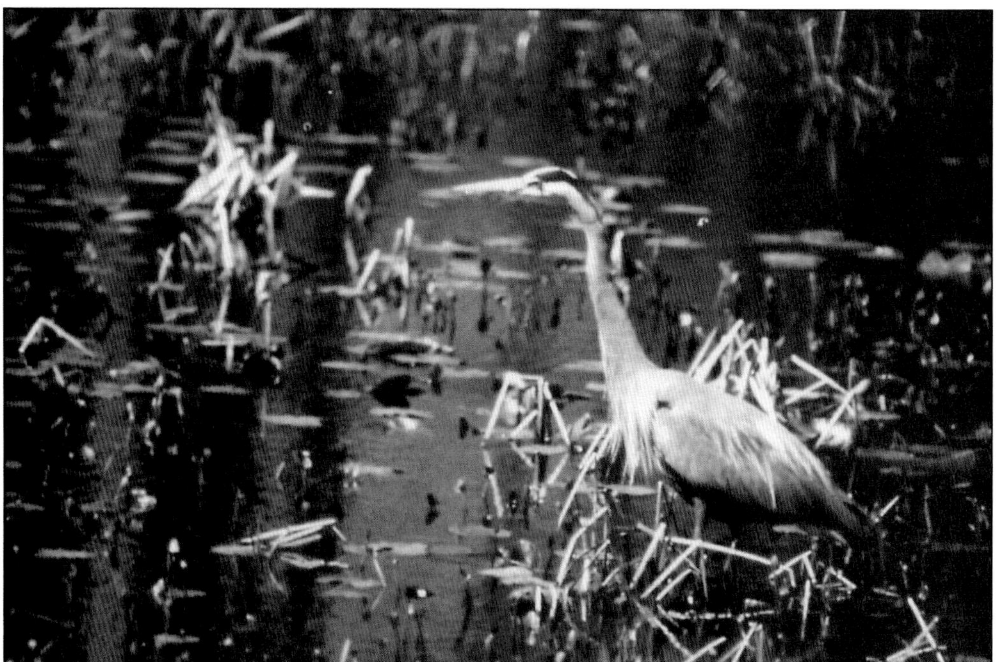

A Great Blue Heron, one of the 150 species of birds who inhabit the Great Swamp Refuge throughout the year. (Paul Becker—Somerset County Park Commission.)

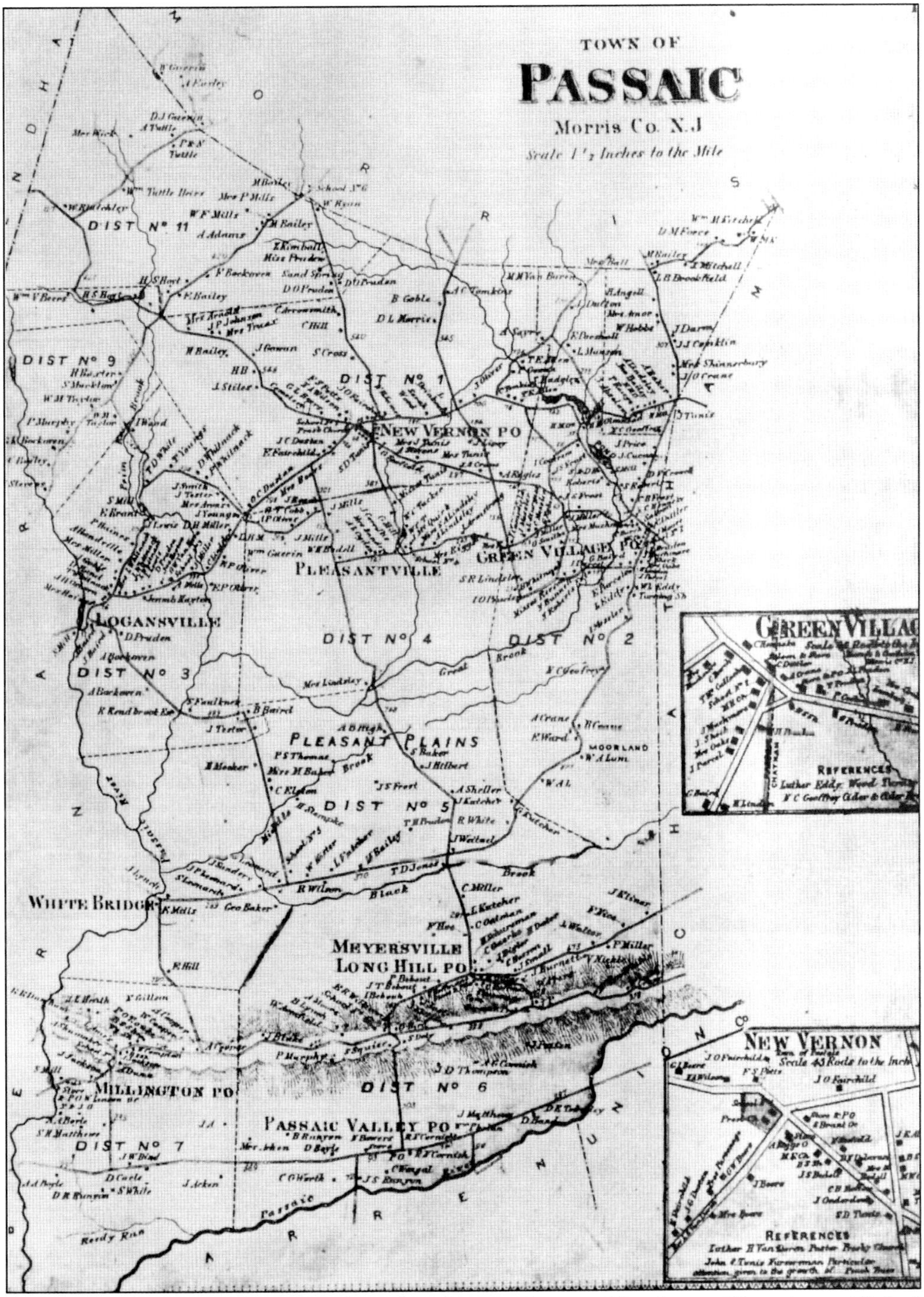

A map of Passaic Township from the *Atlas of Morris County, New Jersey*. The atlas, published in 1868, contains actual surveys by and under the direction of F.W. Beers, assisted by A.B. Prindle and others. John Littell was the first to print a map of the Passaic Valley in 1845; in 1852 he wrote *Family Records and Genealogies of the First Settlers of the Passaic Valley*. (Irma B. Mikulyak.)

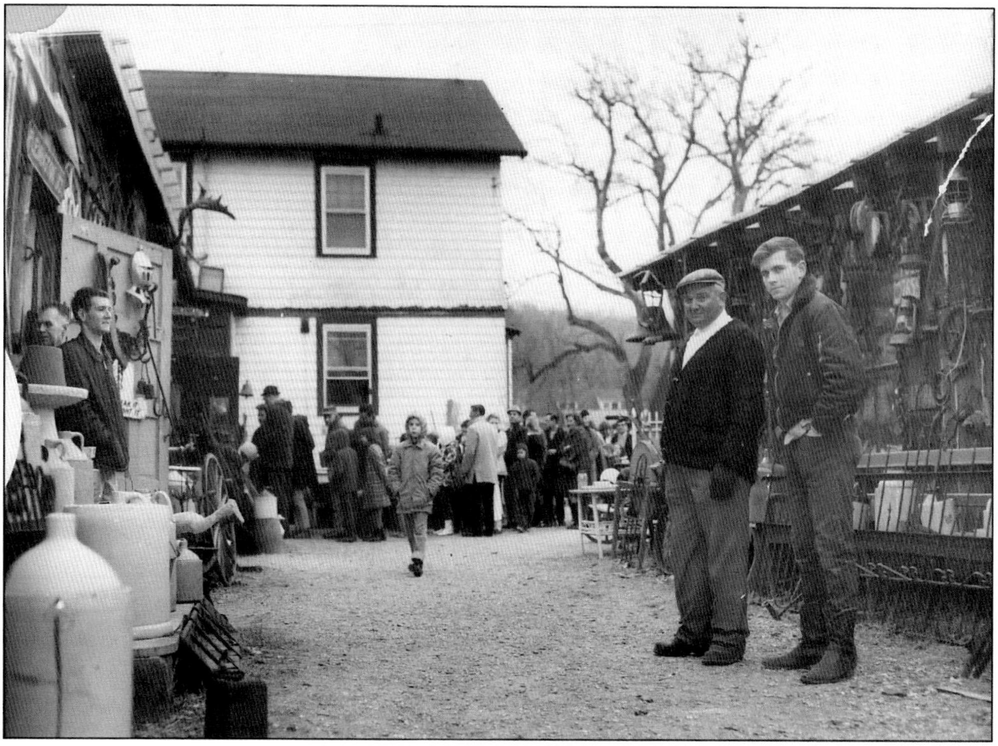

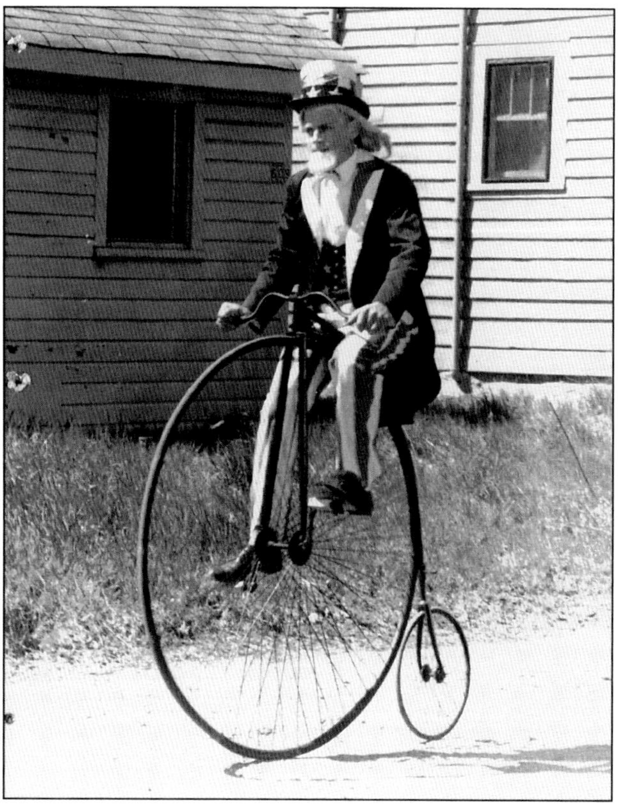

Archie's Resale Shop, at 596 Meyersville Road in Meyersville, in the autumn of 1950. The shop is shown here during one of its numerous "Ice Skate Exchange Days." Archie and his son George are standing to the right in the foreground. Archie's Resale Shop is widely known for their antiques and collectibles. (Emma & Archibald Stiles.)

George Stiles warming up for an entertaining ride on an antique bicycle from the 1880s. The bicycle was owned by his parents, Emma & Archibald Stiles, and George is pictured at their resale shop in the 1950s. George rode the bicycle in many local parades in the area. (Emma & Archibald Stiles.)

Two

Stirling

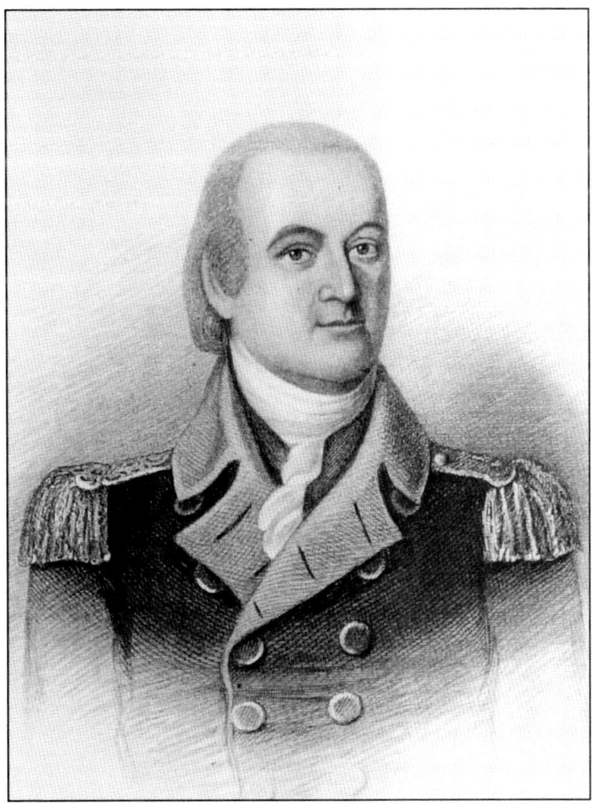

Lord Stirling (1725–1783), a brigadier general in the Continental Army under George Washington. Lord Stirling's real name was William Alexander. He owned a great deal of land in the eighteenth century, and remains of his great estate, which burned in 1920, are still being discovered in Basking Ridge. The town of Stirling was named in his honor. (Paul Becker-Environmental Education Center, Basking Ridge.)

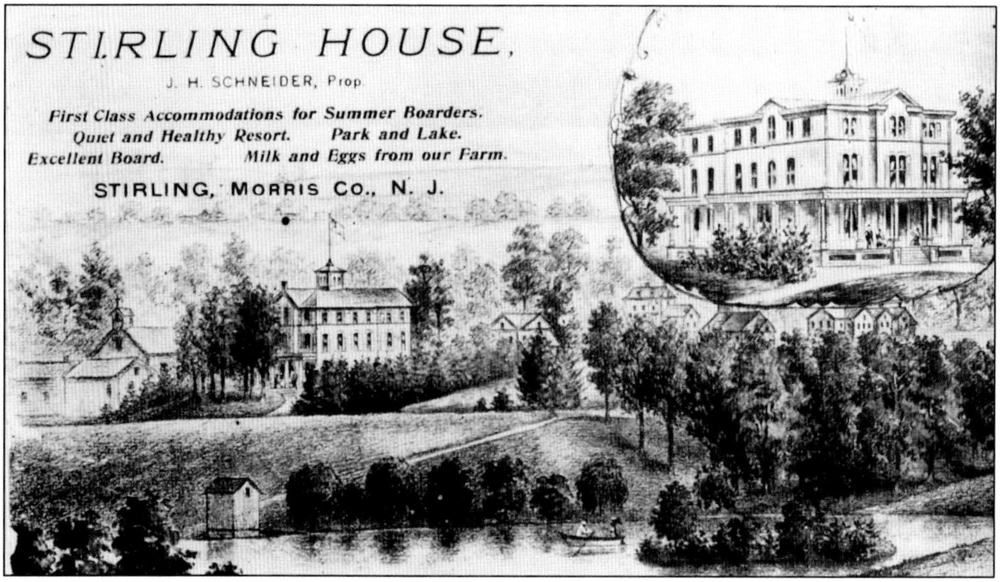

The Stirling Hotel, built in 1890 at the northwest corner of Elm Street and Central Avenue. This beautifully spacious resort hotel was the first big hotel of its kind in Stirling. It had first-class accommodations for summer boarders, and featured a park and a lake within walking distance. It burned to the ground in 1905. (Pam Herrmann Thievon.)

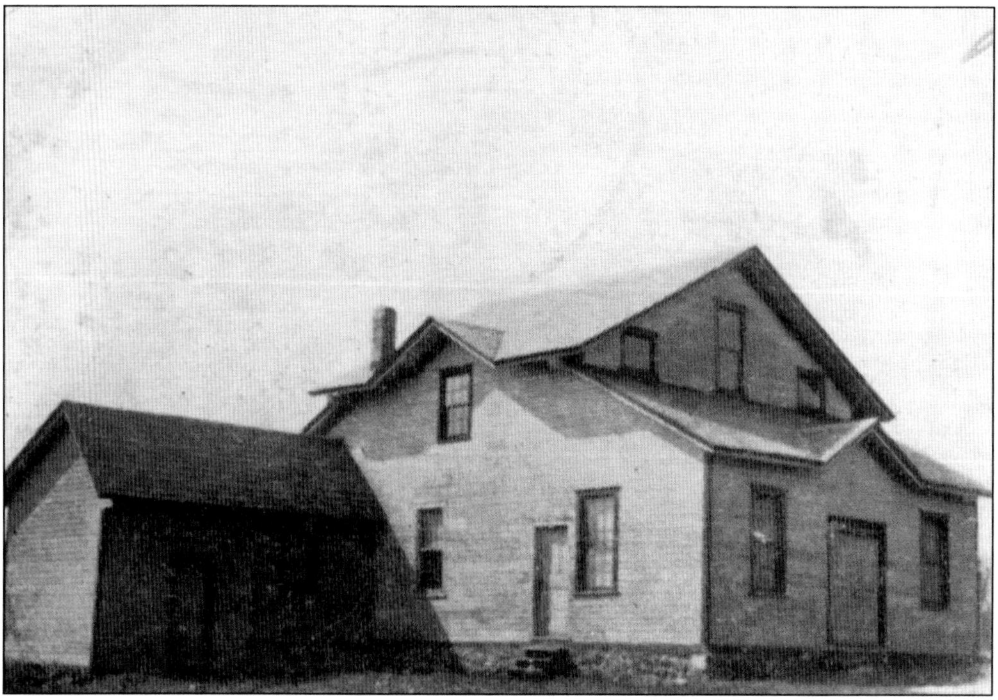

The coach barn, or carriage house, for the original Stirling Hotel. Pictured here c. 1901, it was located across the street from the hotel on Elm Street. After the hotel burned, this building was used for silent movies, Sunday school, meetings, and recreation for the local children in town. It was known as the YMCA, although it had no affiliation with that organization. After sixty-six years of use, it was torn down in 1946. (Lynn Deveney Spurrier.)

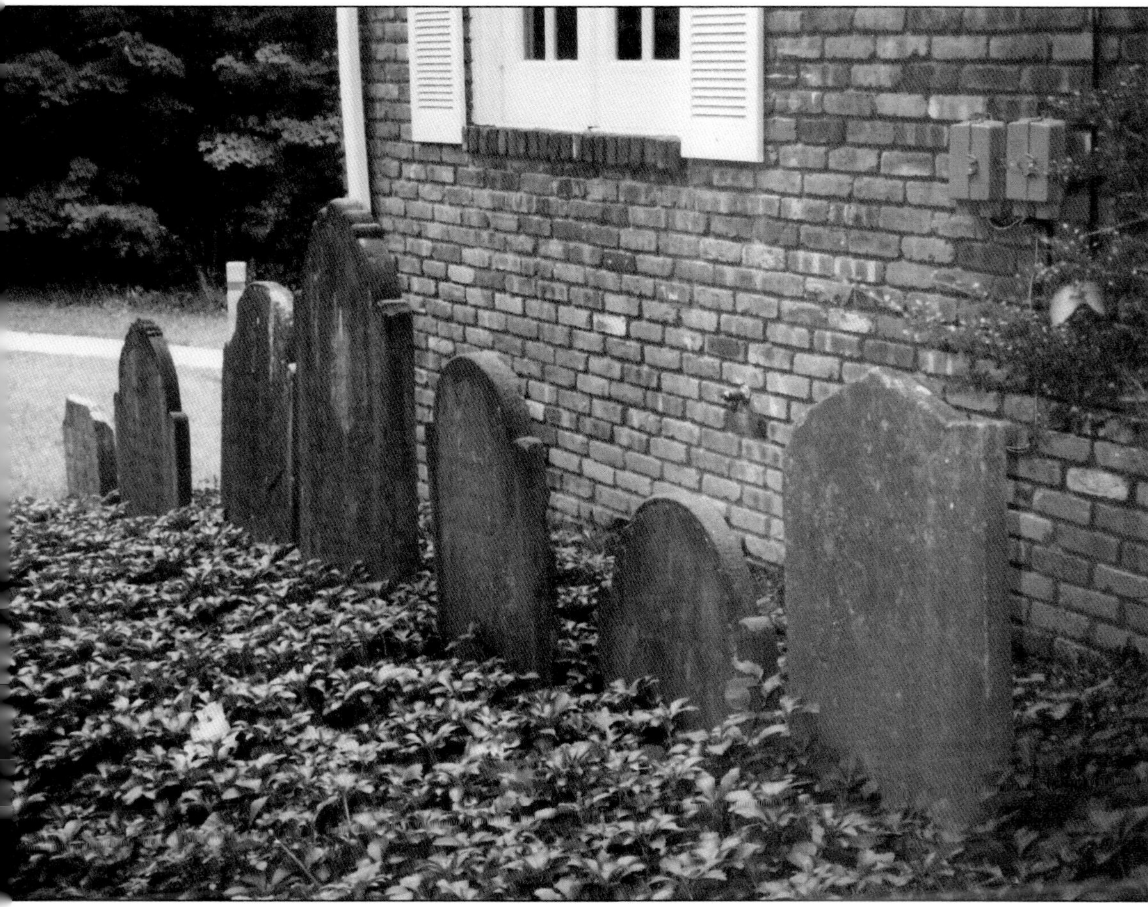

Tombstones from the original Cooper family cemetery. The Cooper descendants came from Holland in the 1700s. They owned vast amounts of land, from Millington to Stirling. Daniel Cooper II, who lived to be 101 years old, married nine times. He was a man of good standing in Morris County. Cooper lived in Stirling in 1755, before Passaic Township was created in 1866, and he established the first public library in Morris County. He achieved the position of high sheriff, and also sat on the bench as a magistrate. The tombstones are from the original cemetery owned by the Cooper family, found in Stirling on Chestnut Street and North Avenue, and later placed at the Long Hill Township Public Library on Central Avenue in 1976. Captain Peter Layton, an early resident of the community who served in the Revolutionary War, is also represented here. The Long Hill Township Historical Society was the key instrument in preserving the tombstones, under the direction of Gwendlyn Thomas at a ceremony on the library grounds on June 26, 1976. (Long Hill Township Historical Society.)

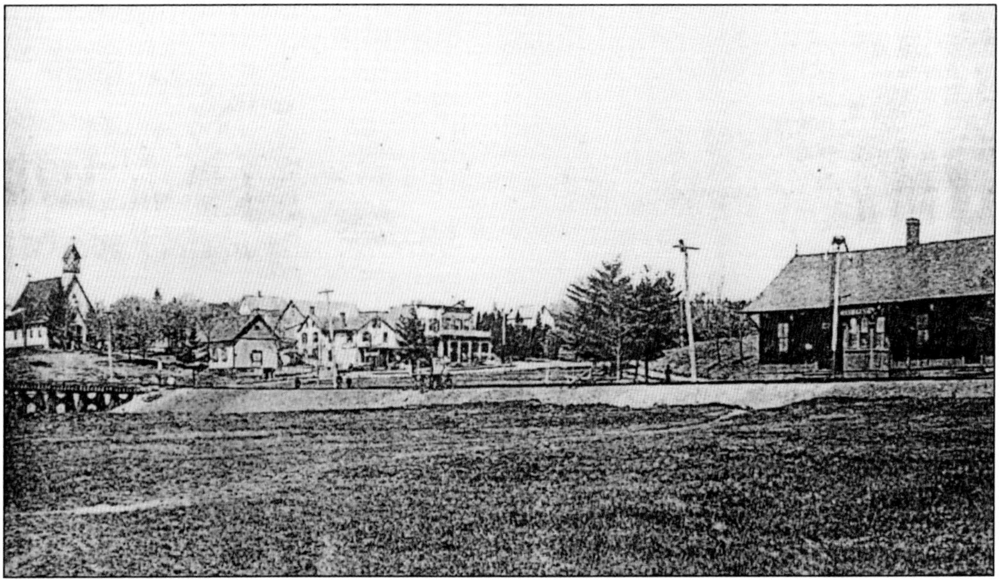

The small country church on the hill where the tennis courts are now located on Elm Street. Built in 1886, this church was named after St. Vincent DePaul, a French Saint. Louis Chaffanjon donated the land for the parish cemetery. He was, at that time, the owner of the Stirling Hotel, and also owned a beautiful home in Long Hill, which was pictorially displayed in *Charm* magazine, c. 1927. (Dale Monetti.)

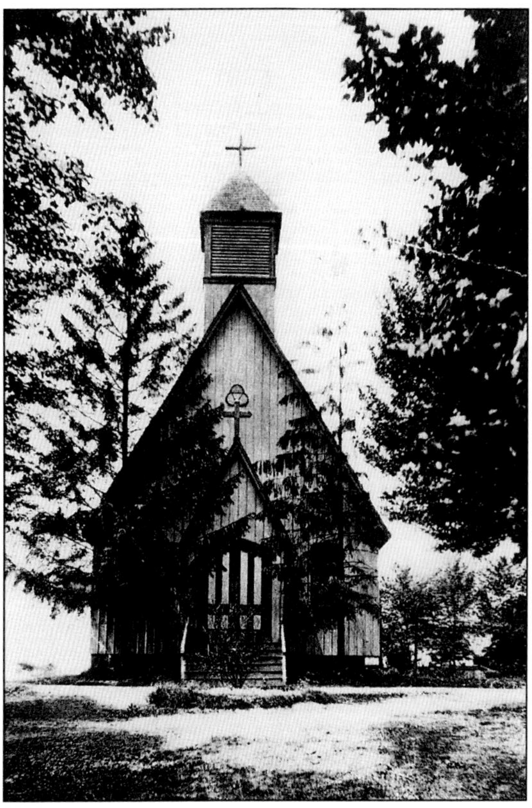

The Street Vincent DePaul Roman Catholic Church, 1914. This photograph taken on its original site, at Elm Street in Stirling. In 1928 the church was moved to Bebout Avenue in Stirling. (Elizabeth Kocisko.)

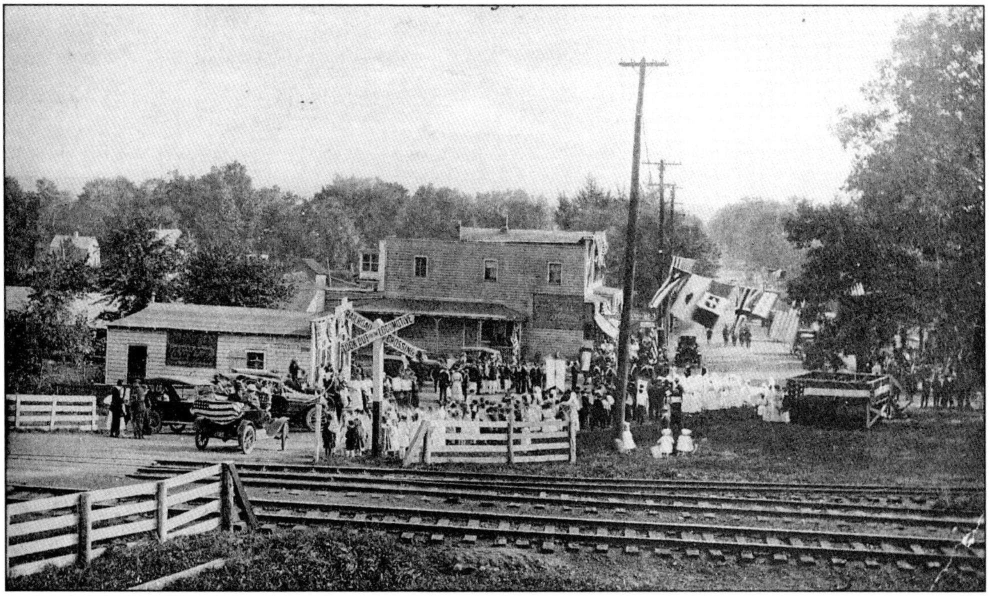

The Assunta Society, *c.* 1900, in a photograph taken at the railroad tracks on Central Avenue, looking south. The society was an Italian men's organization in the Catholic parish, and is shown here dedicating the statue of the Blessed Mother while parading down Main Street during the Feast of the Assumption. People in the street would attach dollar bills to the passing statue as a donation to the society. (Carol Metzler.)

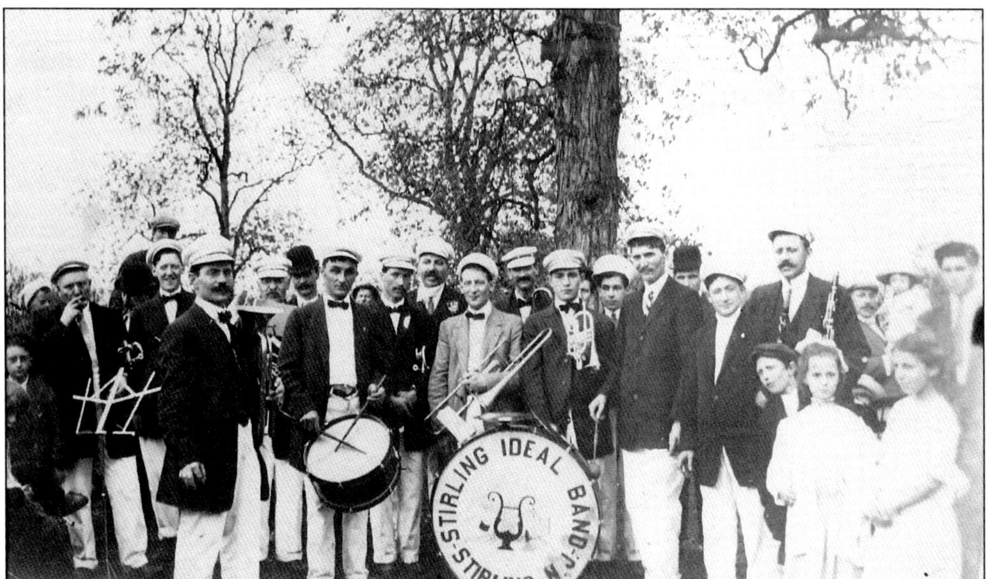

The Stirling Ideal Band preparing for a parade at the turn of the century. Joseph Landwehr holds the drum, while George Harman, wearing a bow tie and white hat, stands in front of the tree. (Mary Harman Gehling.)

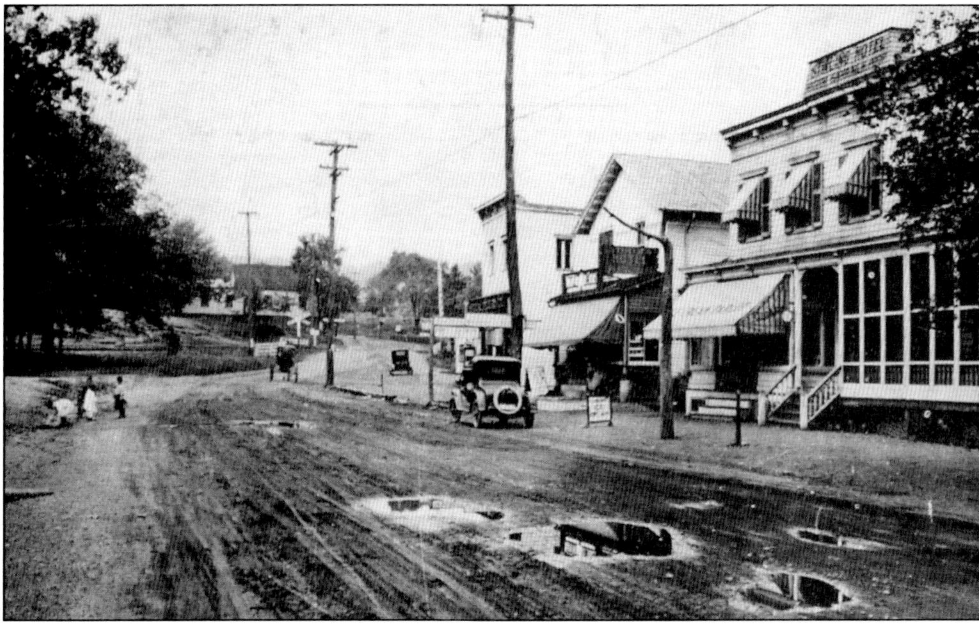

A picture postcard taken facing north onto Main Street, Stirling, *c.* 1910. Note the horse-drawn buggy and 1920 Dodge on the side of the road to the right. What a rare find to have captured the changing technology juxtaposed with a time gone by. (Dale Monetti.)

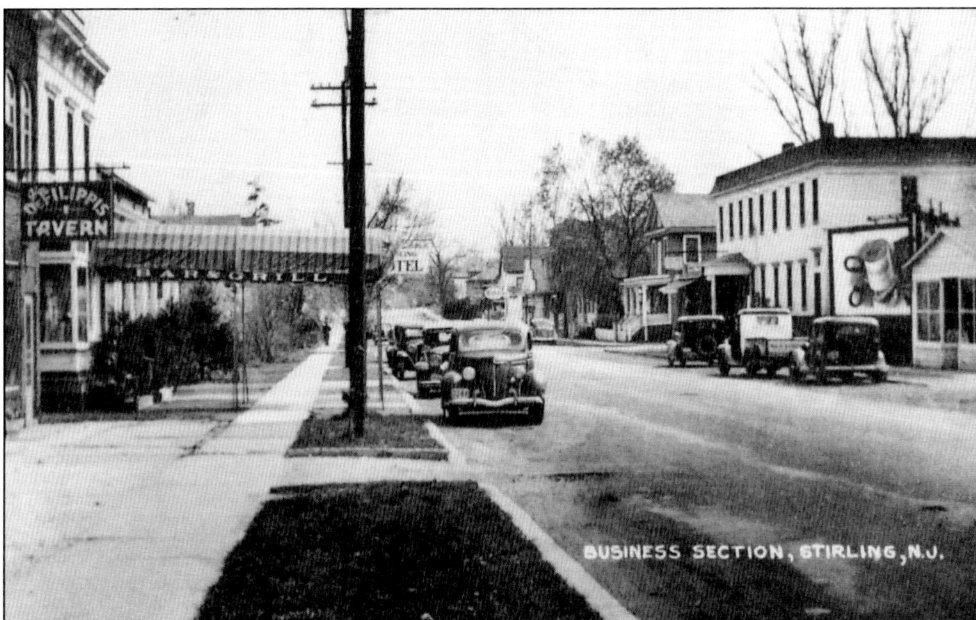

A 1930s photograph of Main Street in Stirling, looking south, showing the more established business district. A 1936 Ford, a Model A Ford, and a Model B pickup can be seen. (Emma & Archibald Stiles.)

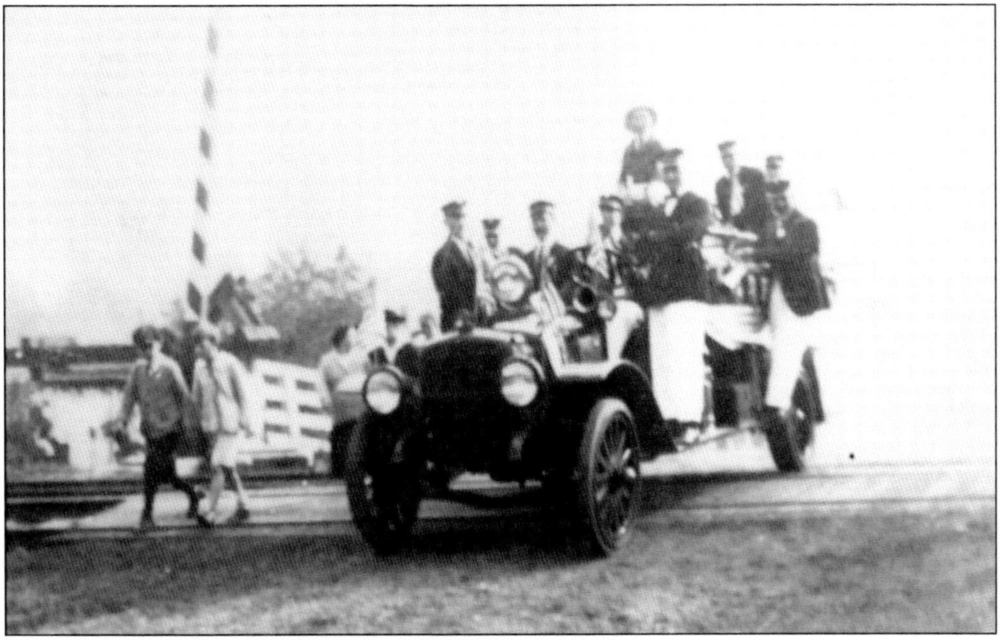

A prize-winning firetruck which took first prize in a parade down Main Street at the turn of the century. Charles Bender's son is seated atop the truck. (Mary Harman Gehling.)

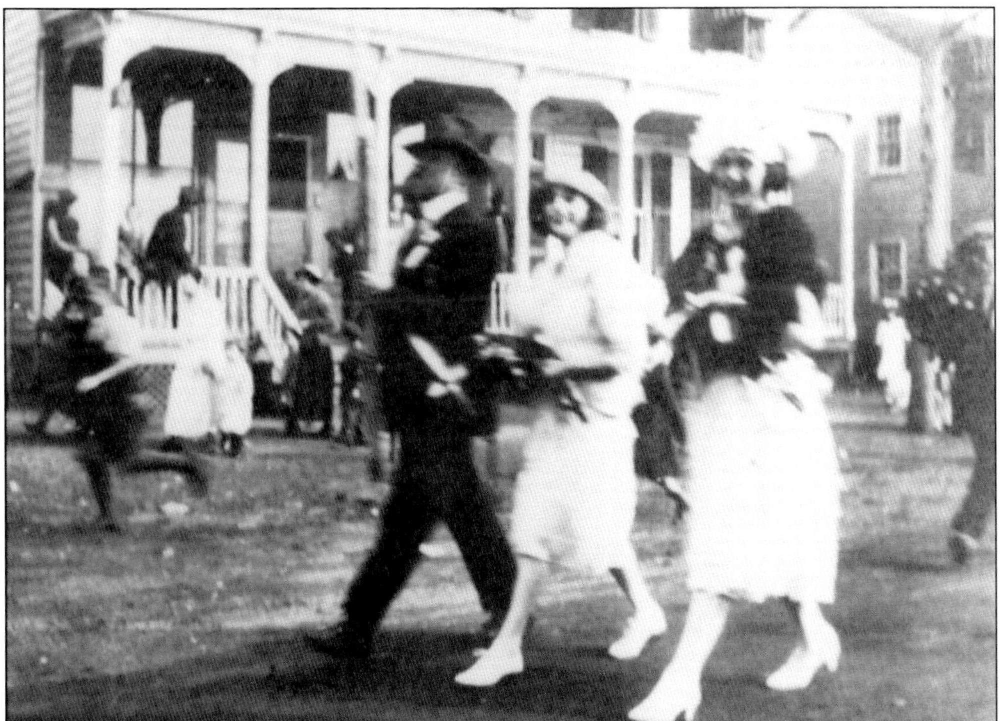

Misses Carrie Balestrini and Mary Tricarico, photographed *c.* 1917 while marching with Ray Alland past the Stirling Hotel on Main Street. (Mary Harman Gehling.)

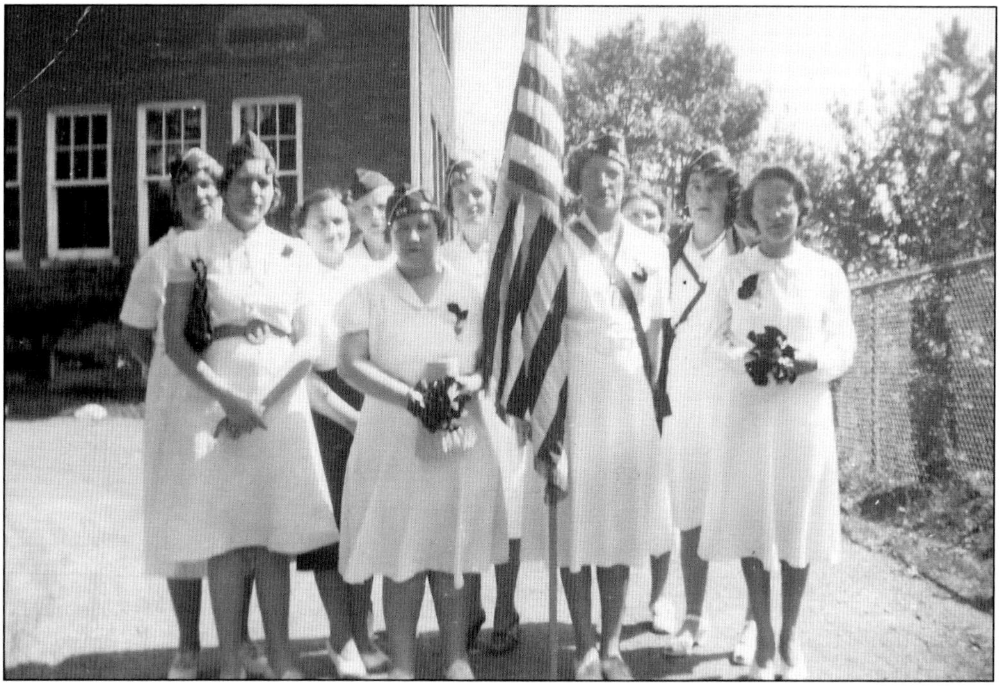

The American Legion Auxiliary #278 of Stirling preparing for a parade down Main Street on May 30, 1941. Some of the members are Emma Fisher, Amelia Terry, Emily Shand, Margaret Landwehr, Marie Wilson, and Myrtle Herrmann. (Barbara Herrmann Corcoran.)

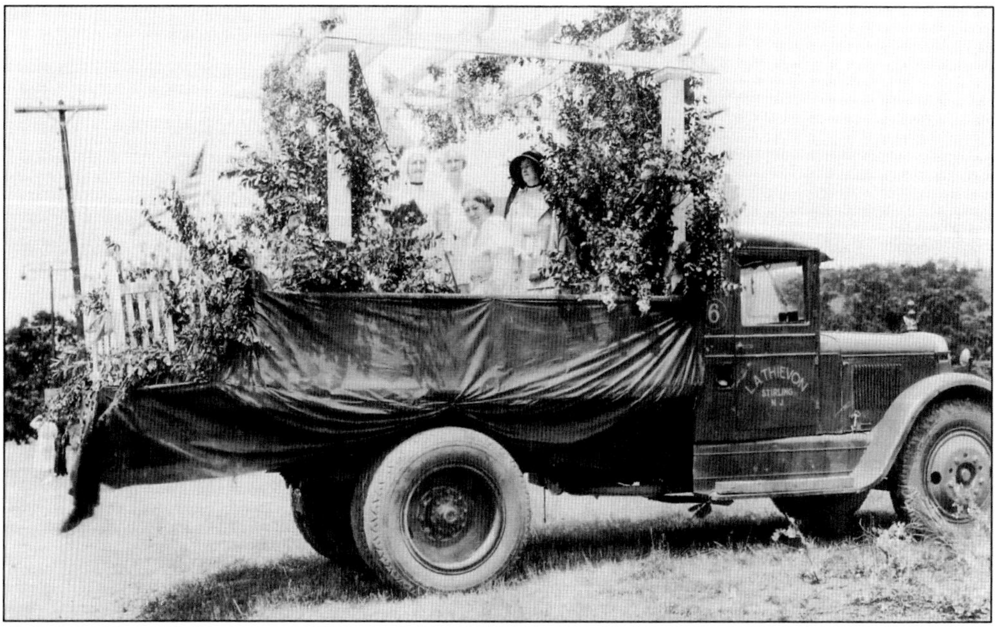

Float members of the Long Hill Women's Club of Long Hill Township, ready for a parade. The truck was owned by Louis Thievon. The club, which was organized to promote neighborhood unity along with cultural and social service, is still active in the community today. On the float are, from left to right, Martha Hall, Caroline Boucher, Marion Pulling, and May Wiegand. (Long Hill Women's Club.)

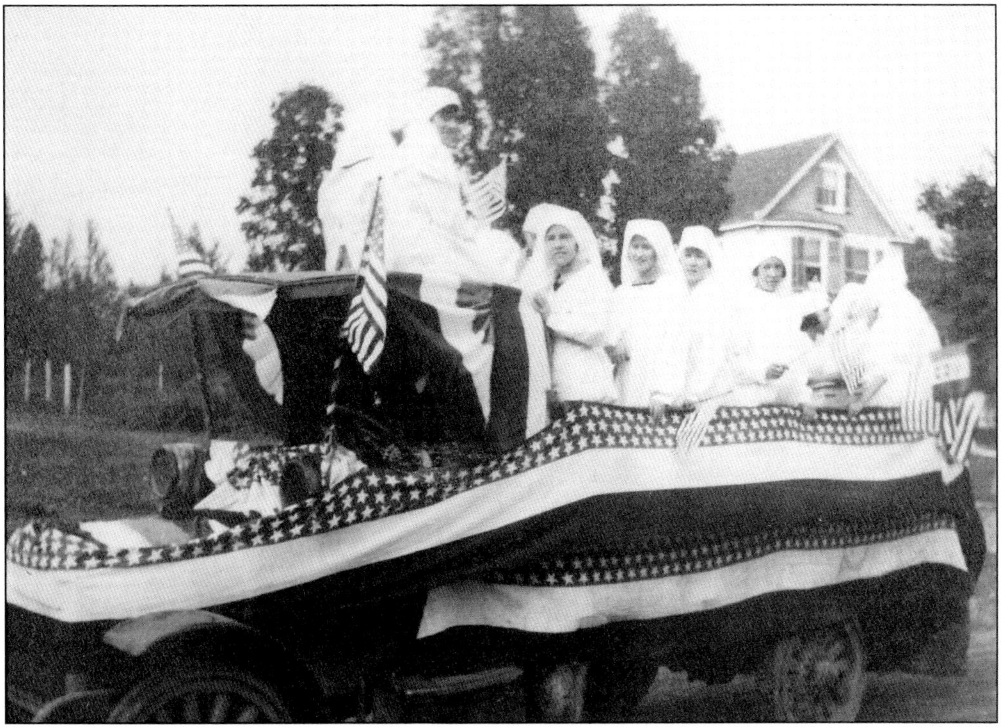

A World War I parade, with volunteers of the Red Cross from the town, headed by A. Swenson. The lady to the far left is Anna Kister. (Mary Harman Gehling.)

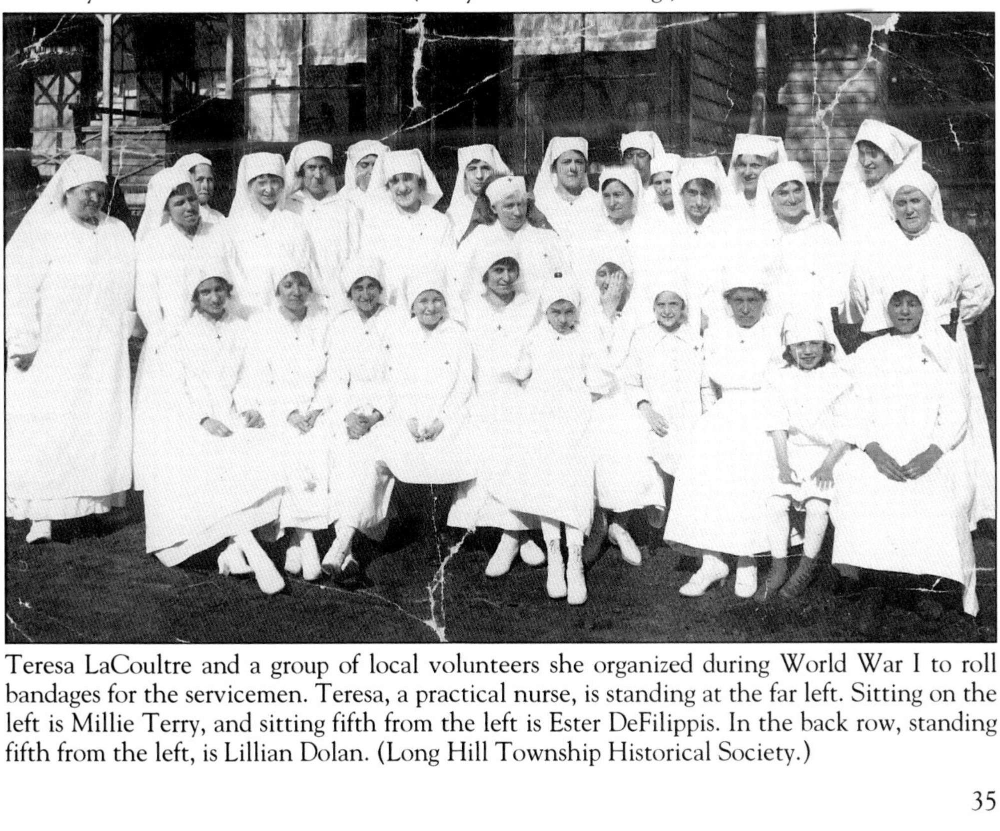

Teresa LaCoultre and a group of local volunteers she organized during World War I to roll bandages for the servicemen. Teresa, a practical nurse, is standing at the far left. Sitting on the left is Millie Terry, and sitting fifth from the left is Ester DeFilippis. In the back row, standing fifth from the left, is Lillian Dolan. (Long Hill Township Historical Society.)

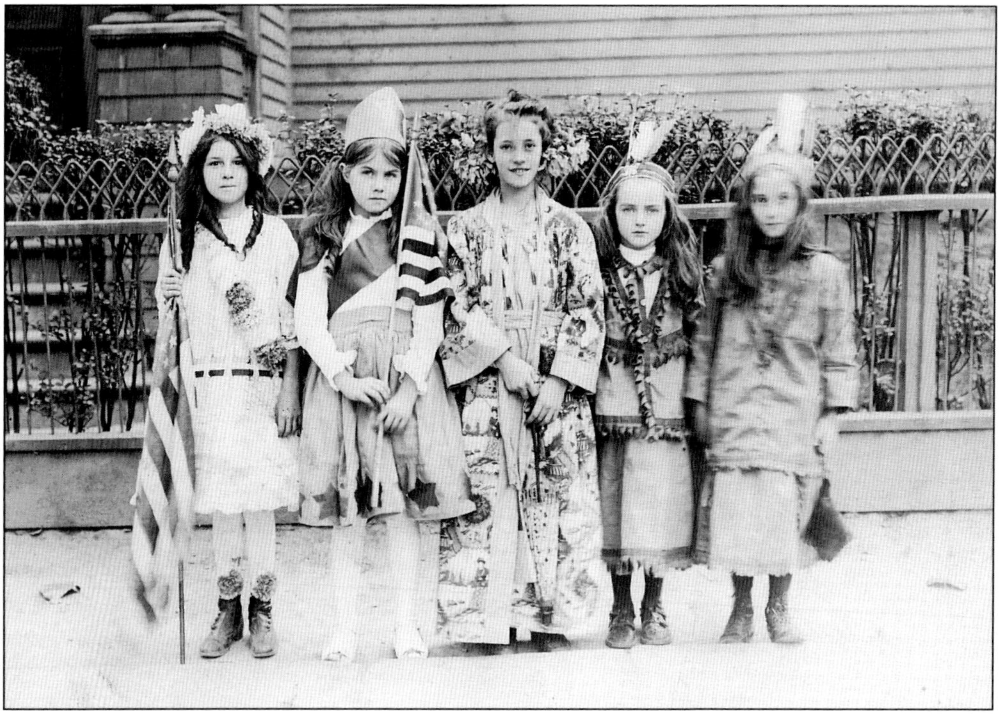

The Arata sisters in all their patriotic enthusiasm, representing the various cultures of America, possibly in an elementary school play. In this *c.* 1900 photograph are, from left to right, Lillie, Edna, Mamie, Florence, and Ida. (Adele Heinz Fellows.)

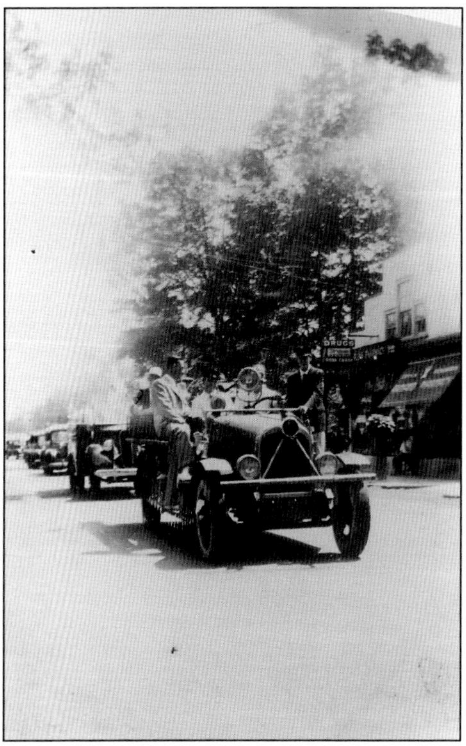

The Stirling Volunteer Fire Department, heading a *c.* 1940 parade in their 1925 Larabee firetruck. Seated are Frank Landwehr (left) and Albert Richter, with Ike Wilkesmann (at the wheel) and Bill Metzler (standing). Bill was a longtime resident and member of the department for fifty years. (Mary Lou Landwehr Weller.)

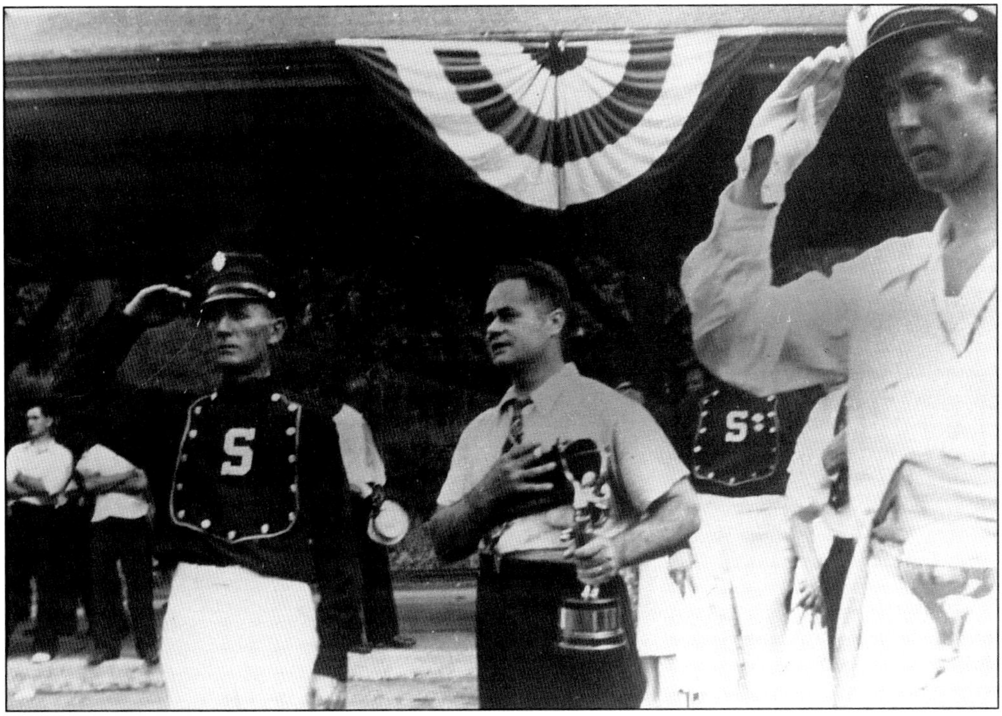

Holly Shand receiving a trophy after seven years of duty from the Exempt Firemen at a parade near Central School in 1929. (Jean DeFilippis Falzarano.)

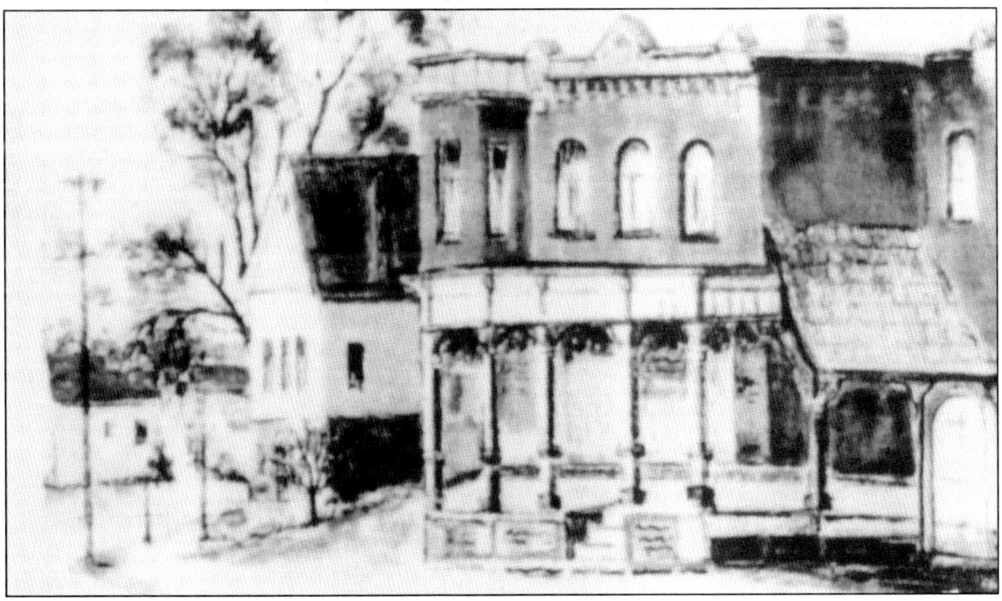

Dorsi's store, located on the corner of Elm Street and Central Avenue. This Stirling landmark served as a church for the Presbyterian congregation from 1872 to 1873, as well as a general meeting place for the town. After being discharged from the Air Force in World War II, Bob Dorsi bought the building to launch his business, and has since added a pharmacy. He and his wife, Stella, recently celebrated being both married and in business for fifty years. (Stella & Robert Dorsi.)

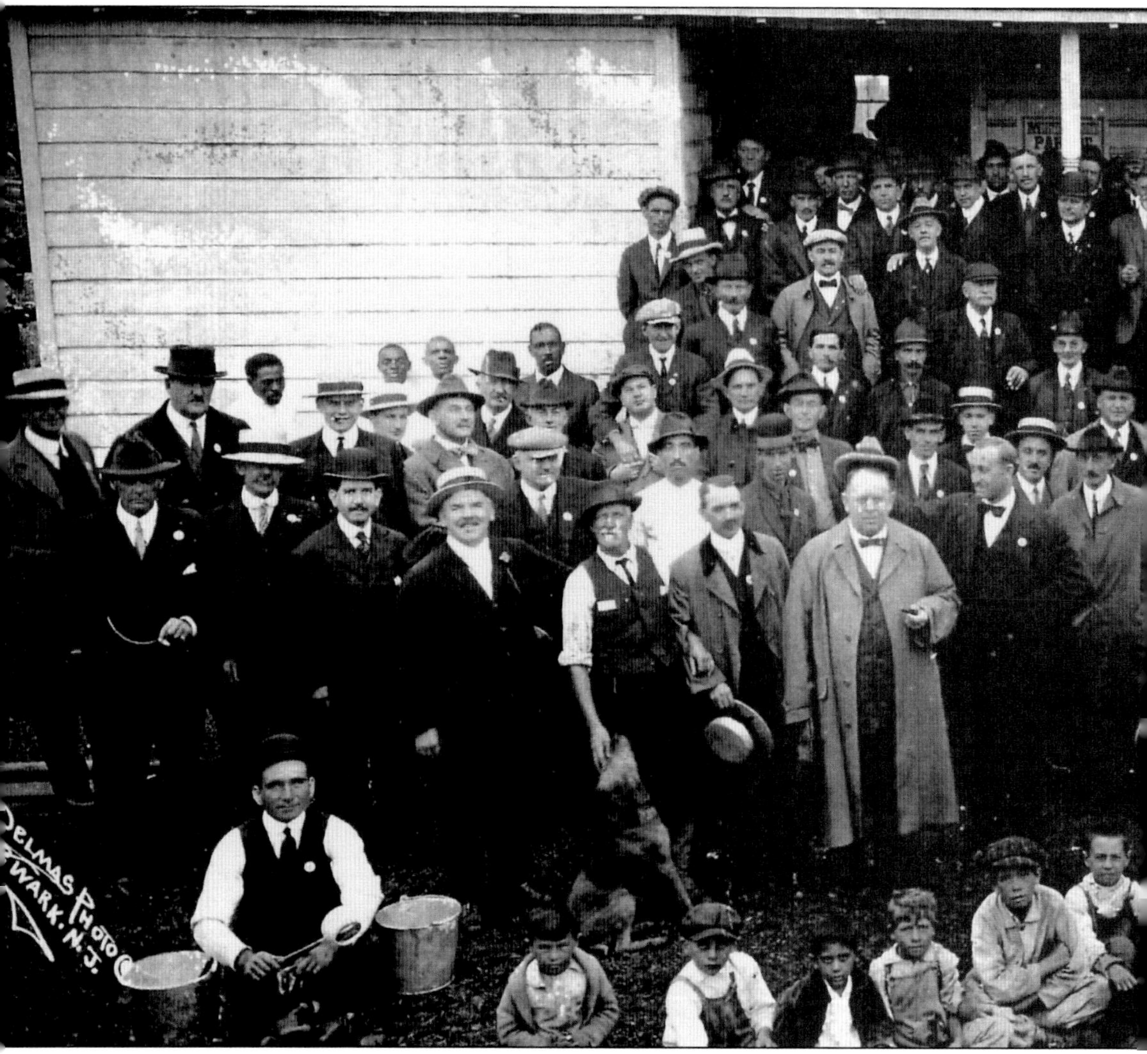

A clambake at the German Hall in Stirling, held by the Passaic Township Republican Executive

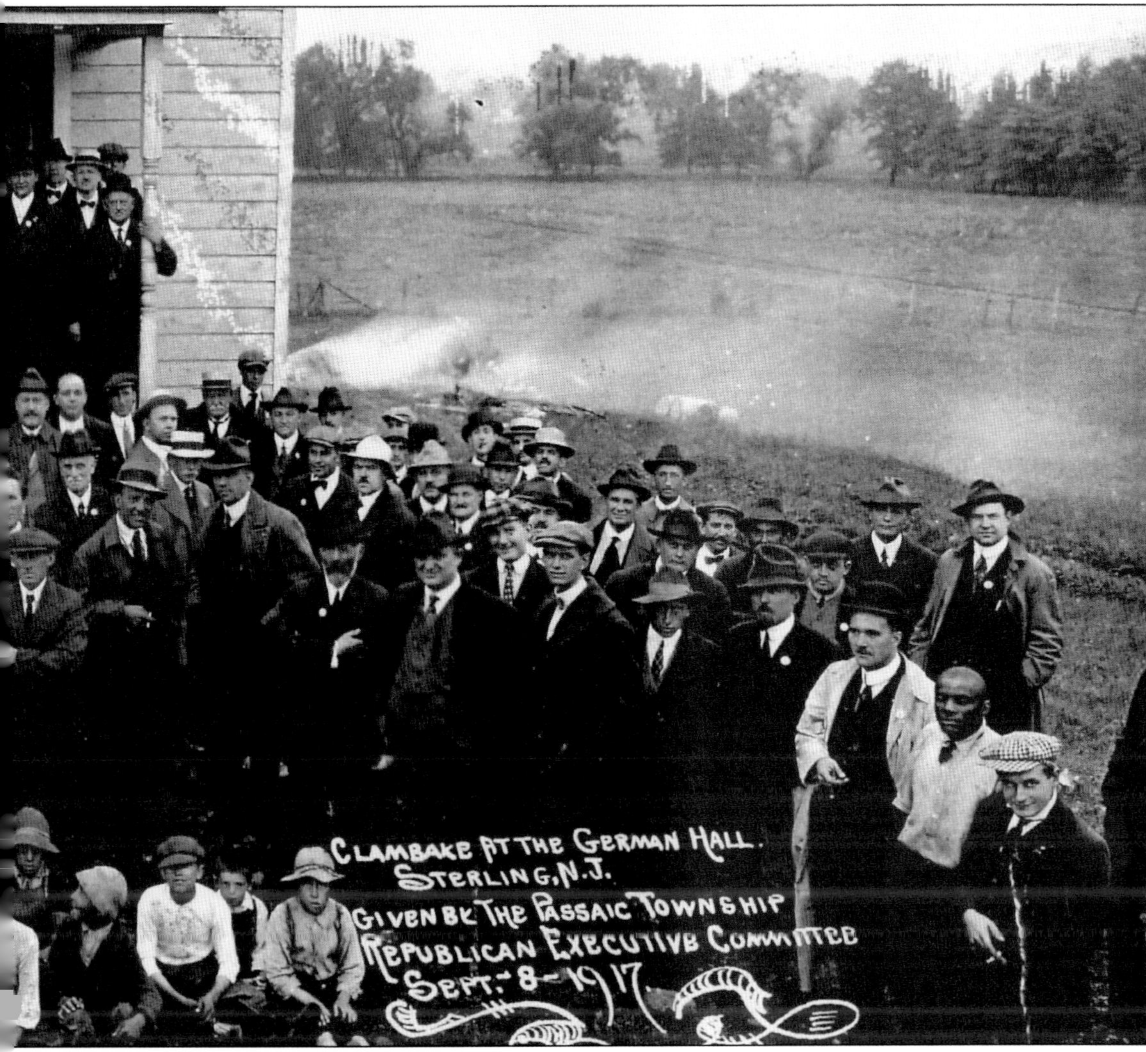

Committee, September 8, 1917. (Karg Fuel Oil Company, Inc.)

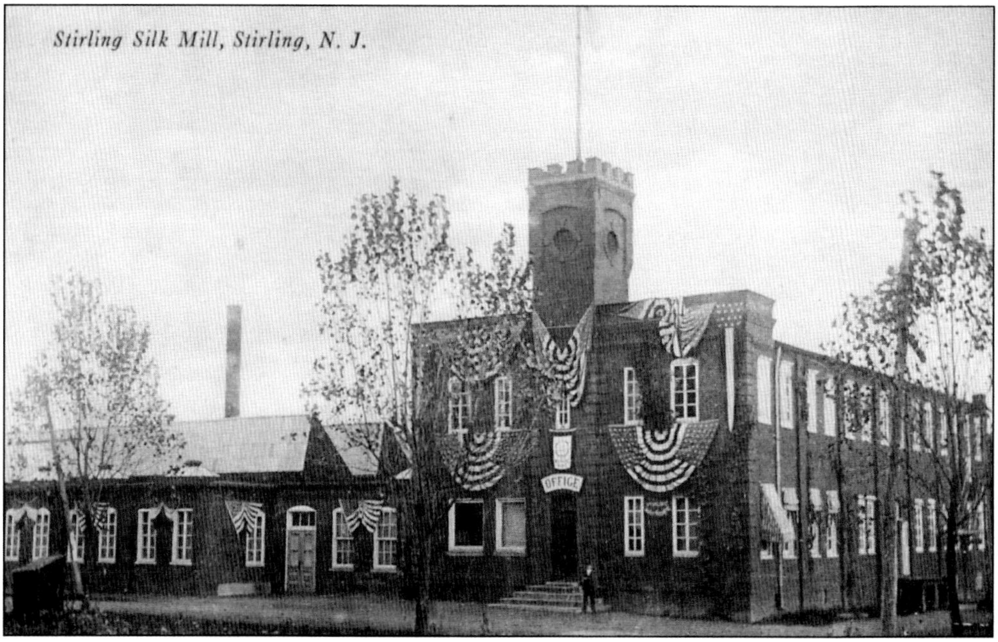

The silk mill. Located along the railroad, this was one of Stirling's largest industries at the turn of the century. Established by Charles Chaffanjon, it was first a button factory in 1878, and was later developed into the silk mill. The building burned in 1896 and a new one was built in its place. Lastly, it became a piston ring factory, which closed shortly after World War II. (Frank Cerulli.)

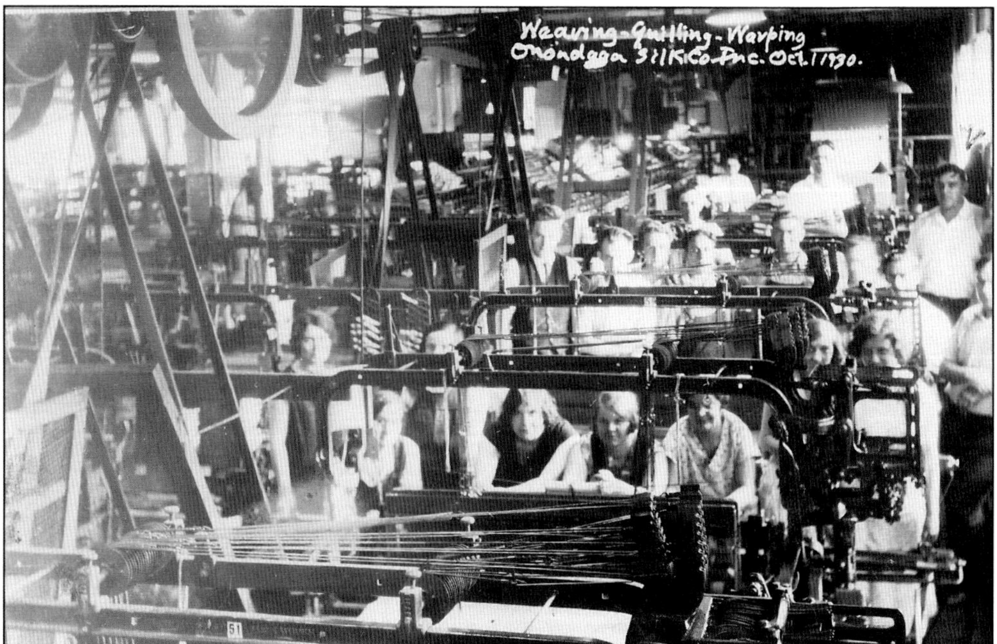

The interior of the silk mill, with the employees at work weaving, quilling, and warping. This is Lou Maresca's work group from October 1, 1930. Lou is standing in the back on the right. (Carolyn & Ralph Malfatone.)

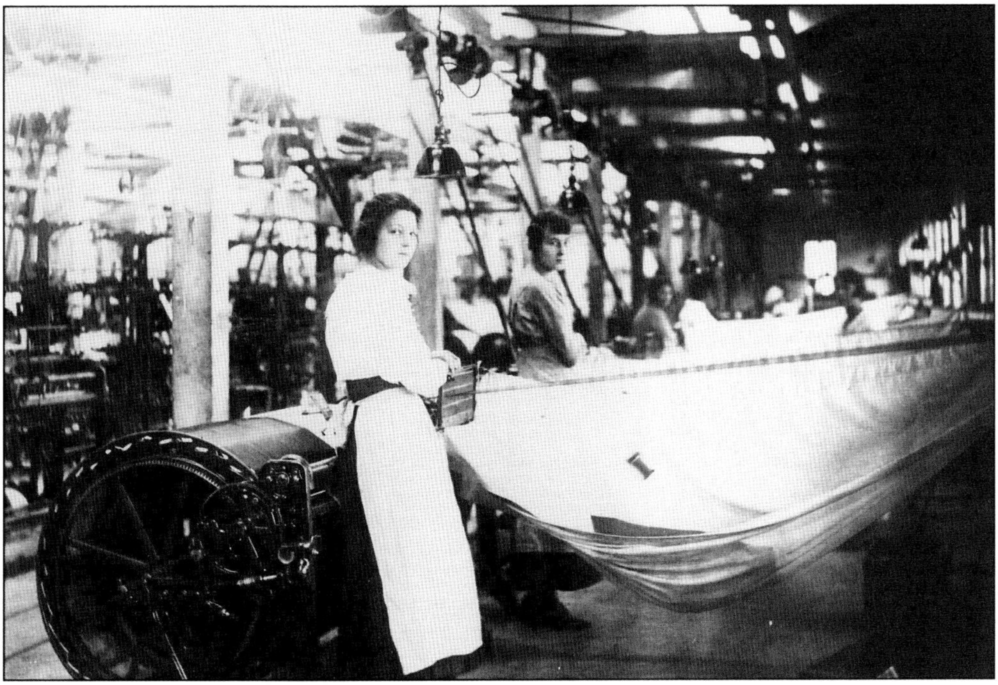

Mary Kocisko, in her long white apron inside the silk mill in Stirling, c. 1920s (Winifred Shimol.)

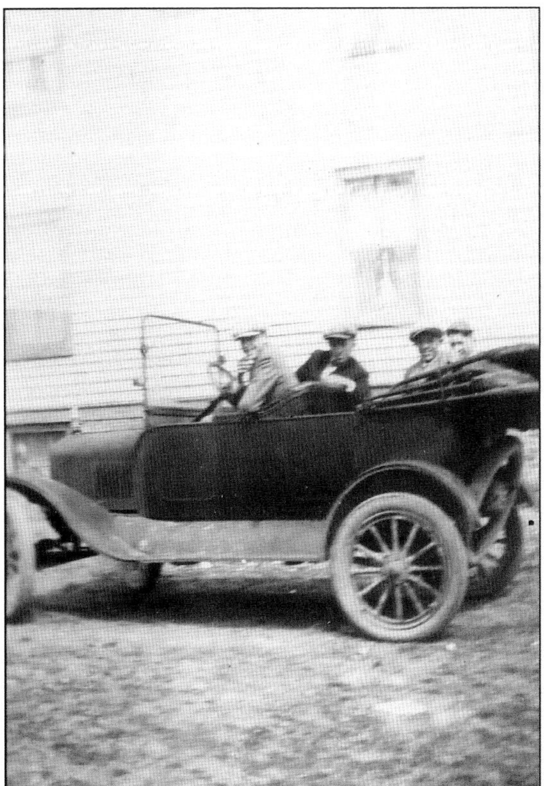

A *c.* 1930 photograph taken behind the silk mill of, from left to right, Steve Harman, Clement Falzarano, and Joseph Byelick. The 1920 Model T Ford was otherwise known as "The Junk." (Ann Manailovich.)

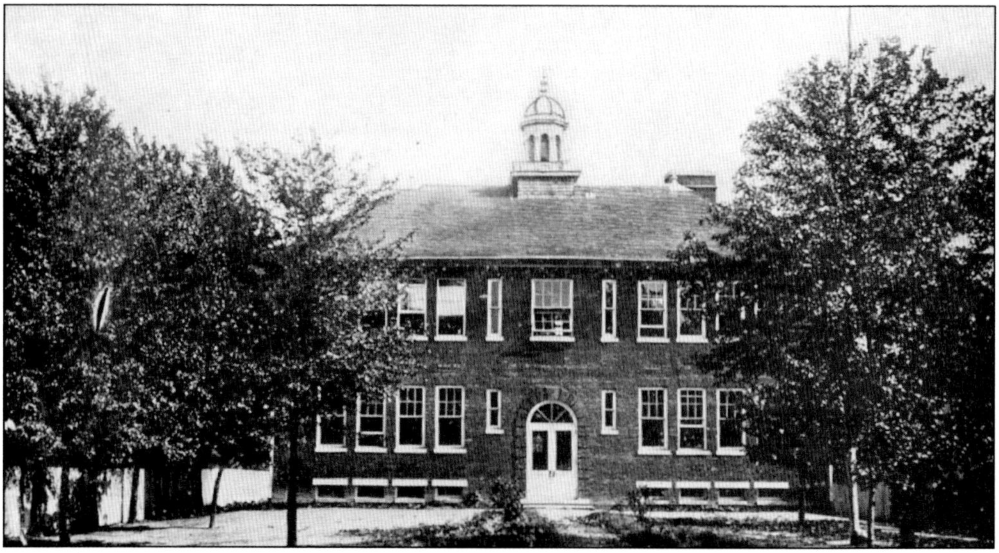

An early picture of the Elm Street School. This structure was built in 1908 as a four-room schoolhouse holding eight grades. Note the cupola on the roof, which no longer decorates the building. Many residents of the community who attended the school and still live in the area reflect upon their education here. (Mary Falzarano Thoms.)

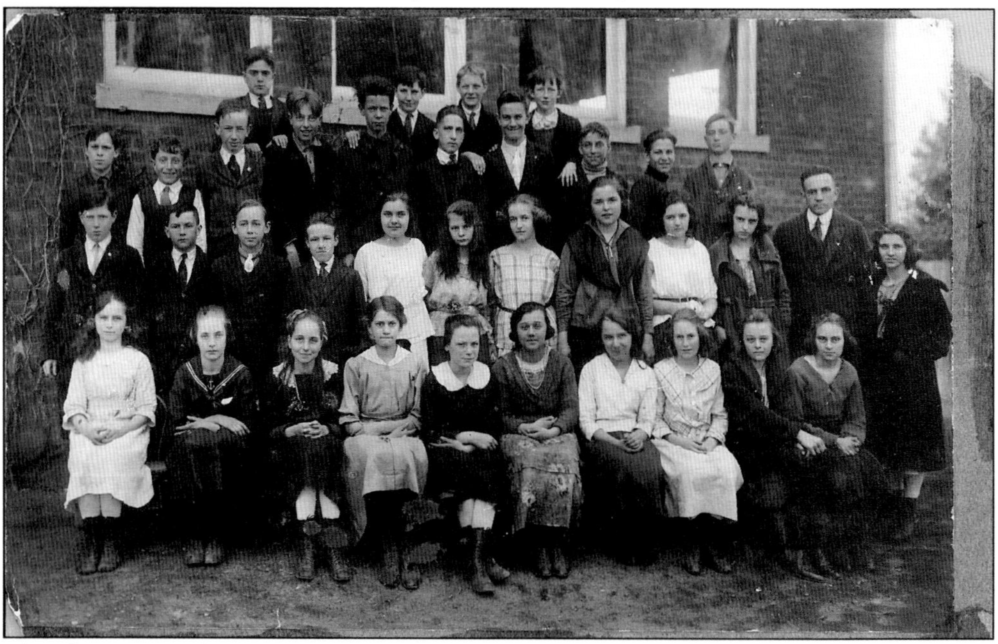

The Elm Street School Class of 1918. From left to right are as follows: (front row) Florence Estock, Catherine Duncan, Cullinan, Ethel Wilson, Rose Restivo, Truppi, Harman, Mary Bianco, Anna Horwith, and Margaret Horwith; (second row) George Osborn, Frank Landwehr, Wurmser, Michael Domanski, Lucy Gennaro, Mauser, Wurmser, Wolfe, Florence Arata, Emma Metzler, school principal Mr. Matteson, and Madeline Montrassio; (third row) Richard Barkalew, Nicholas Bianco, Harry Randall, Emil Yannuzzi, Jean Cornish, Louis Toll, Fred Schaan, Fred Lindenmeyer, Edward Ananson, and Harold Mosher; (back row) Armando Rossi, Alphonse O'Reilly, William Schuerman, and Edward Thievon. (Mary Lou Landwehr Weller.)

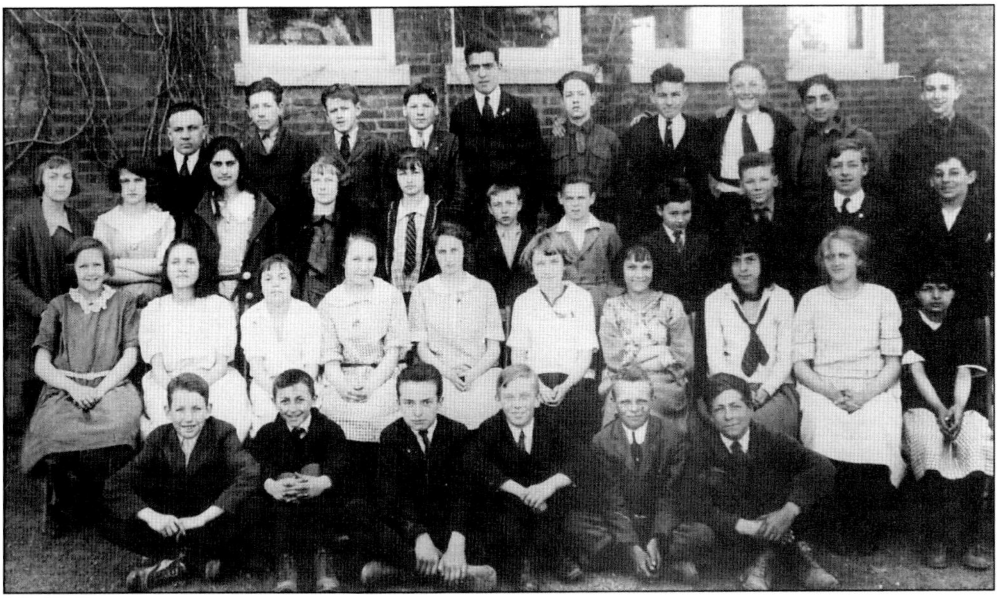

The Elm Street School Class of 1923. From left to right are as follows: (front row) Louis Thievon, Stephen Harman, William Metzler, Robert Ortman, William Oheley, and Alphonse Volpe; (second row) Katherine Cornish, Helen Cullinan, Mary Gennaro, Edna Besmer, Anna Havriluk, Betty Bebout, Helen Chrenko, Pearl Yannuzzi, Cecelia Denharty, and Mary Falzarano; (third row) Agnes Clarke, Helen Domanski, Allegra Falzarano, Agnes Rippert, Mary Byelick, William Corcoran, Eugene Miozzi, Earl Faulker, Kenneth Moffett, August Schmidt, and Donato Dorsi; (back row) principal and teacher Mr. Matteson, Anthony Volpe, Warren Missing, James McDonough, Walter Helreigel, Thomas Melee, Bernard McDonough, Paul Thievon, Joseph Bahoosian, and Harold Wolf. (Mary Falzarano Thoms.)

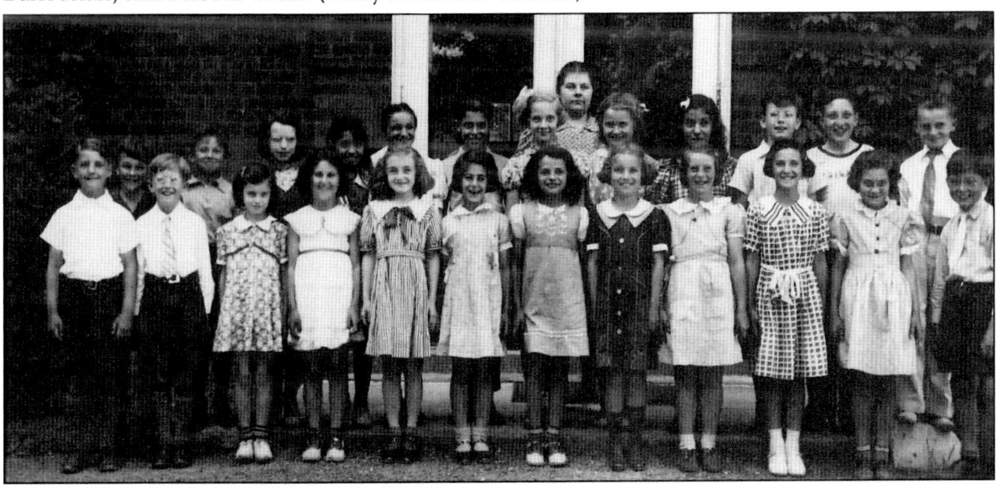

The Elm Street School Class of 1938. From left to right are as follows: (front row) Henry Rademacher, Merill Hedden, Anita Byelick, Betty San Giovanni, Mary Achille, Jean DeFilippis, Dorothy Groppi, Edith Kishpaugh, Gertrude Sherman, Millie Melise, Phyllis Bender, and Francis Cerulli; (back row) Donald Ralph, Steve Mihal, Florence Dougherty, Ramona Cortese, Clementine Malfatone, Angelo Ruggerio, Barbara Herrmann, teacher Katherine Allocco, Barbara Ann Gliesner, Luy Melise, Hugh Monteith, Charles Bianco, and Morgan Lucas. (Barbara Herrmann Corcoran.)

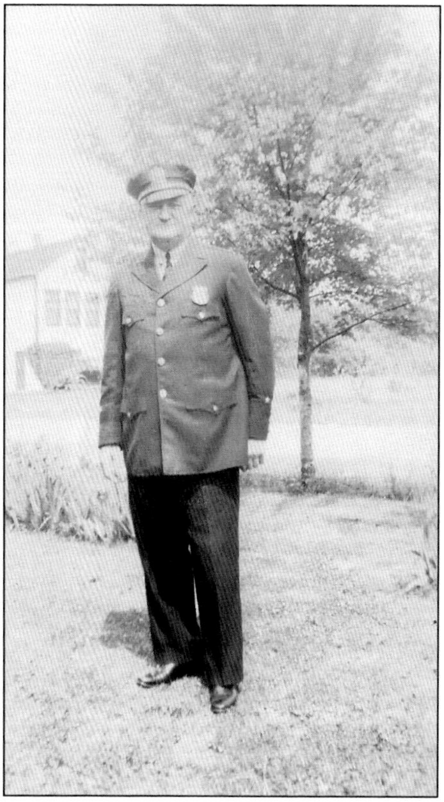

Thomas Rhein, one of the chiefs of police in Long Hill Township. The police department was organized in 1922. For a number of years Tom was "a one-man police department." Later on, special police were hired. Tom retired in 1951. (Patricia Rhein Cunningham.)

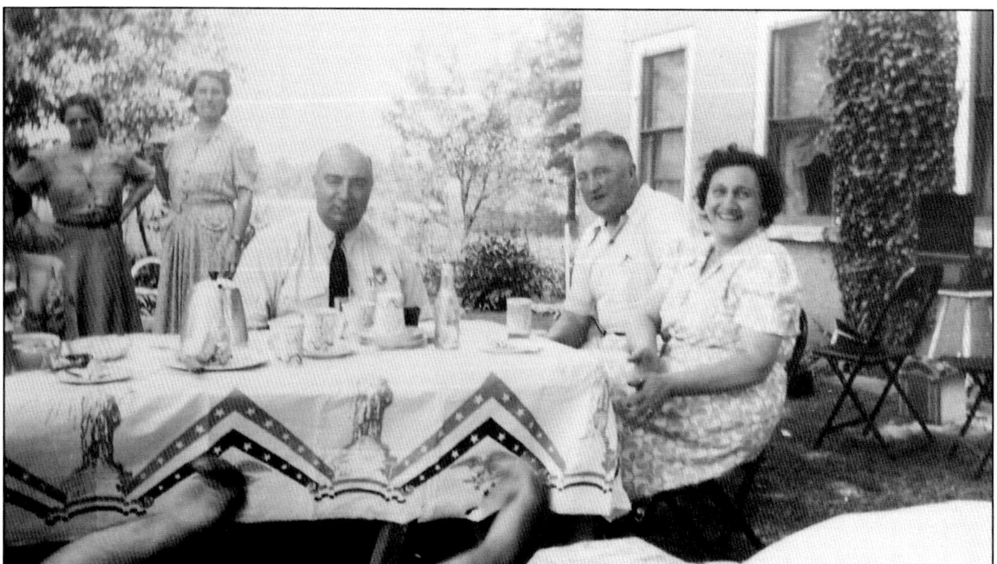

Berkeley Heights Chief of Police Dominick Russo, Long Hill Township Chief of Police Thomas Rhein, and Margaret Landwehr at a picnic on Laurel Avenue in Stirling, *c.* 1940. Picnics were held annually for police and their families on the Fourth of July. (Patricia Rhein Cunningham.)

John Dolan. John joined the Long Hill Township Police Department in 1948 as a special officer, and in 1951 he was appointed lieutenant in charge. In 1954 he started his term as chief of police, which lasted to 1966. Howard L. Runyon Sr. was chief from 1966 to 1986. Our present chief is Robert Falzarano. He has twenty-four full-time officers and four full-time dispatchers. (Eleanor Lamson Dolan.)

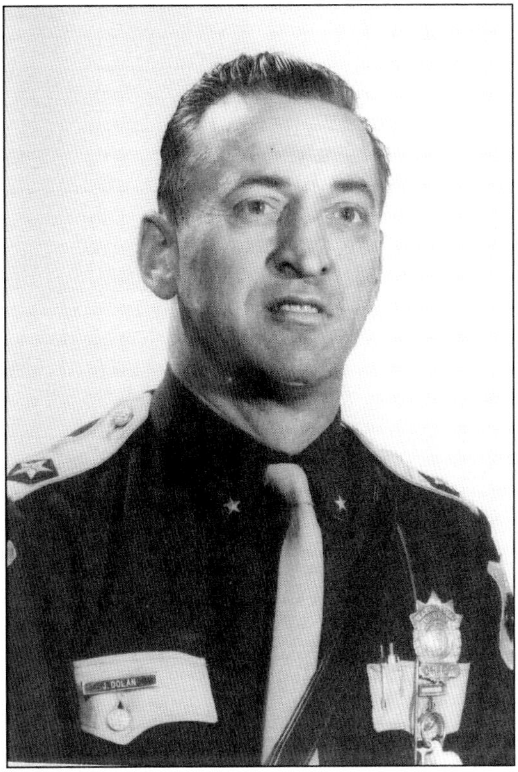

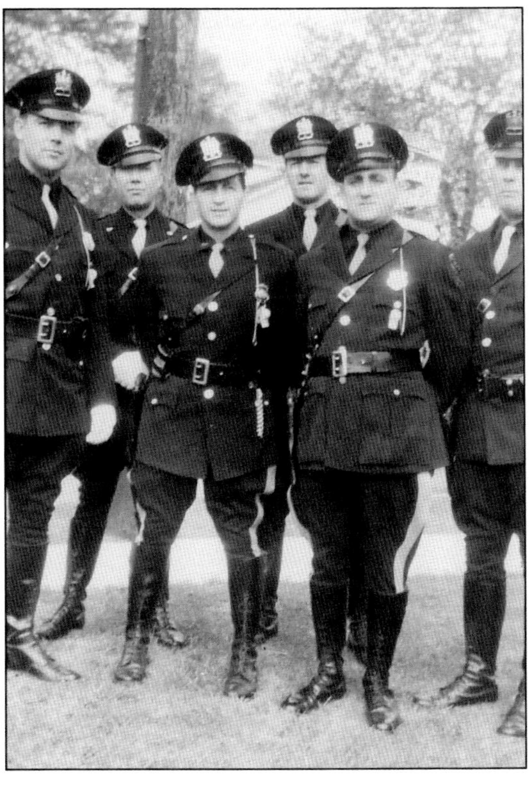

Our township's special officers. In this May 17, 1958 photograph are, from left to right, Raymond Compton, Robert Steward, Albert Landwehr, Charles Dropp, George Armenti, and Joseph Nowak. (Eleanor Lamson Dolan.)

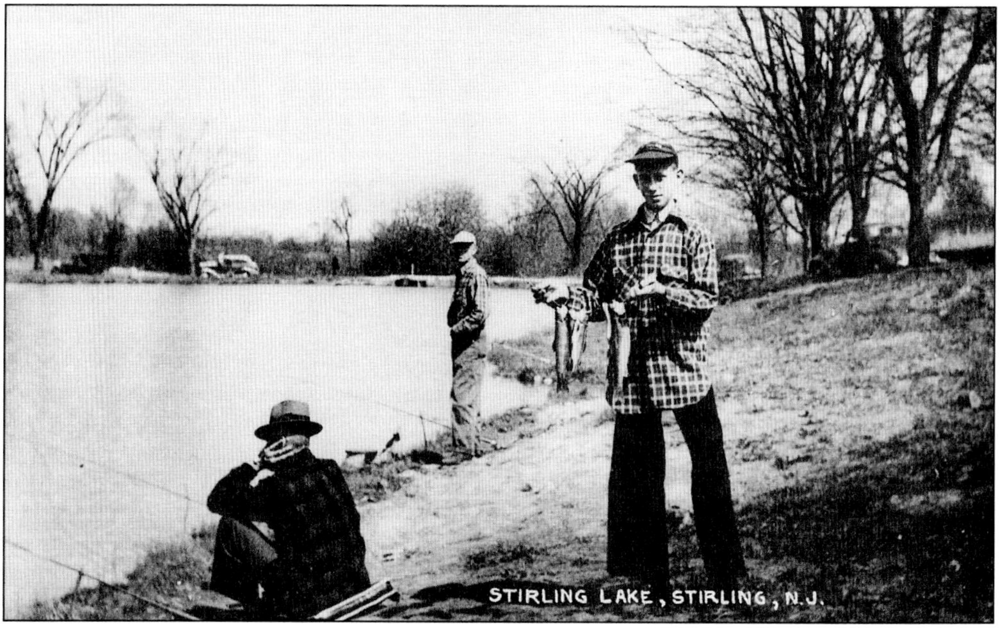

Stirling Lake, known as Springwater Lake at the turn of the century. This group of local fishermen are taking time out during the day to see what's biting. From left to right are Ernest Herrmann (seated with pole), Chris Lindenmeyer (standing by the water's edge), and John Dubets (holding a fresh catch). (Eleanor Murphy.)

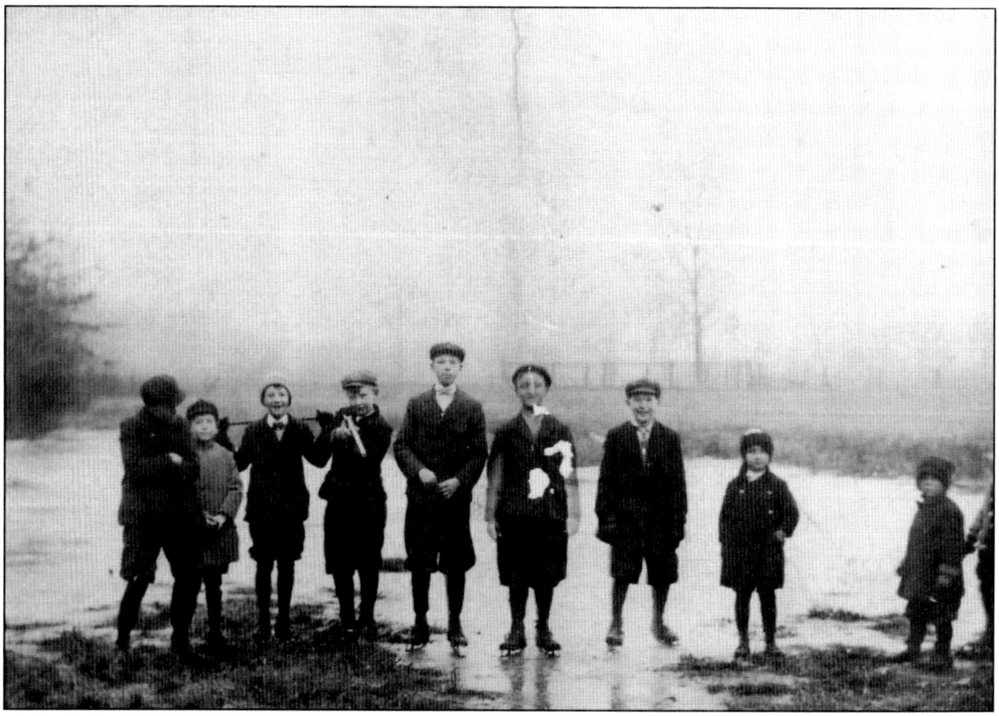

Playing hooky, perhaps? A spirited bunch of young skaters expressing the timeless, wide-eyed innocence that is universal in all children, on a winter's day on Stirling Lake, c. 1917. The tallest boy is Ike Wilkesmann. (Ann Wilkesmann Barta.)

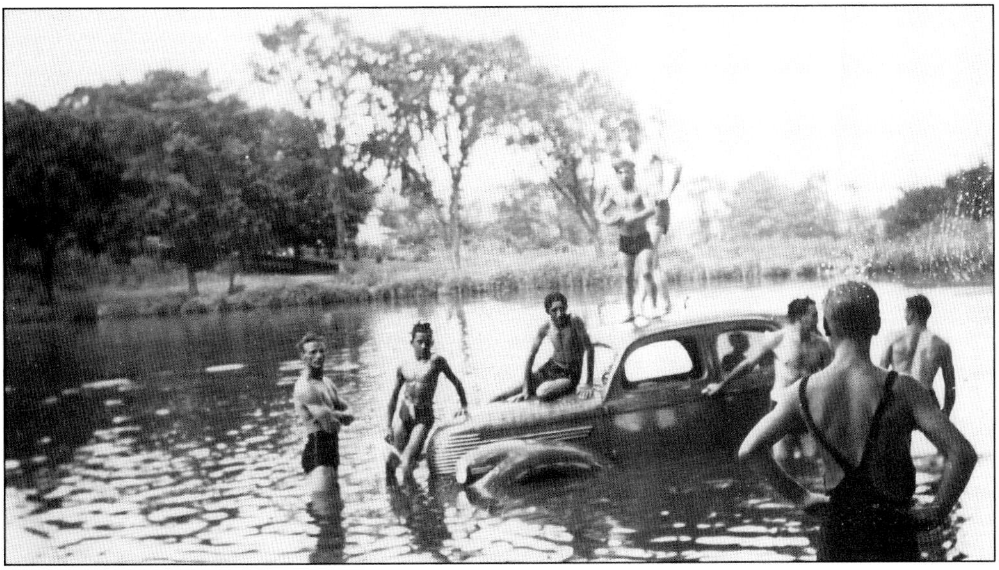

What excitement! These young boys have discovered a 1935 Willys bobbing in Stirling Lake. Notice the back of the bathing suit of the boy nearest the foreground. Jessie Domanski is at the far left. (Ralph Malfatone.)

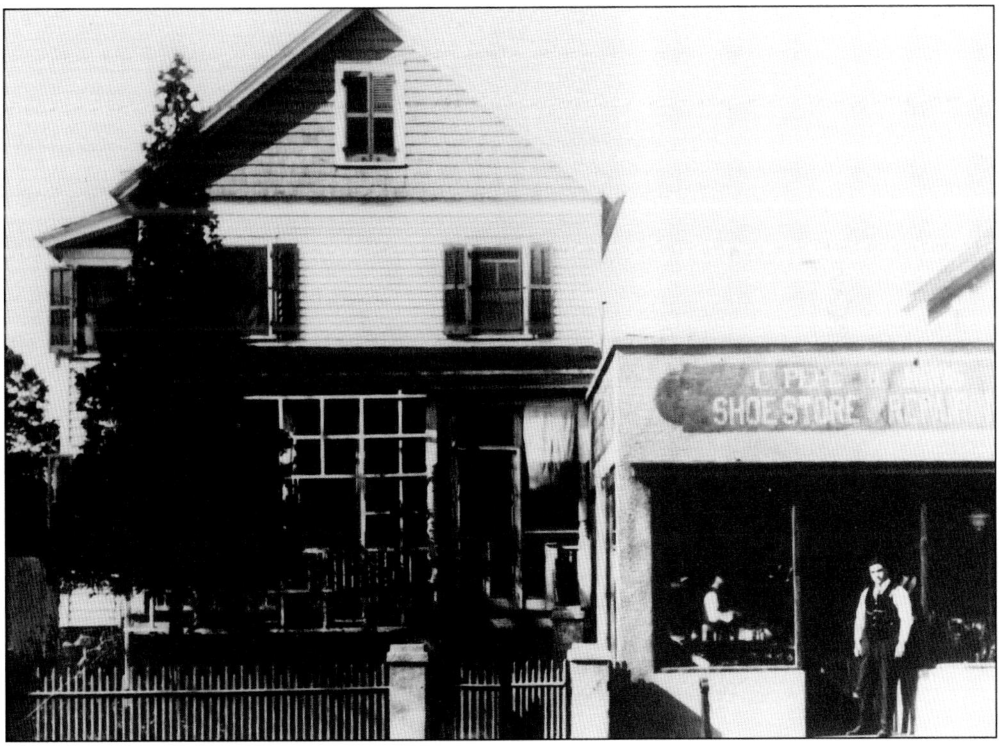

The shoe store of Carmine Pepe and brothers, the finest shoe repair business in town in the 1920s. Grandfather Pepe is pictured outside his shop. Two stores have since been built in front, covering what was once the store. The Pepe family continues their original craft of repairing shoes in Bernardsville. (Vincent Pepe.)

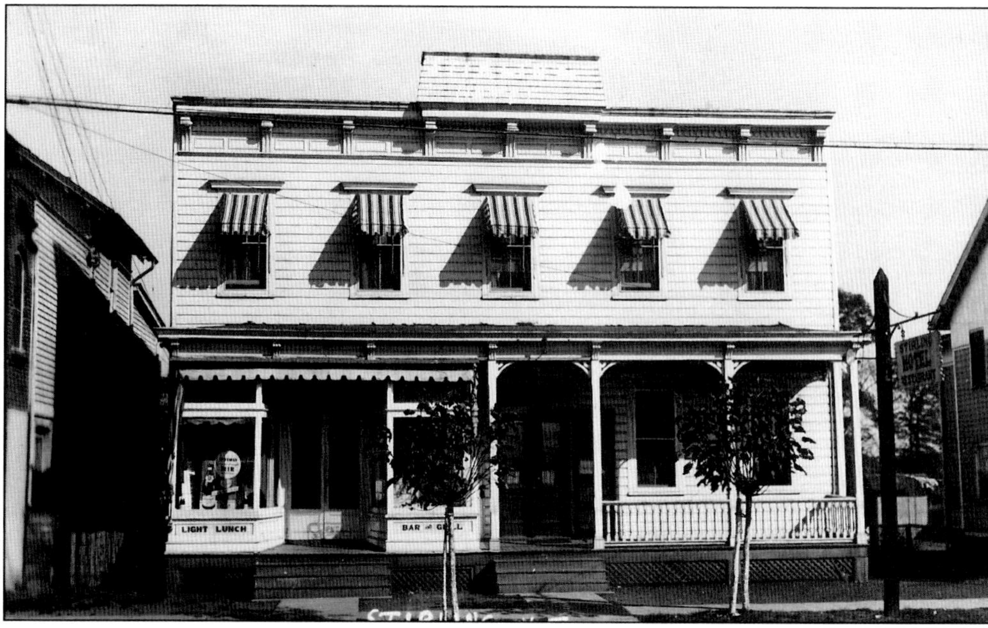

The Stirling Hotel on Main Street, *c.* 1930. This hotel, built in the early 1900s, has always been a landmark and a widely known eatery in Long Hill Township. Victor Sarrailh owned it early on, and Dave Achille and family purchased it in the 1940s. Homemade turtle soup, clams on the half shell, and frog legs were the specialty items on the menu. (Jennie & Louis Delli Paoli.)

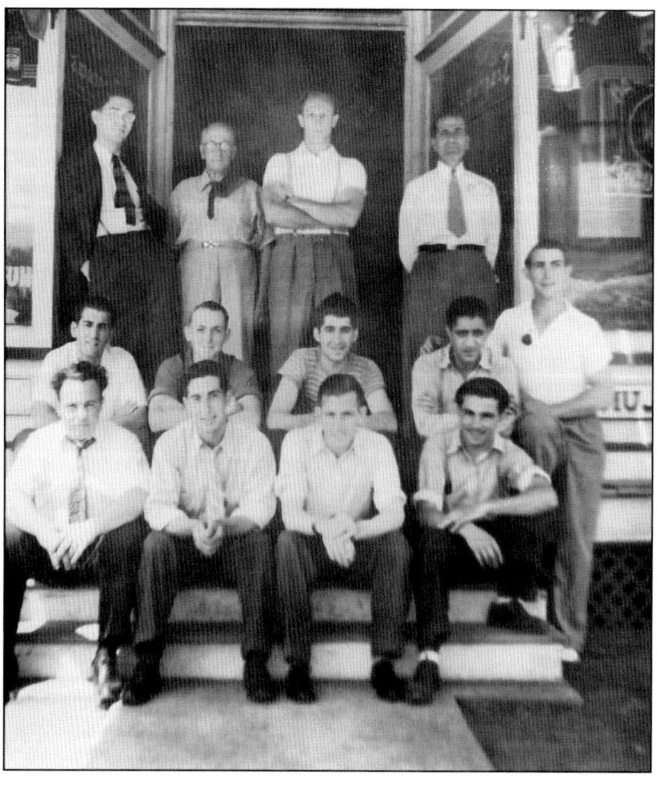

Sitting on the steps of the Stirling Hotel. When the American Legion parade, an annual affair, was in full swing, many residents would use the steps of the Stirling Hotel as a front row seat. In this *c.* 1938 photograph are, from left to right, as follows: (front row) Dan Cerulli, Mario Dorsi, Louis Thievon, and Frank Cerulli; (middle row) Pat Di Giammatteo, Leonard Clark, Louis Esoldi, John Bahooshian, and Vincent Clark; (back row) Dr. Alpert, Victor Sarrailh, Nick Manailovich, and Dick Ananson. (Frank Cerulli.)

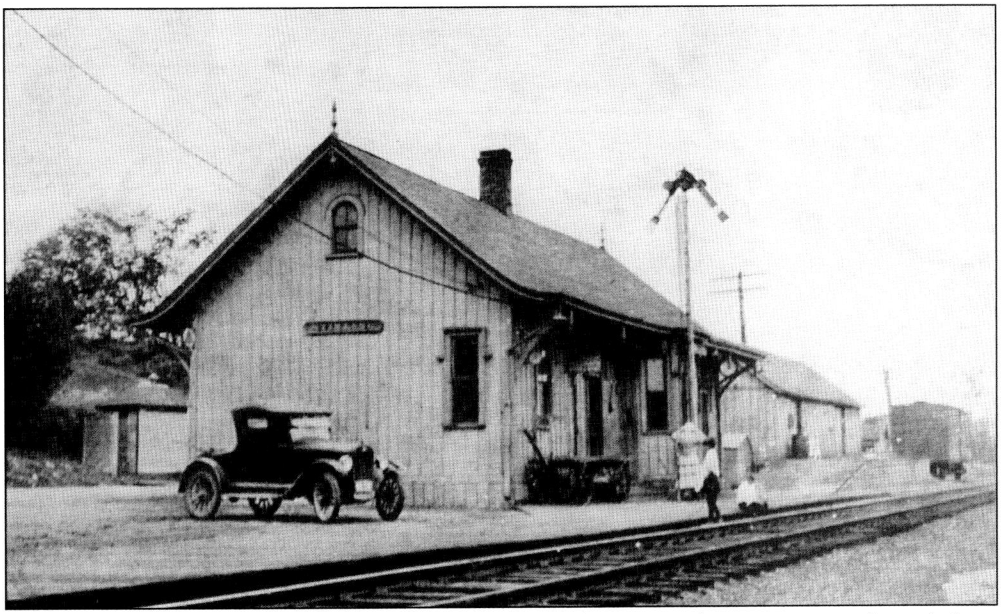

The Stirling Train Station in the 1920s. At that time the Erie Lackawanna came through from Summit to Bernardsville. Note the Chevrolet Roadster. The ticket agent for the station was Eddie Osborne, who was also the town tax collector. (Frank Cerulli.)

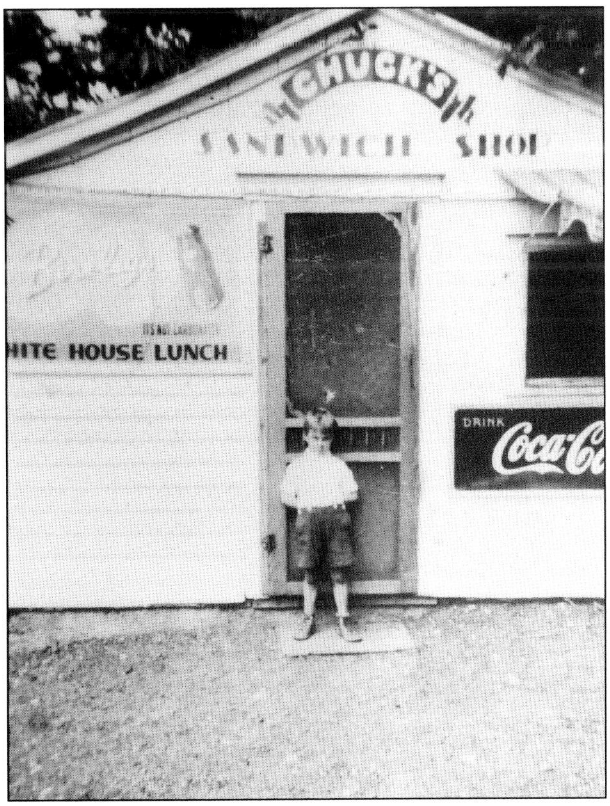

Chuck's Diner, *c.* 1942. The diner was owned by Chuck Wall Sr., and was located across the street from the Stirling Hotel, on Railroad Avenue. It was one of the first diners in town, and was open twenty-four hours a day, in order to serve the workers from the silk mill. (Jo Ann Wall.)

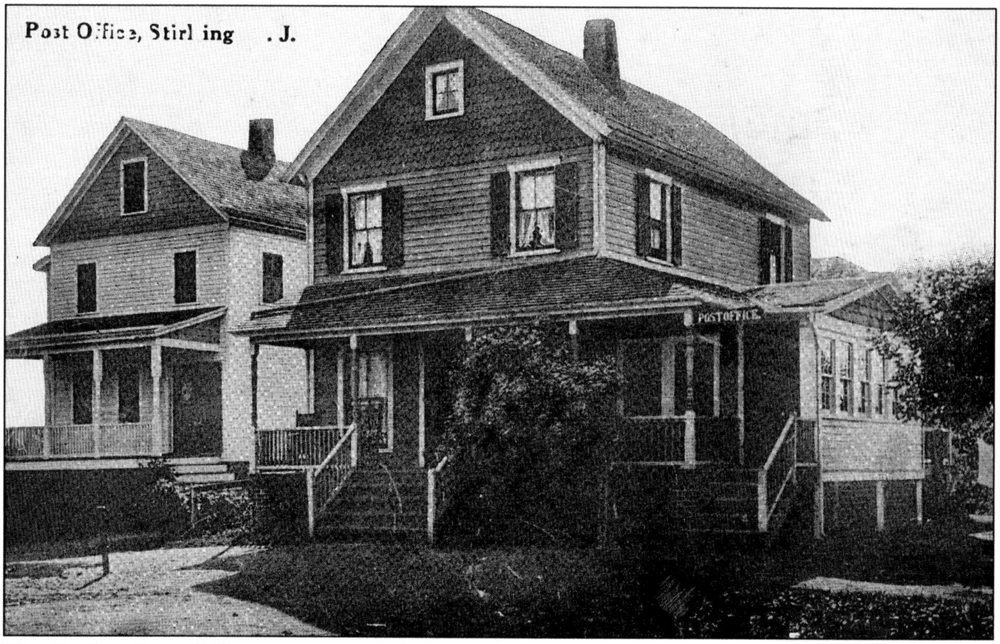

The Stirling Post Office in 1919. At this time the post office was in a portion of the Monteith family home. Later the Metzler family bought the house and lived there fifty years. Bill Metzler was an active resident of Stirling, and a devoted member of the fire department. (Carol Metzler.)

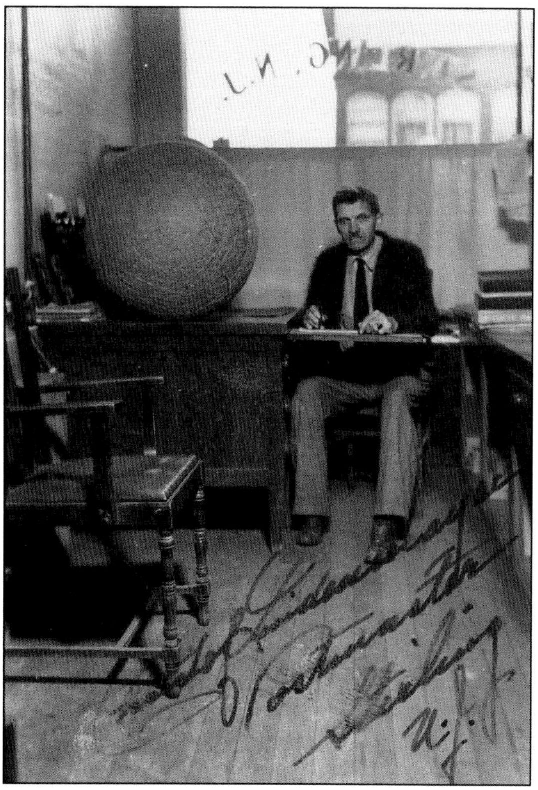

Postmaster Christof Lindenmeyer working behind his desk. The post office was located across the street from the Stirling Hotel. "Fury" Romeo and "Chamber" Vincent Rossi were employed at the post office as well. Note the large ball of string, a conversation piece at that time. (Ralph Malfatone.)

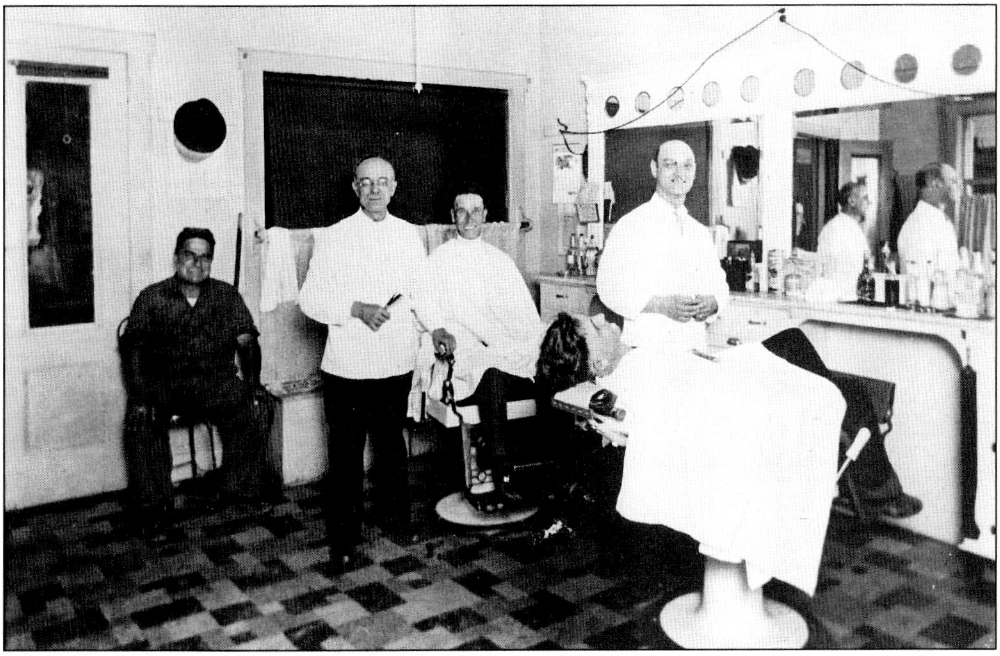

A c. 1935 photograph of the well-known barber shop on Main Street owned and run by Pete and Emido Truppi. Seated is Joseph Rossi. I am told trims and cuts at that time were 35¢. The family lived in the building and continued the business up until the 1990s. (Jennie & Louis Delli Paoli.)

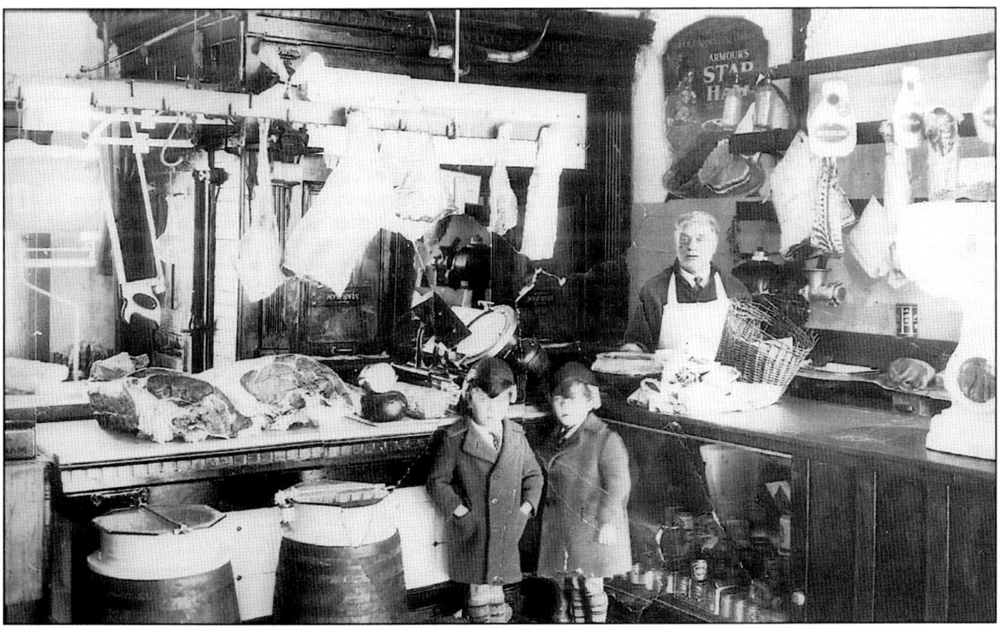

Shand's Butcher Shop on Main Street in the early 1900s. Owner James Valentine Shand is pictured with his twin grandchildren, Roy (left) and William. James made his own sausage and had three meat trucks which would deliver his homemade products to the extent of Far Hills. After he retired, the shop became the office of Dr. Palakoff, M.D., Dr. Alpert, D.D.S., and Dr. Abraham Baumann. (Paula Shand Ross.)

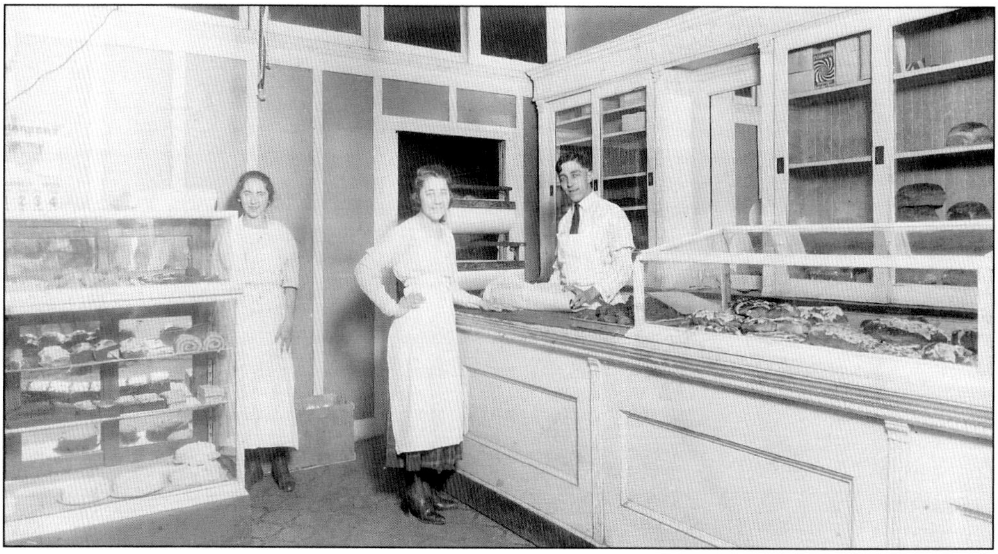

Hedden's Bakery, founded and located on Central Avenue, between Dorsi's store and the silk mill. The proud owners were Alfred S. Hedden and Annie Hedden. Their entire family—son Alfred and wife Florence, son Patrick and wife Viola, and daughter Betty—contributed in helping with production. They had two delivery trucks that would cover all the surrounding areas. Their Washington House Cakes, which sold for a penny a piece, are still talked about by residents. The bakery closed in the early 1930s. Betty Hedden went on to teach in our school system for many years. (Barbara & Robert Hedden.)

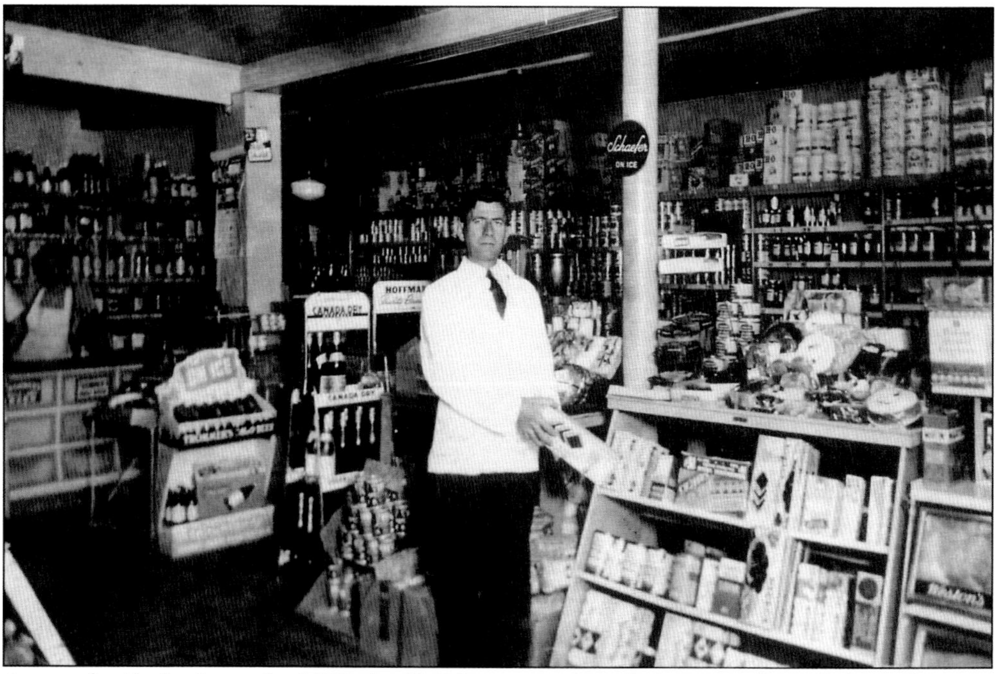

A true family business. In 1923 the DeFilippis purchased the store from Robert Ortman. They had six children, who would all share in working there from time to time. The store flourished for many decades. Most of the family have remained in the township. (Jean DeFilippis Falzarano.)

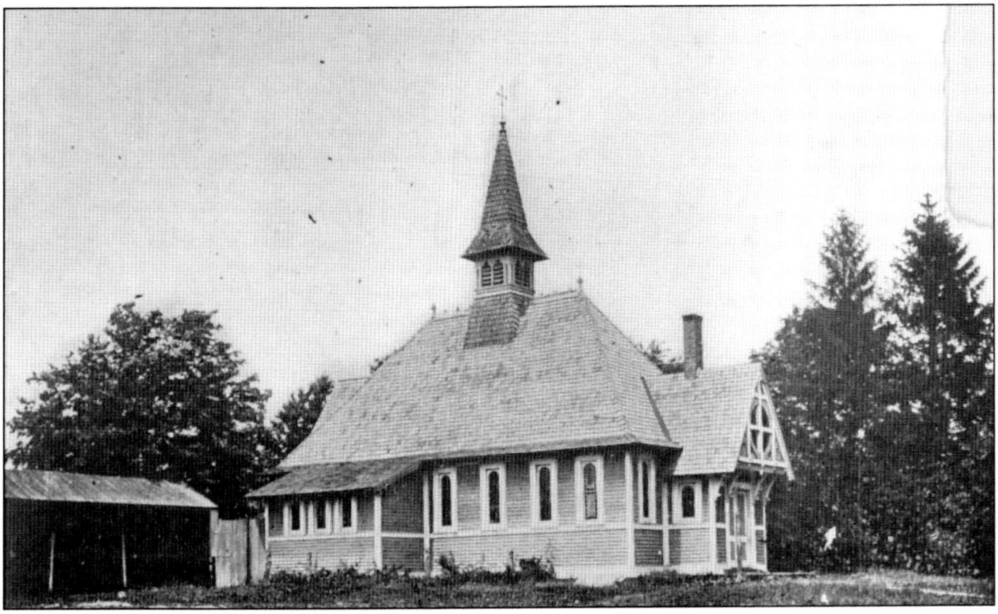

The Stirling Presbyterian Church. This church started with a handful of dedicated members who met in Dorsi's store on the corner of Elm and Central Avenue. In 1872, the cornerstone was laid on the northwest corner of an acre of ground on Central Avenue and Chestnut Street. Through the years the church grew, and in July 1974 the chapel was completed and dedicated. (Carol Metzler.)

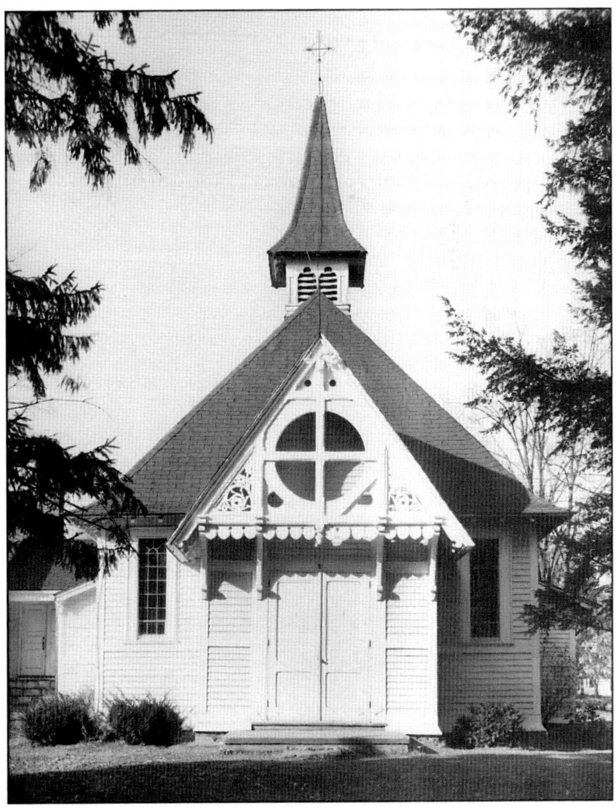

The Presbyterian church. The history of this church centers around the original building discussed in the previous picture. The minister's house was built in the late 1930s. After numerous ministers presided throughout the years, the 1950s and '60s saw growth, and the shape of the church changed and expanded. (Stirling Presbyterian Church.)

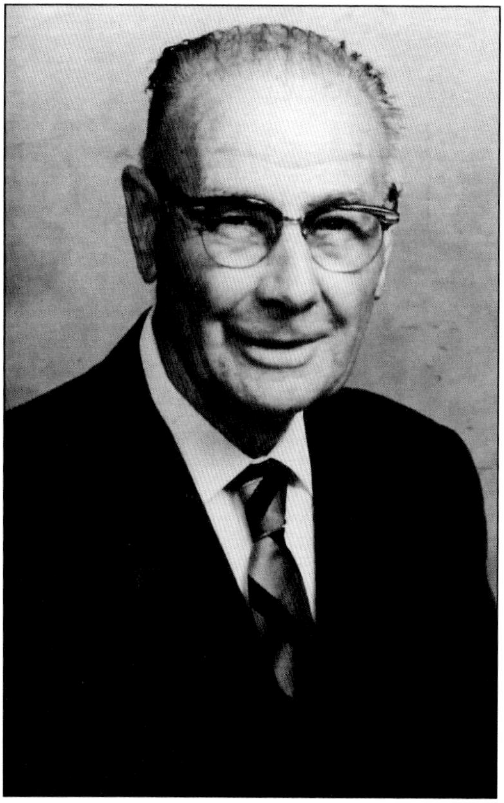

Albert H. Richter (1889–1985). Mr. Richter was a lifelong resident of 334 Main Street, Stirling, along with his wife, Louise, and their five children. He had his own painting and decorating business, was the first president of the Stirling Volunteer Fire Company #1, and was the oldest member and elder of the Stirling Presbyterian Church. (Josephine and Robert Richter.)

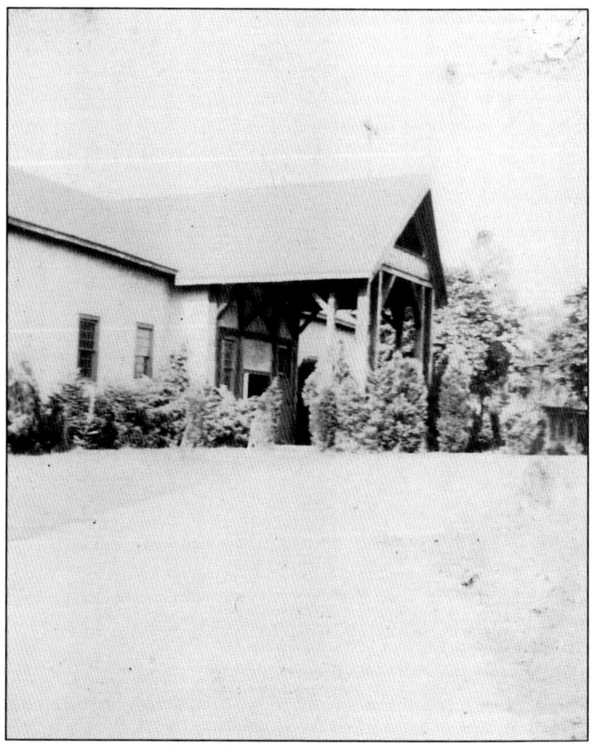

The St. Joseph Shrine. The site of the original chapel on Long Hill Road was predominantly farmland and barns into the early 1800s. After 150 years, it succumbed to weather and rot. The new building is a mecca for modern-day pilgrims to find inspiration, retreat, and a breathtaking site. Mass is held daily for the public. (Sister Genevieve Hartmann M.S.B.T.)

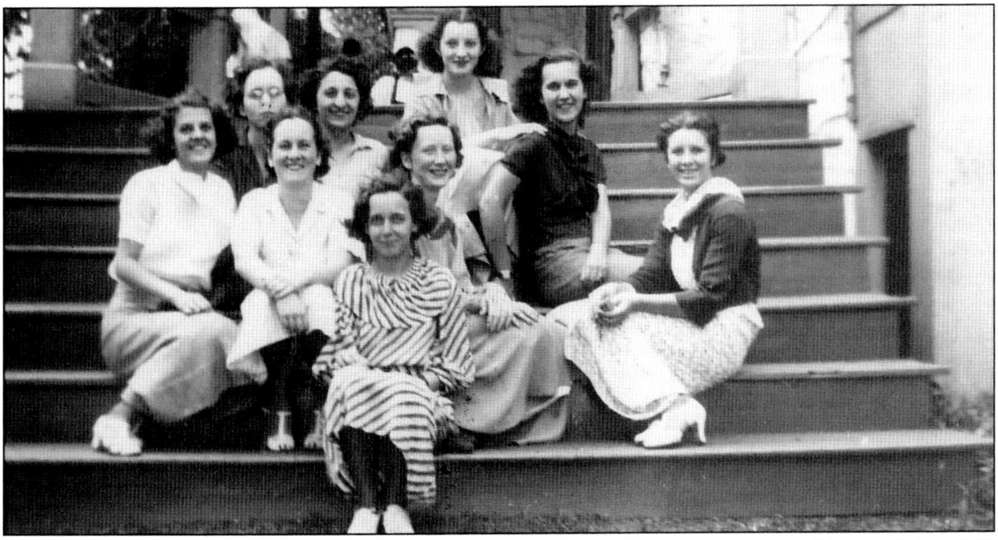

Posing on the steps of the Blessed Trinity Missionary Cenacle on 1190 Long Hill Road. In 1935 a group of young women, who would become future nuns and mission sisters, met here for a retreat. At the turn of the century the building was the estate of Herbert Torry, a geologist and metallurgist. It was later called the Middle House because it is between the St. Joseph Shrine and the Trinity Ministries Center on Long Hill. The center, known as Sentinel Elms, was once the home of Cornelius Ludlow, a colonel in the Morris County Militia. (Sister Genevieve Hartmann M.S.B.T.)

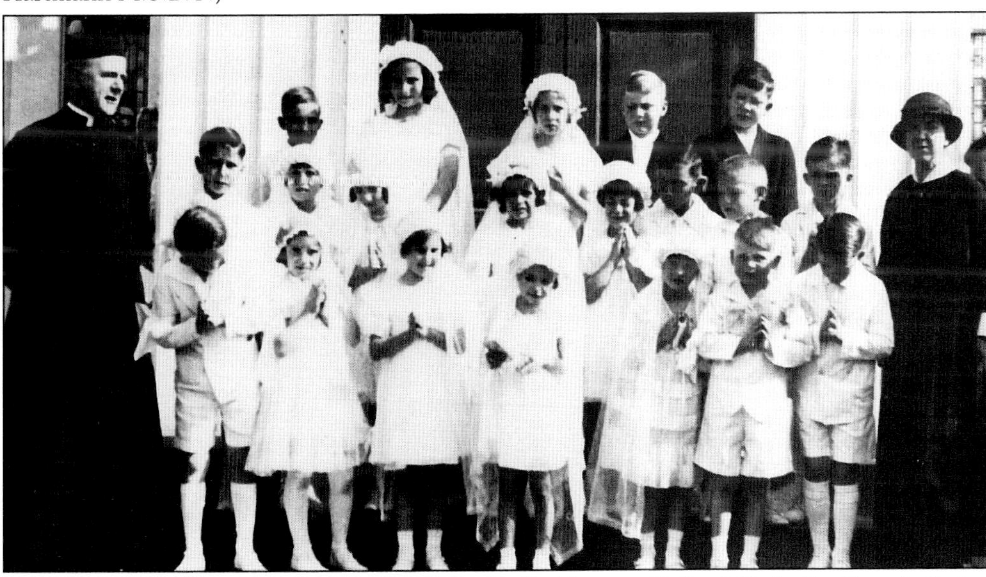

The First Holy Communion Class of 1938 at the St. Vincent DePaul Catholic Church. Father Doogen and Sister Agnes Claire are shown with this group of young students. From left to right are as follows: (front row) Henry Rademacher, Merill Head, Annita Byelick Chiappa, Betty San Giovanni, Mary Achille Russo, unknown, Dorothy Groppi Vincent, Edith Kishpaugh, Gertrude Schuman, Millie Melise Felice, Phyllis Bender, and Frank Cerulli; (back row) Donald Ralph, Steve Mihal, Florence Dougherty, Romma Cortese, Tina Malfatone, Angelo Ruggerio, Barbara Gliesner, Lucy Melise, Hugh Montieth, Charles Bianco, and Morgan Lucas. (Jean DeFilippis Falzarano.)

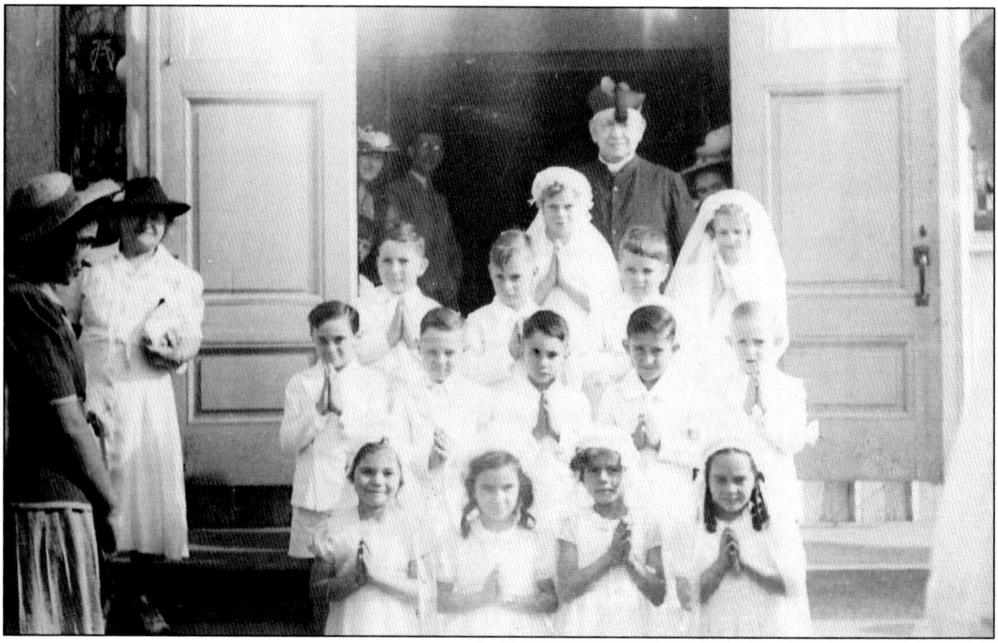

First Holy Communion, c. 1942, at the St. Vincent DePaul Catholic Church. From left to right are as follows: (front row) Joan Suiter, Roseanne LaGuardia, Ann Thoms, and M.L. Landwehr; (middle row) Ralph Malfatone, Angelo Ruggerio, Victor Quinto, Ernest Piano, and Robert Hedden; (back row) Sam Maglione, unknown, and Charles Wall. (Mary Lou Landwehr Weller.)

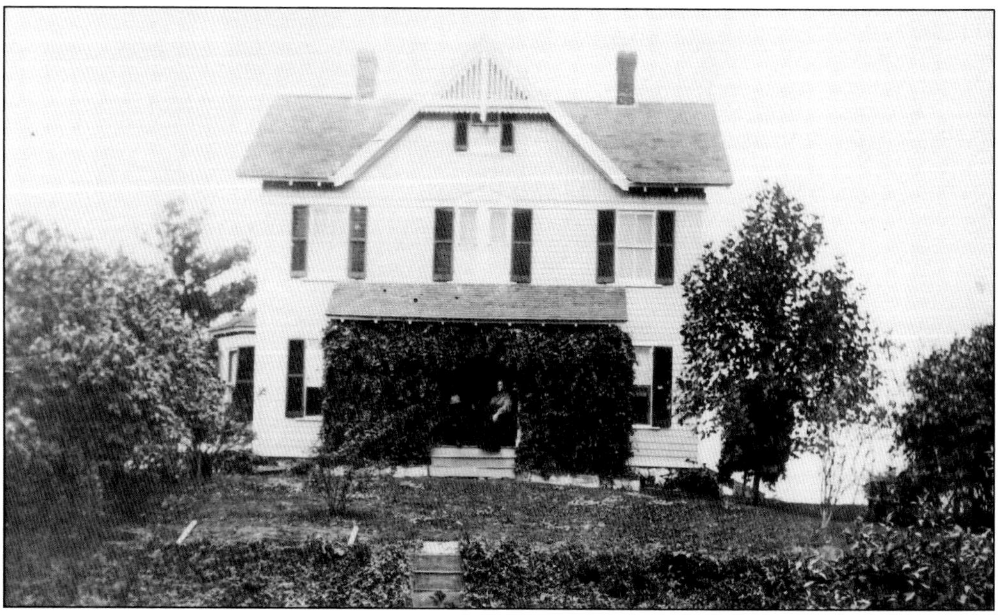

The Herrmann homestead at the turn of the century, on the north side of Valley Road in Stirling. Barbara Herrmann's grandfather owned the 7-acre farm for many years. Later, in 1926, the Groppi family bought it. They opened a restaurant called the Picccadilly, which offered home-cooked food, and also had a dance hall and bocci court for entertainment on the grounds. It is now the Elks Club. (Barbara Herrmann Corcoran.)

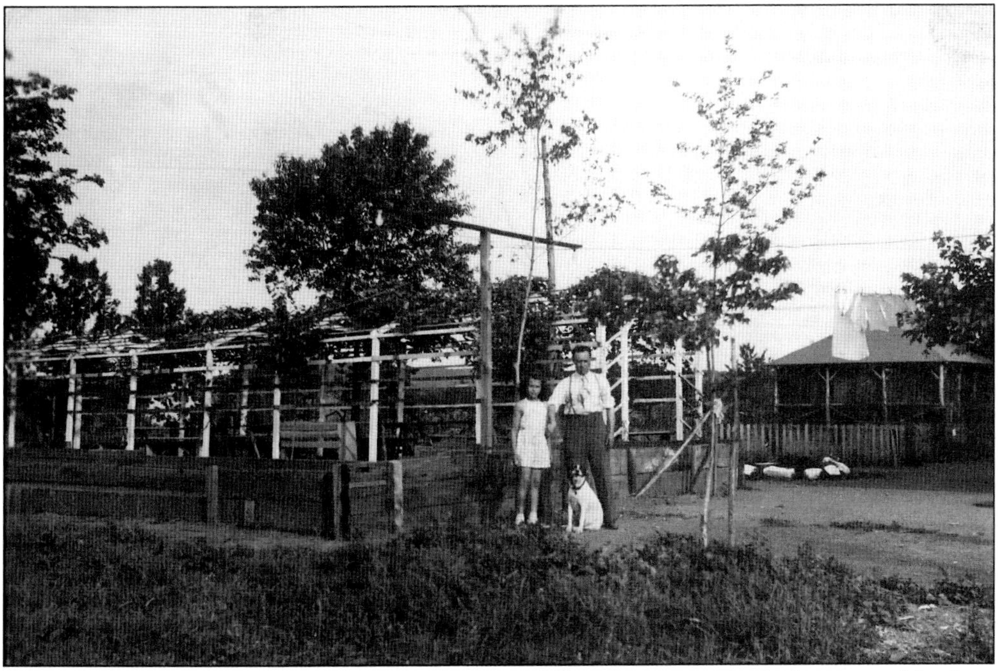

The bocci court on the side lawn of Groppi's Piccadilly Restaurant, which they owned for forty years. Mr. Groppi and his daughter Dorothy are standing in front of the courts with the family dog, *c.* 1939. (Dorothy Groppi Vincent.)

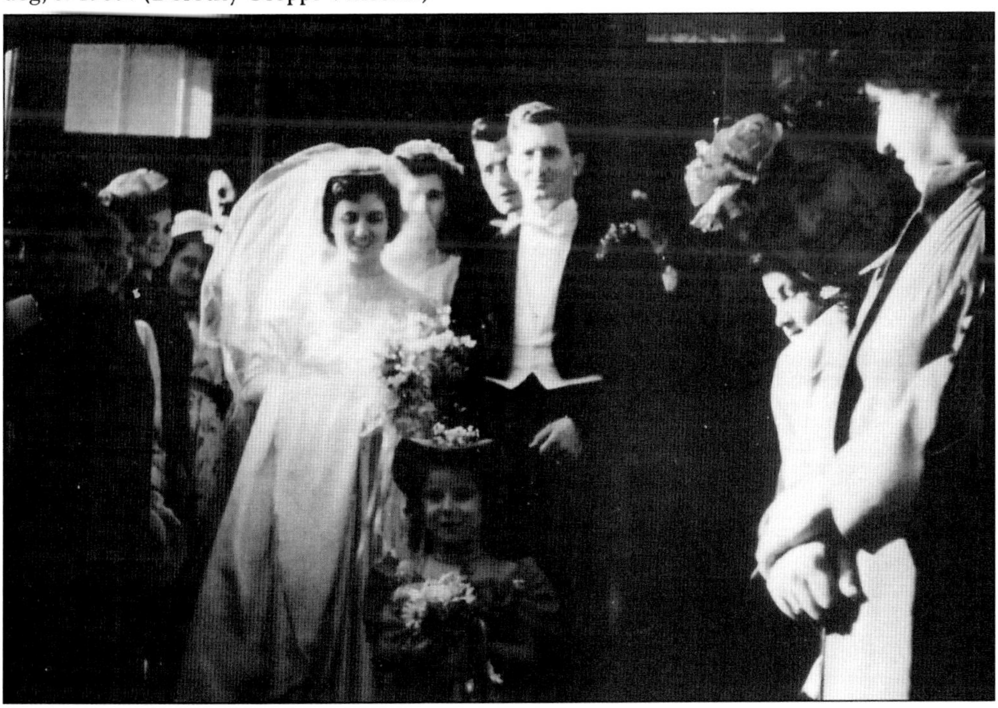

Louis "Red" DeFilippis' wedding, April 25, 1948, at the St. Vincent DePaul Catholic Church. Vincent (Chamber) Rossi was the best man, Marie Farina was the maid of honor, Mary Lou Esoldi was the flower girl, and Theresa Rossi was the bride. (Jean DeFilippis Falzarano.)

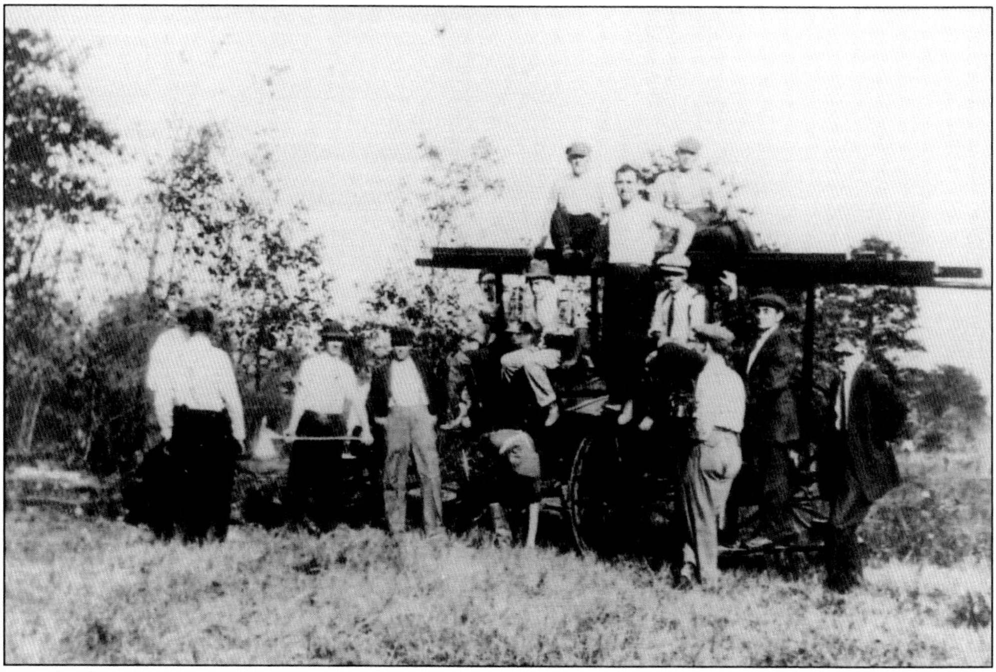

The Stirling Volunteer Fire Company #1 in 1913, shown with their first horse-drawn fire wagon. At that time, the firehouse was on the corner of Main and Morris Streets. The steam whistle at the silk mill was the only fire alarm at the time. (Stirling Volunteer Fire Co. #1.)

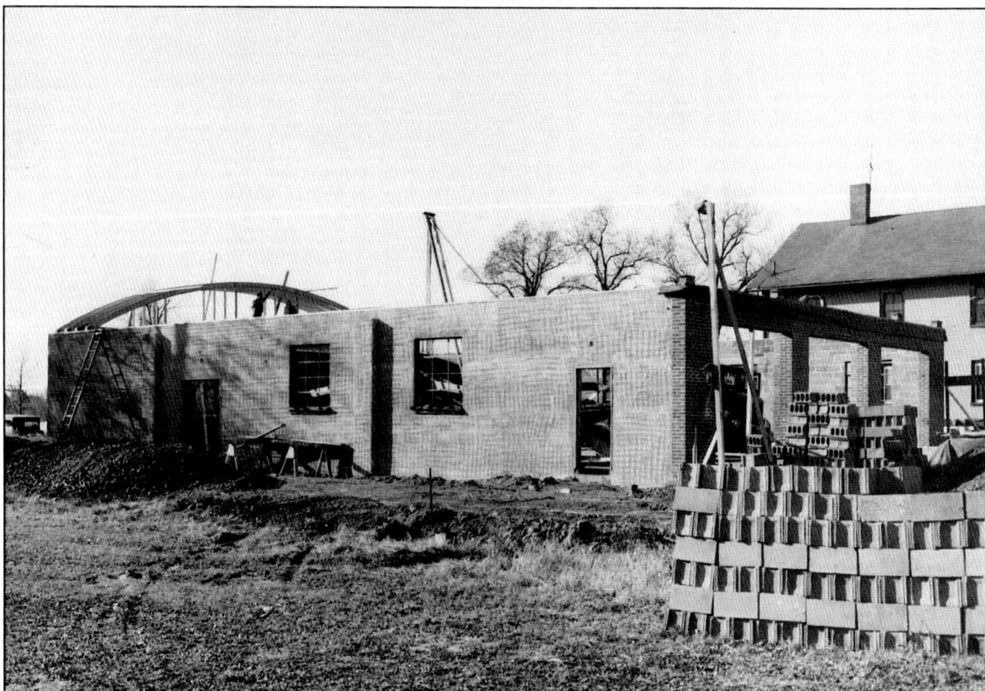

The new building of the Stirling Volunteer Fire Company #1 under construction in 1949, on Somerset Street. The building was completed in 1952. (Leo Maren.)

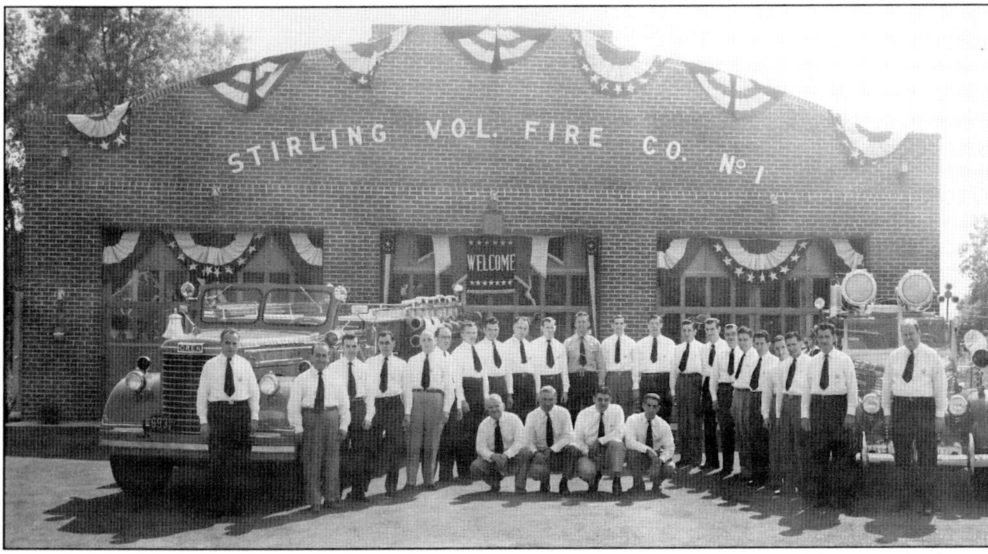

A proud day on Somerset Street. On September 21, 1952, the dedication of the new firehouse for the Stirling Volunteer Fire Company #1 took place. The fire chief at that time was Daniel P. Cerulli. (Leo Maren.)

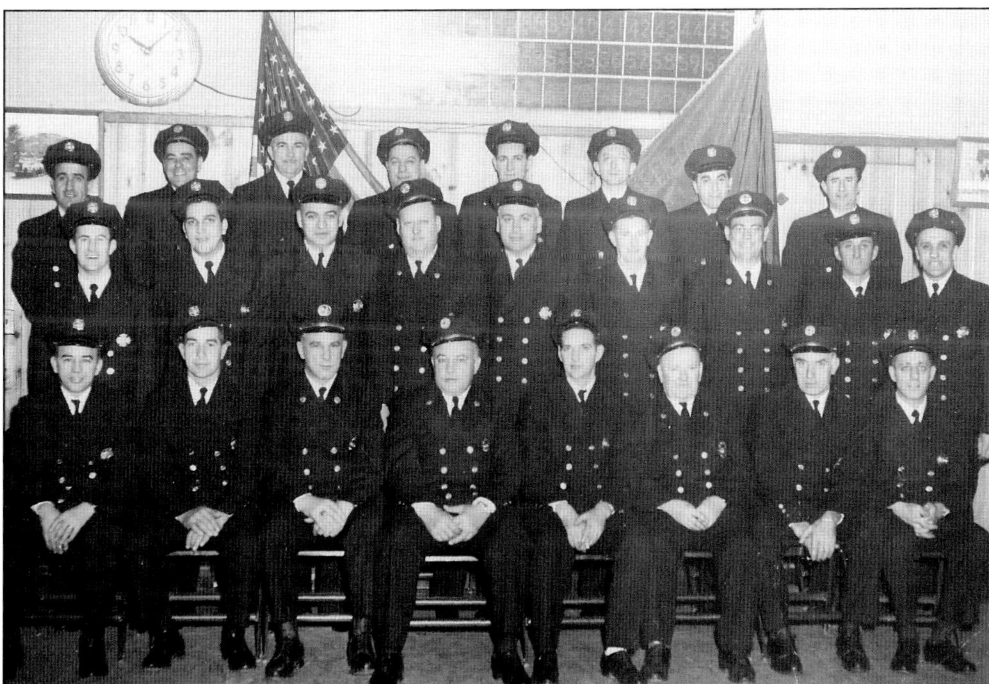

The Stirling Volunteer Fire Company #1 at their best, honoring Chief Dan Cerulli in 1958. From left to right are the following: (front row) Joe Cerulli, Mario Dorsi, Angelo Cerulli, Dan Cerulli, Bob Dorsi, Leo Maren, Bill Metzler, and Nick Mortarono; (middle row) Andy DeFilippis, Anthony Maldonato, Herbert Pattberg, John Falzarano, Lou DeFilippis, Vito Armenti, Jim Sangiovianni, and Tony Falzarano; (back row) Italo Quinto, Ralph Maresca, Frank Cerulli, Tony DeFilippis, Ernie DeFilippis, Henry Mihal, Al Pepe, and Frank DeFilippis. (Leo Maren.)

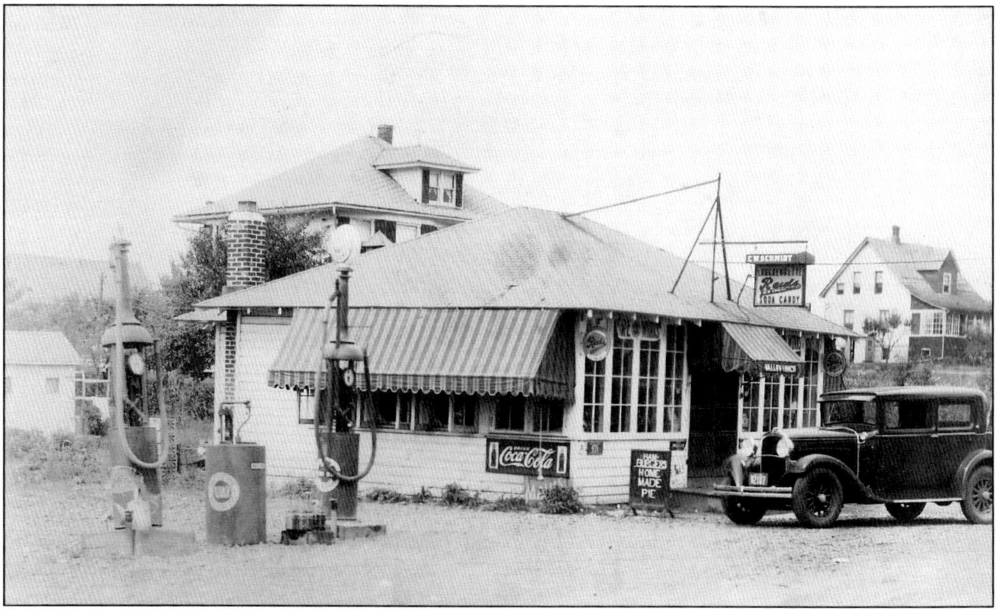

The Valley Tavern. This building on Valley Road was built within the years of 1926–28. Clara Schmidt operated it as a luncheonette. Not only was there a gasoline station on the side, but "Ma Schmidt" secured one of the first liquor licenses in town. It was always a favorite spot for music, dancing, and homemade food. Later, a banquet hall was added. The building was sold in 1954. It has since been totally redesigned, and remains a restaurant today. Note the 1929 Plymouth automobile. (Lilas & Charles Schmidt.)

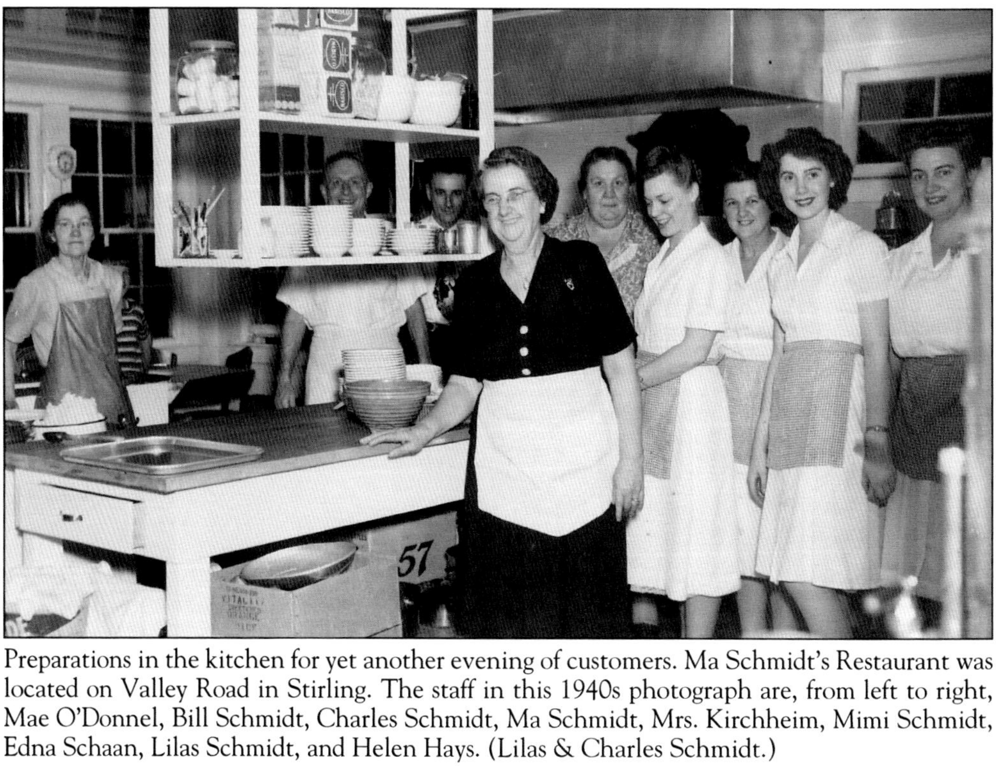

Preparations in the kitchen for yet another evening of customers. Ma Schmidt's Restaurant was located on Valley Road in Stirling. The staff in this 1940s photograph are, from left to right, Mae O'Donnel, Bill Schmidt, Charles Schmidt, Ma Schmidt, Mrs. Kirchheim, Mimi Schmidt, Edna Schaan, Lilas Schmidt, and Helen Hays. (Lilas & Charles Schmidt.)

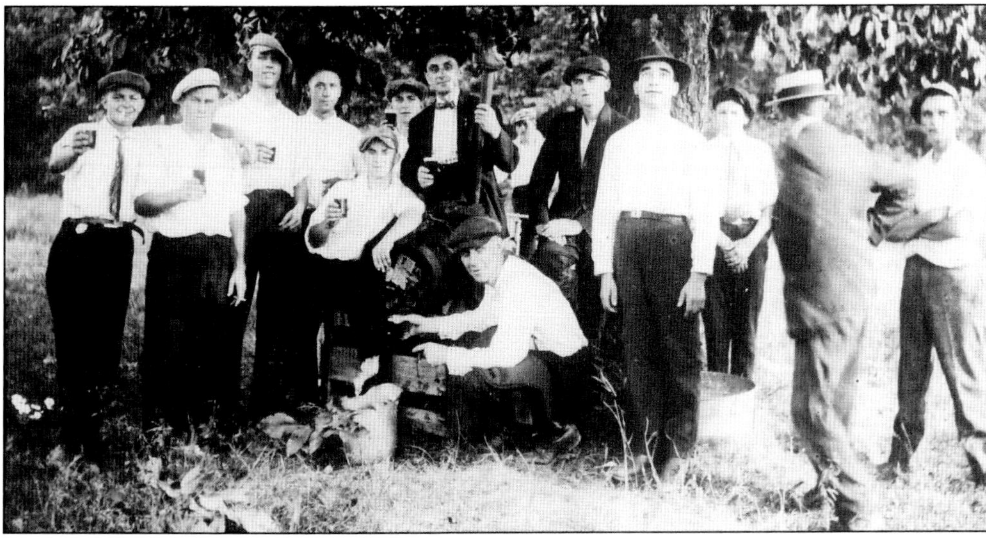

The Thoms Eagle Gun Club, one of the first gun clubs in Stirling in 1931. Land was leased and stocked for hunting. This picture was taken from a picnic area behind Ma Schmidt's Restaurant. From left to right are Tony Simet, Richard Thoms, Ike Wilkesmann, Bill Simet, Dave Achille, unknown, Joseph Landwehr, Frank Landwehr, Lour Thievon Sr., unknown, Dan Cerulli, Nick Manailovich, unknown, and Lou Mauro. (Long Hill Township Historical Society.)

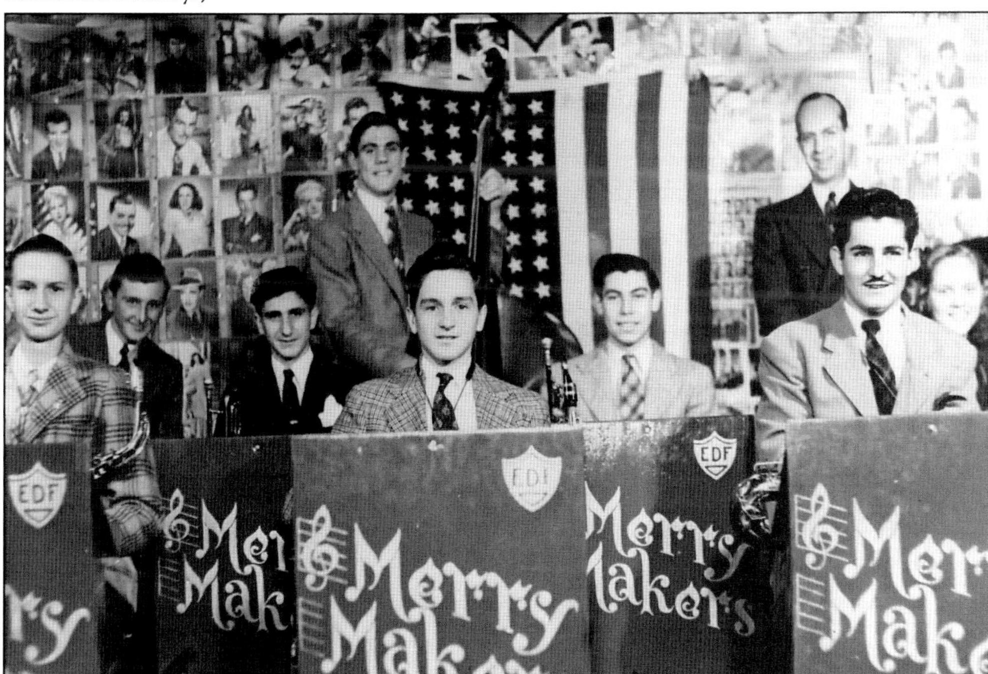

The Merry Makers Band of 1943–44. Local students from town comprised the band. Shown here, from left to right, are Raymond Wall (sax), Raymond Lillis (drums), Peter Agostino (trumpet), Vito Armenti (bass), Albert Landwehr (sax), Leonard Mocerino (trumpet), leader Charles (Chuck) Wall, Ernest DeFilippis (sax), and Barbara Herrmann Corcoran (piano). (Mary Lou Landwehr Weller.)

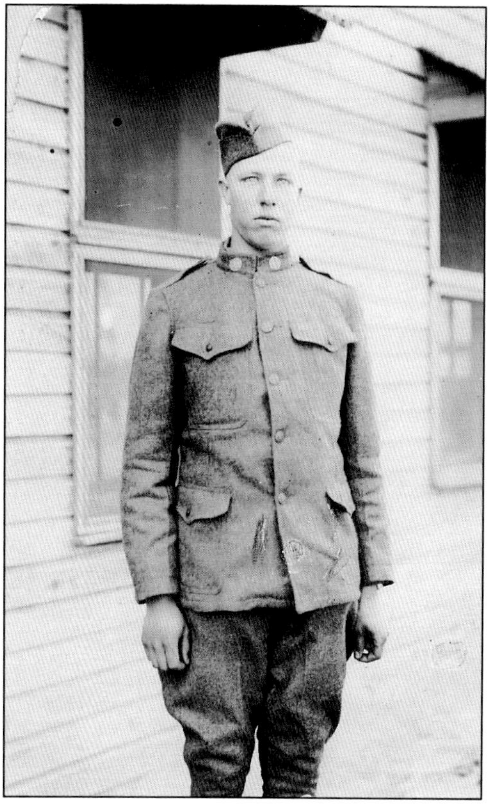

Ike Wilkesmann, from Essex Street in Stirling, in uniform during World War I. (Ann Wilkesmann Barta.)

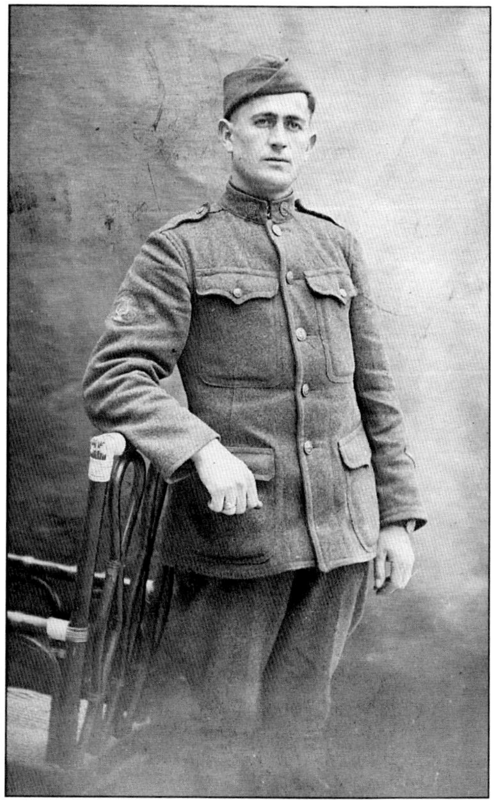

Frank DeFilippis, who owned Defilippis' General Store on Main Street for many years, in uniform during World War I. (Jean DeFilippis Falzarano.)

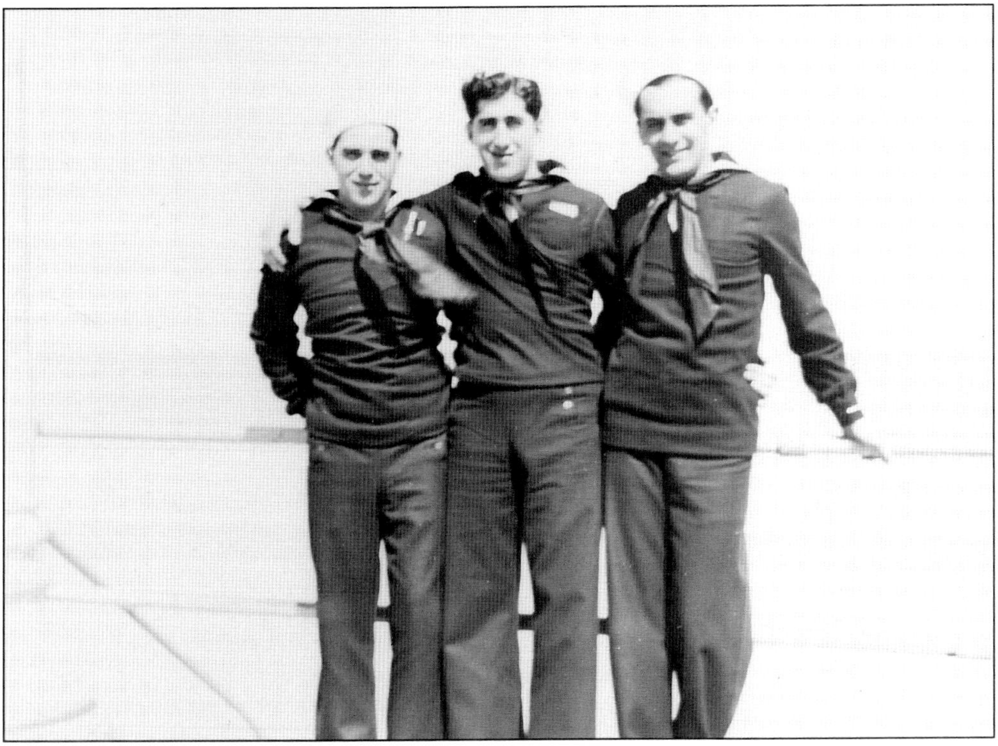

Local sailors on leave in Stirling during World War II. From left to right are Mike Maresca, Lou "Rail" Esoldi, and Lou Truppi. (Ralph Malfatone.)

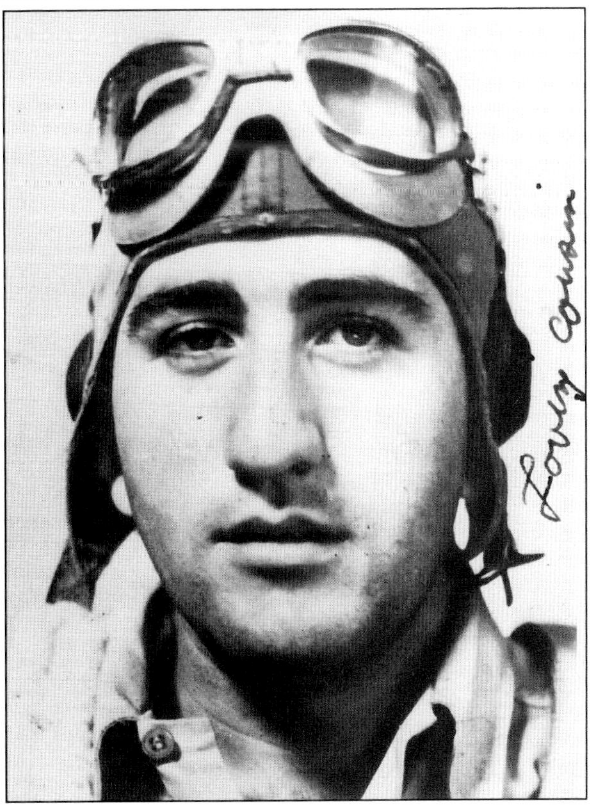

Italo Quinto, an aerial gunner in the European Theater in World War II, *c.* 1943–45. After the war he organized annual Memorial Day parades down Main Street for many years. (Italo Quinto.)

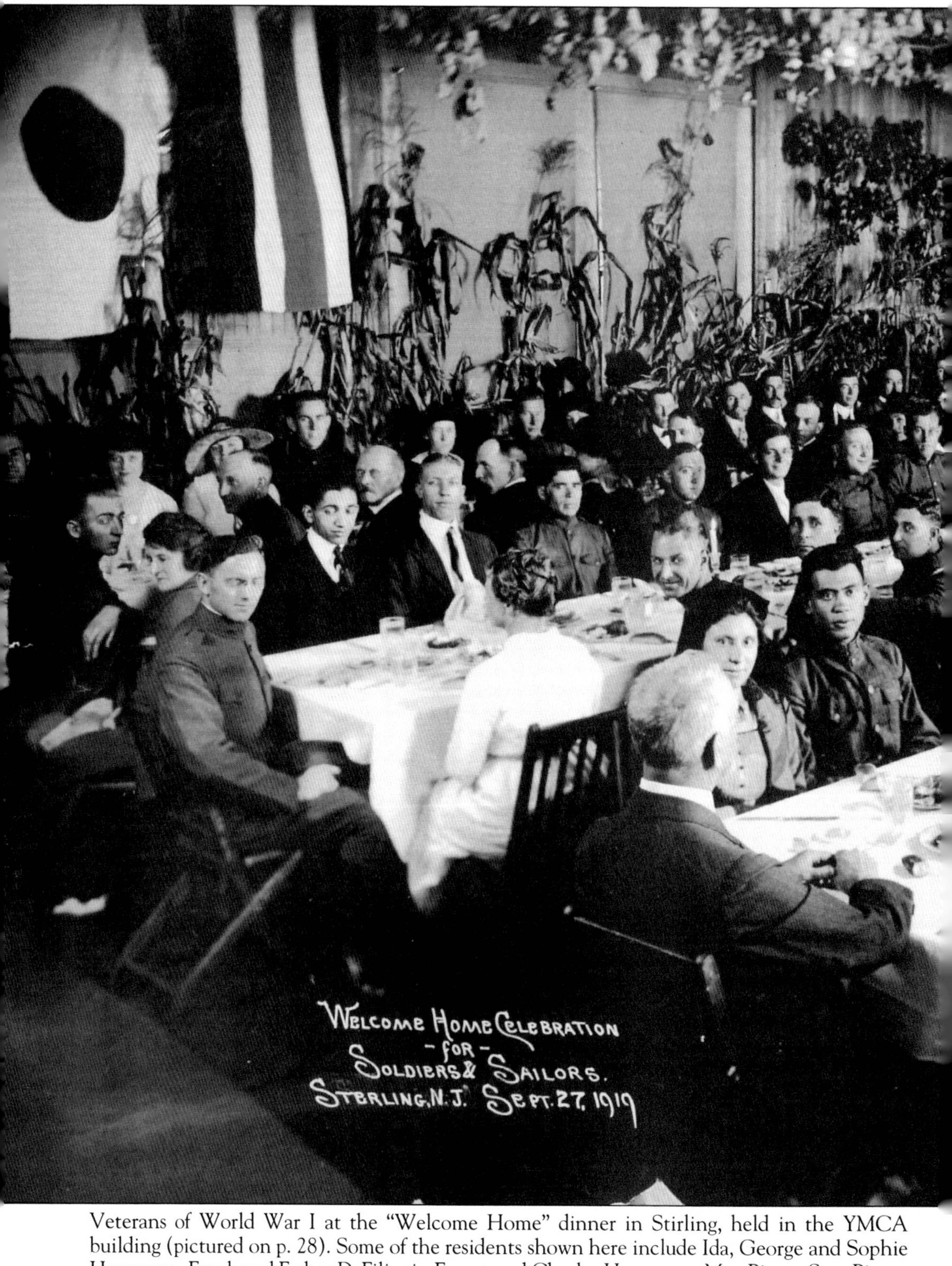

Veterans of World War I at the "Welcome Home" dinner in Stirling, held in the YMCA building (pictured on p. 28). Some of the residents shown here include Ida, George and Sophie Herrmann, Frank and Esther DeFilippis, Ernest and Charles Herrmann, Mrs. Piano, Sam Piano,

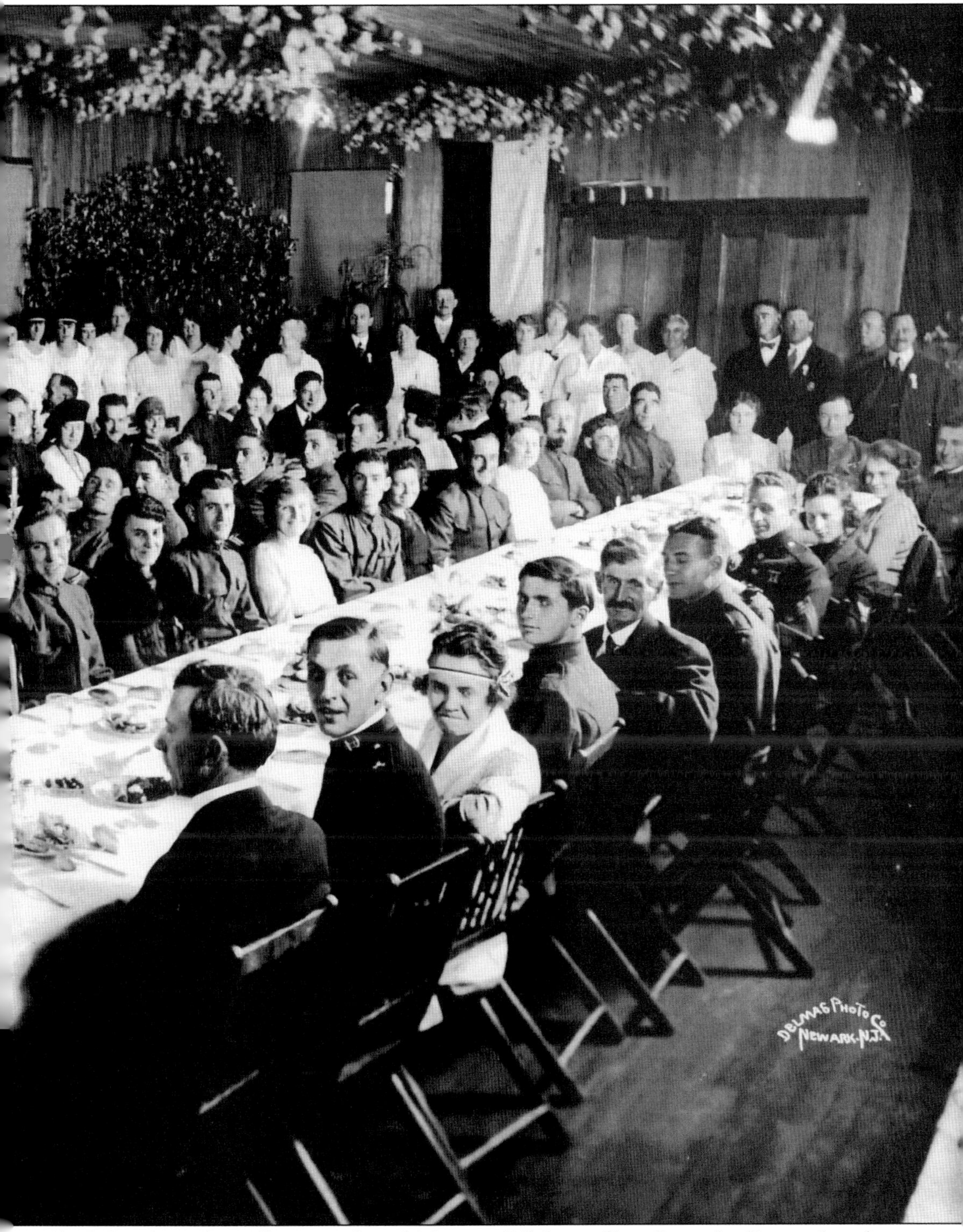

Abe Bahooshian, Ike Wilkesmann, Joseph Massano, Bill Simet, Tony Simet, Joe Besmer, Joseph Landwehr, Dr. George Freeman, Mrs. Lillis, Jim Lillis, Lillian Bianco, Tony Bianco, and Cora and Ray Alland. (Mary Falzarano Thoms.)

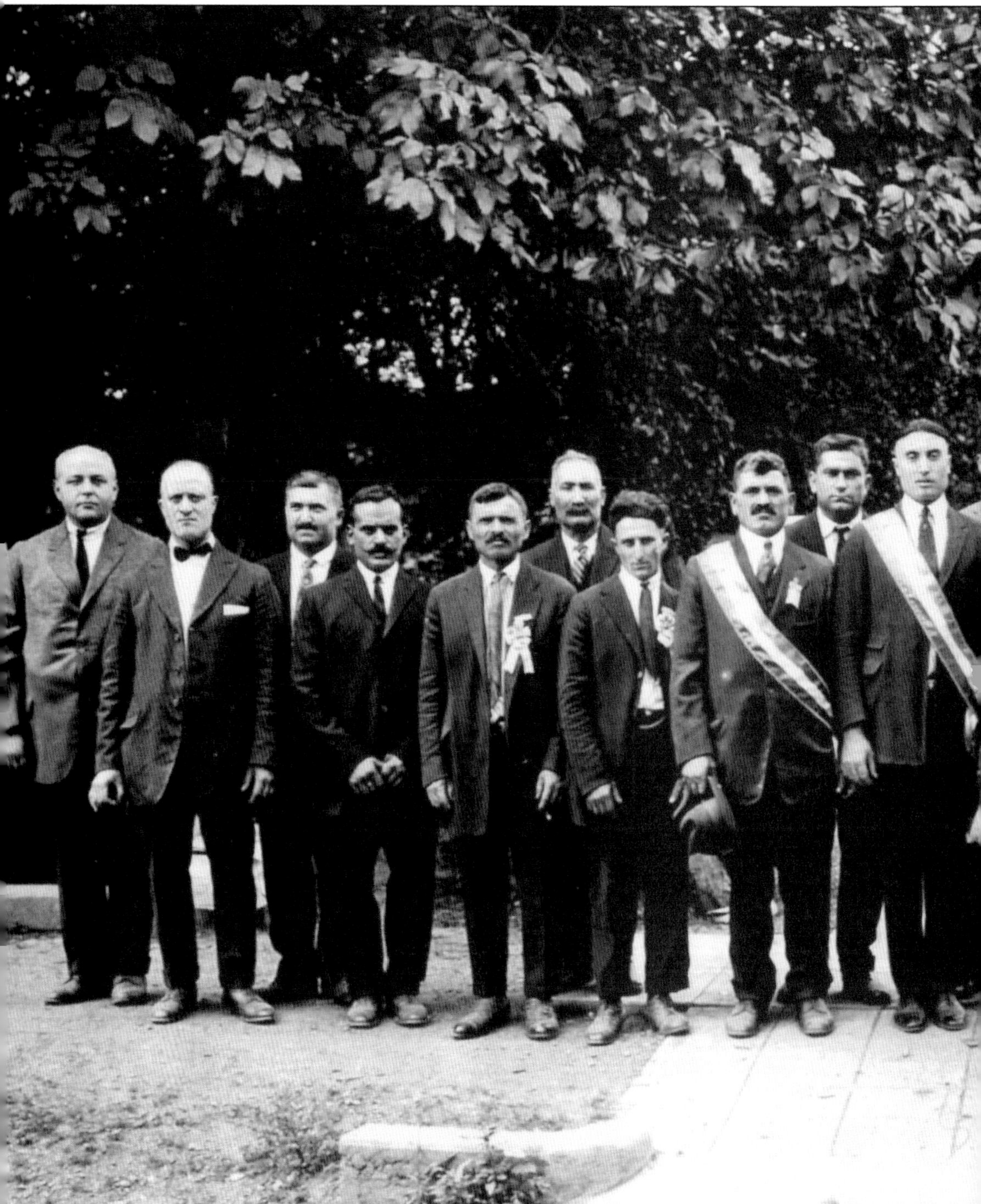

The Columbus Club. Raymond A. Alland was the advisor to this popular Italian organization. They met at Carmine Pepe's hall on Main Street in Stirling. Columbus Day was celebrated with a parade on October 12 each year. Organized in 1924, the club lasted ten years. From left to right are Cosmo Dorsi, Benny Nunzio, Carmine San Giovanni, Joseph Truppi, Anthony

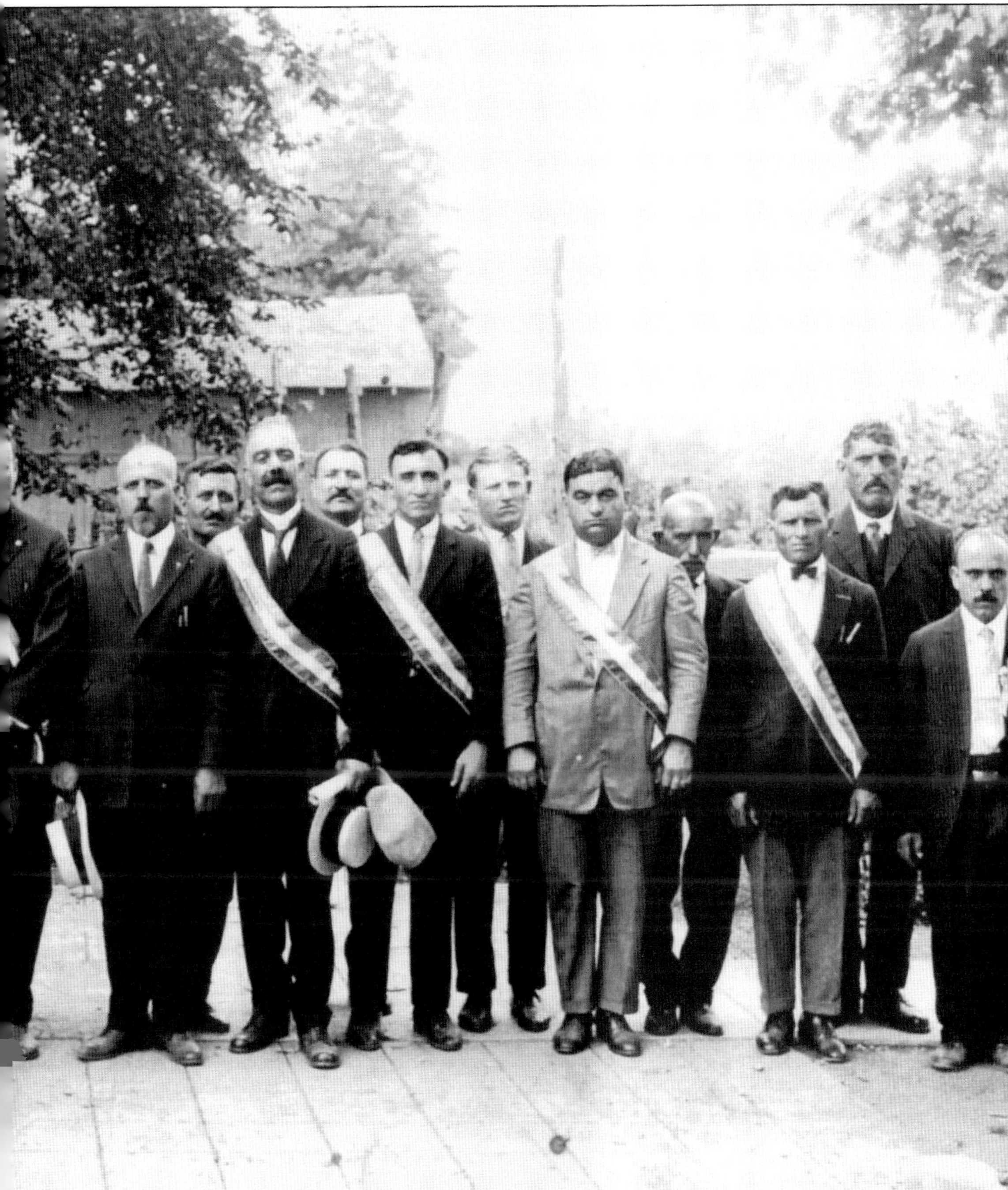

Falzarano, unknown, unknown, Salvatore Carfaro, unknown, Mike Fucci, unknown, unknown, Raymond A. Alland, Ralph Ferraro, Serafino DeGiammattio, unknown, unknown, James Maglione, Carmine Pepe, Angelo Truppi, James Ruggerio, Clement DiMasi, and Peter Melise. (Mary Falzarano Thoms.)

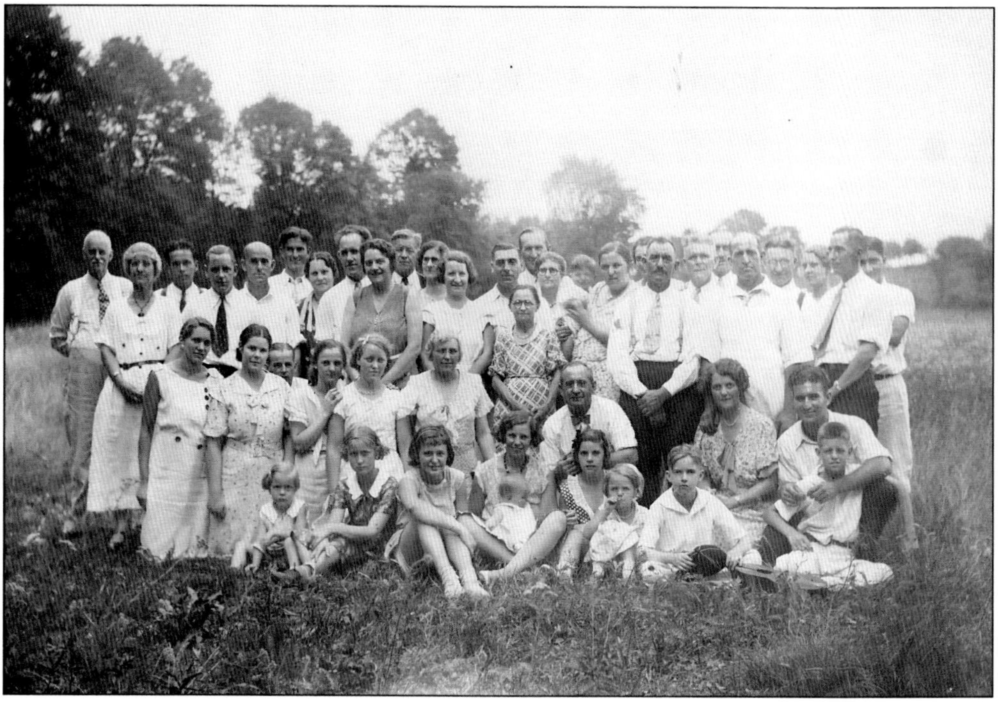

A Saturday reunion. In 1933 forty-three members of the Herrmann family from Stirling gathered in Schmidt's Grove, on Valley Road in Stirling, for a reunion. (Barbara Herrmann Corcoran.)

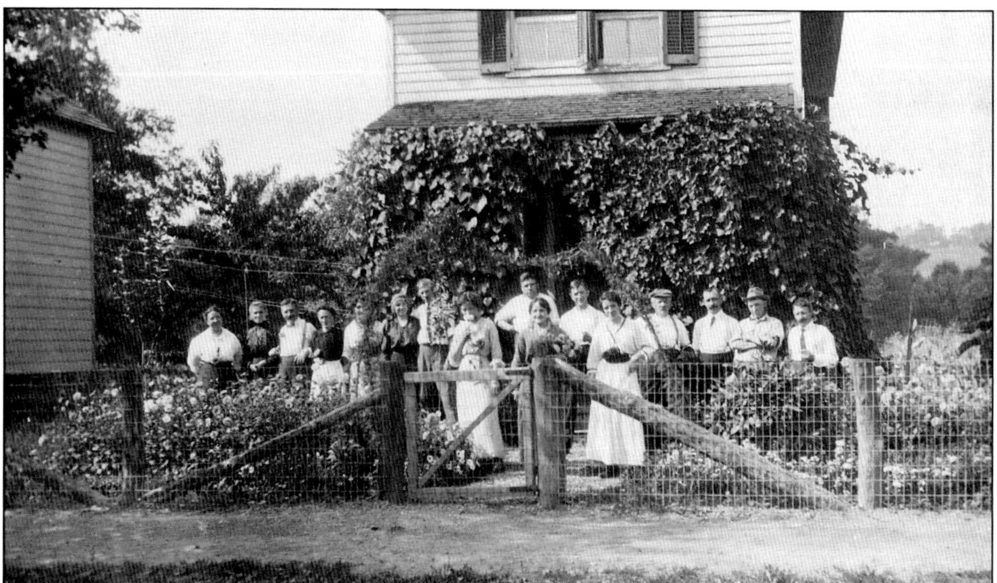

An early 1900s summer gathering of the Wilkesmann family, in front of their home on Essex Street. (Ann Wilkesmann Barta.)

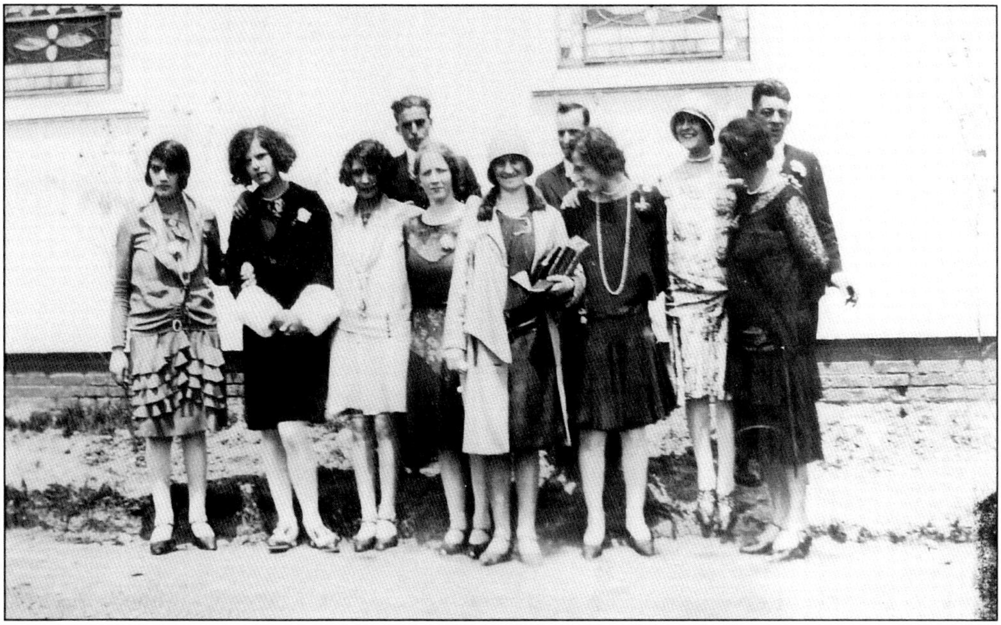

Members of the Kocisko family and friends possibly going or coming from a Sunday mass, on the grounds of the original Catholic church on Elm Street, c. 1917. (Winifred Shimol.)

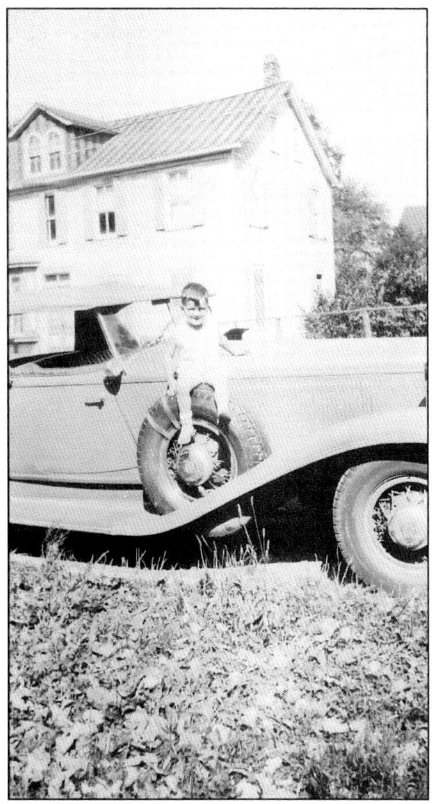

Albert Landwehr and a 1932 Auburn Roadster, a truly fancy car of its day, on Main Street heading north, c. 1935. (Mary Lou Landwehr Weller.)

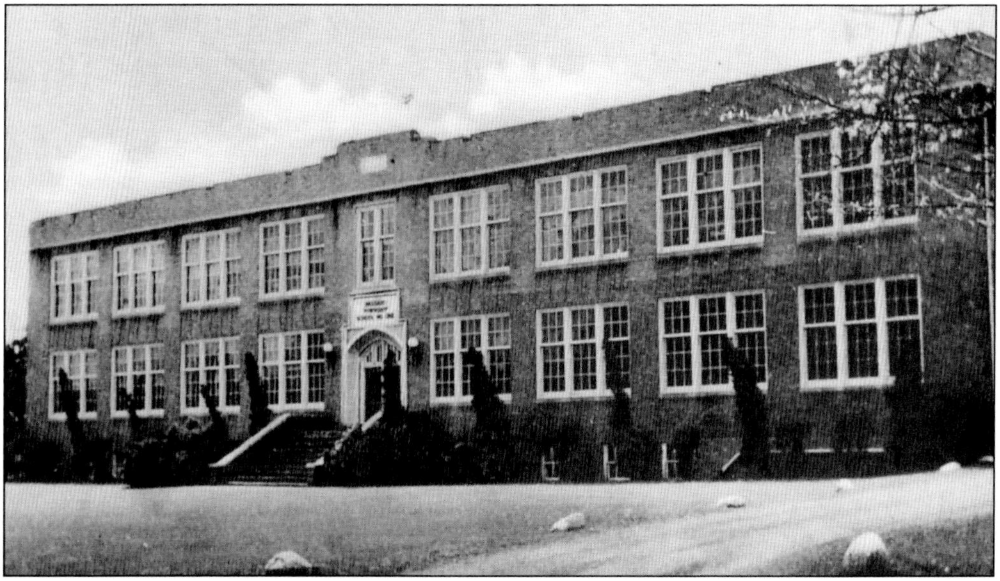

Stirling Junior High School, 1950. In 1926, Stirling Junior High School, as it was called at that time, was built on Main Street, across from where the library stands today. Comprised of seventh, eighth, and ninth grades, the graduates started at either Bernardsville or Morristown in their sophomore year. That changed over the years, and in 1957 the Watchung Hills Region High School was built at 108 Stirling Road, in Warren, for the regions of Long Hill Township, Warren, Watchung, and later, Greenbrook. (Dale Monetti.)

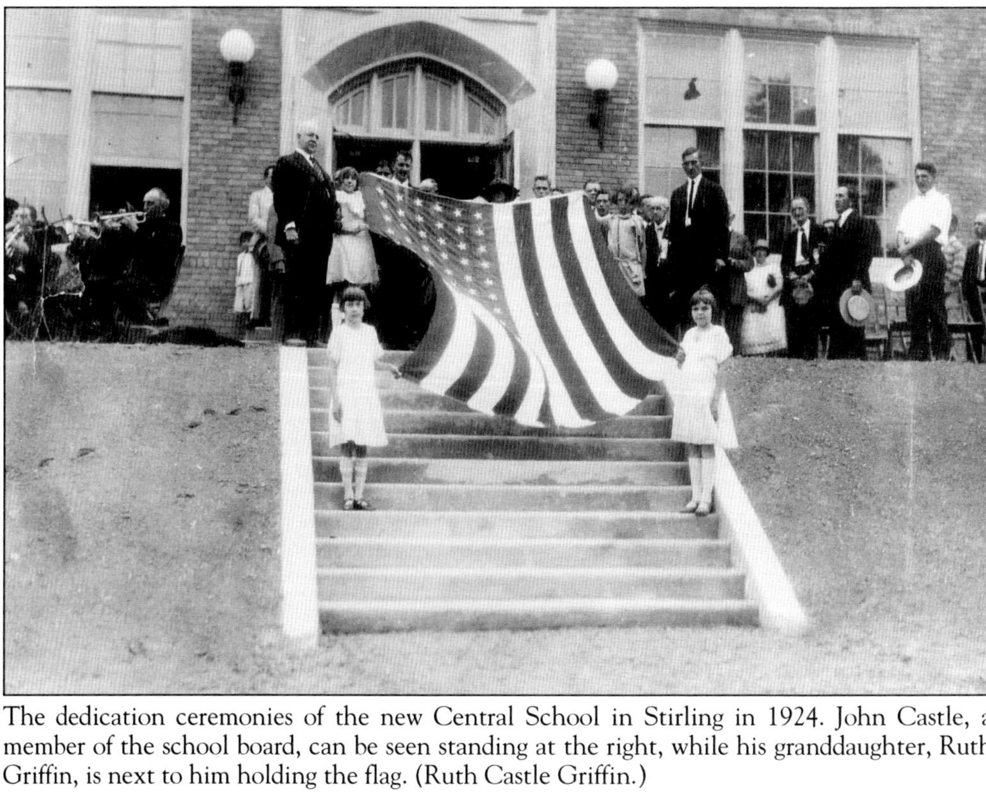

The dedication ceremonies of the new Central School in Stirling in 1924. John Castle, a member of the school board, can be seen standing at the right, while his granddaughter, Ruth Griffin, is next to him holding the flag. (Ruth Castle Griffin.)

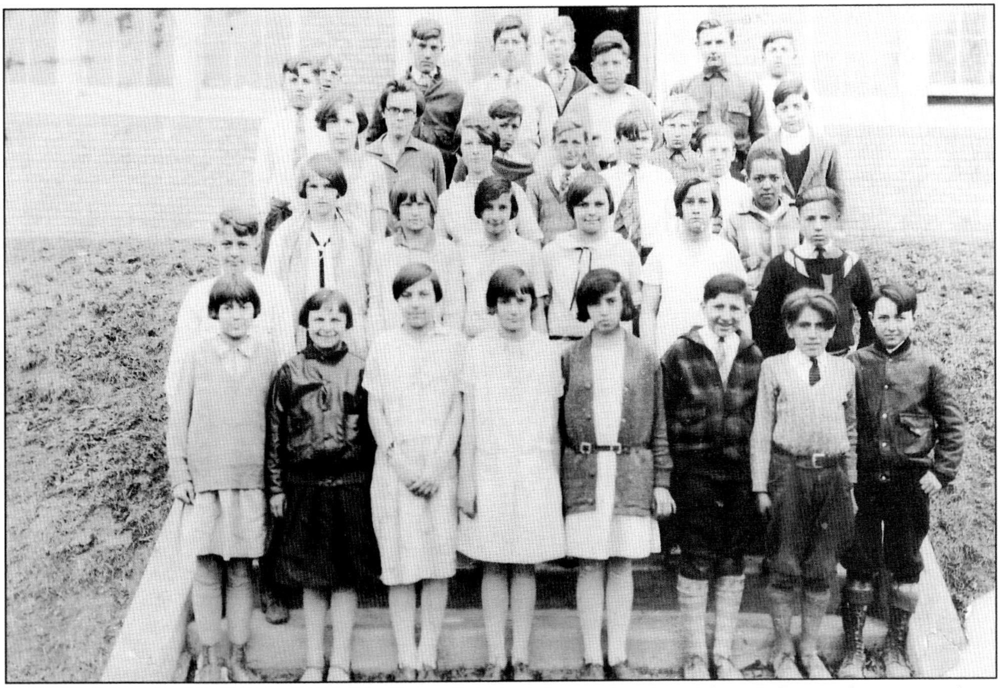

The Central School Graduating Class of 1929. Among the students shown here are Ann Skrobacz, Connie Dorsi, Dorothy Bogart, Julia Quinci, Andrew Kocisko, John Ananson, Richard Ananson, Florence Cortese, Sally Kocisko, Jennie Truppi, Alex Groppi, Jessie Domanski, Robert Smith, Joseph Dorsi, and James Falzarano. (Lynn Deveney Spurrier.)

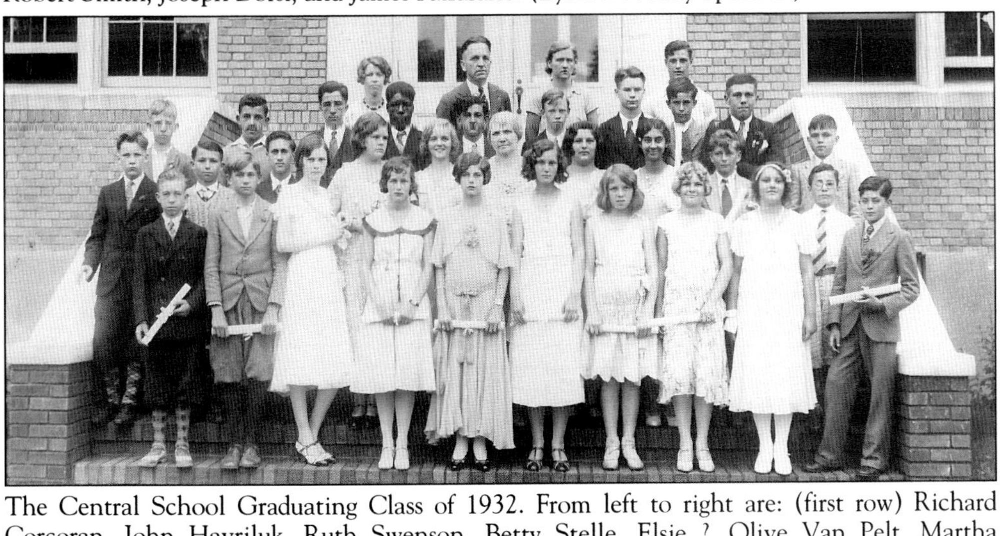

The Central School Graduating Class of 1932. From left to right are: (first row) Richard Corcoran, John Havriluk, Ruth Swenson, Betty Stelle, Elsie ?, Olive Van Pelt, Martha Whalley, Ginny Geoginski, Ruth Rhein, and Joseph Truppi; (second row) "Winkie" Brown, John Yurkovic, Ralph Wolf, Helen Merritt, Doreen Swanson, Miss Parsons, Mary Romeo, Irene Rossi, Joseph Jacenty, Tony Cortese, and Nick Angelapoulos; (third row) William J. Ziegelmeier, Henry Fiske, Michael Cerulli, Robert Smith, Dominick Reillo, Robert Swenson, Everett Faulkner, Felix Norosic, and Charles Meeker; (back row) gym teacher Miss Paul, superintendent Edward Applegate, teacher Edith Jones Cashman, and Joe Fernicola. (Joseph Jacenty.)

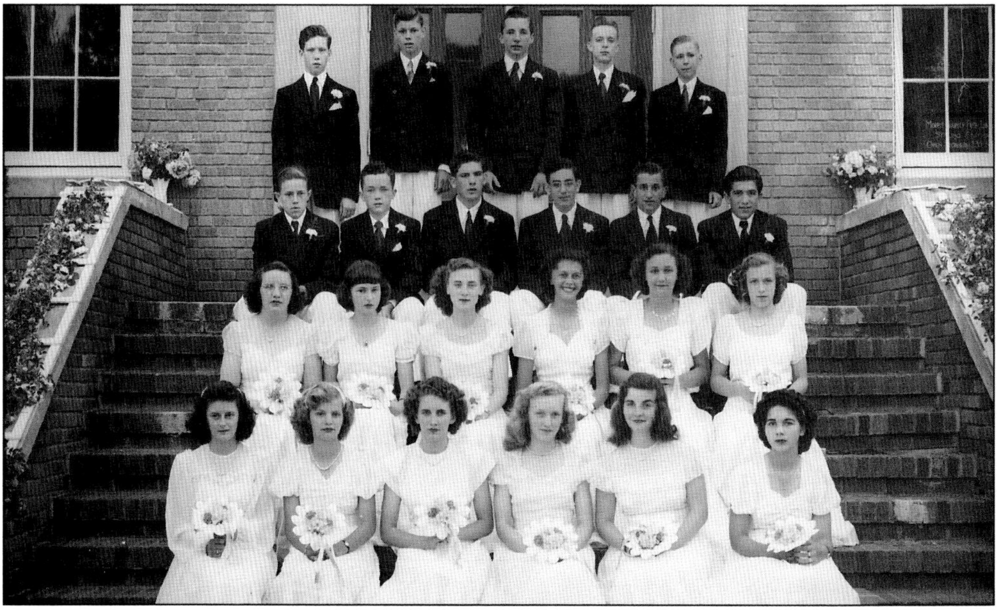

The Central School Graduation Class of 1947. From left to right are: (front row) Mildred Hunt, June Lund, Joan Thievon, Addy Radder, Gloria Schaible, and Anna Falzarano; (middle row) Martha Cox, Lorraine Lange, Gertrude Lamson, Janet Mauro, Eleanor Schaefer, and Helga Grundling; (back row) John Van Wettering, Donald Morgan, Harry Weigan, Joseph Melisi, Louis D'Agostino, Frank Massaro, Edward Scheick, Roger Fennimore, Frank Swertsfeger, Alan Rydell, and Arnold Kruth. (Eleanor Castle Groves.)

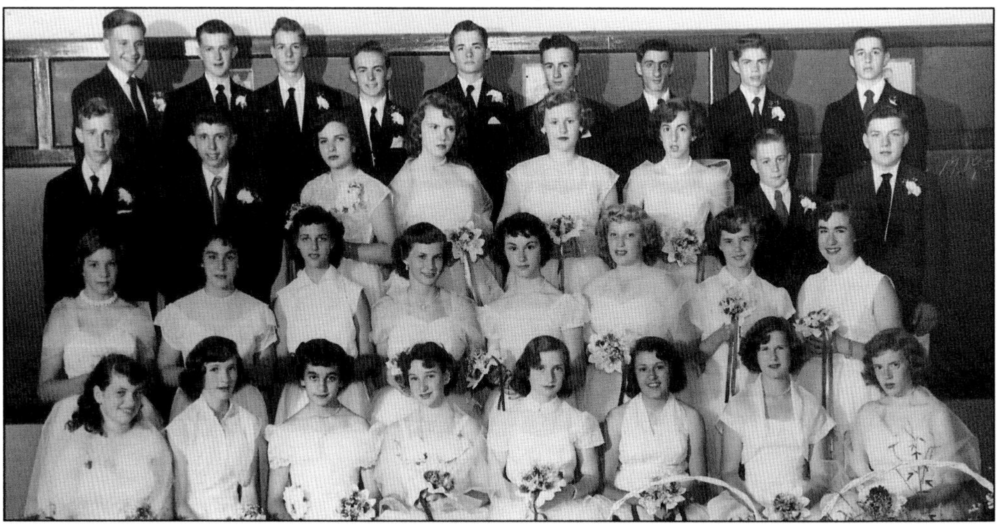

The Central School Graduating Class of 1953. From left to right are: (front row) Claire Plunguin, Eleanor Graef, Carmela Gomez, Carol Bauerle, Bethany Ann Bylick, Edith Patterson, Barbara Woodruff, and Barbara Ortman; (second row) Hilda Mueller, Leonora LaGuardia, Diane Minikus, Kaye Leppo, Inge Rist, Rose Maglione, Lillian Wilkinson, and Jean Leishe; (third row) Robert Krause, Robert Piano, Lorraine Williams, Elaine Fairhurst, Joan Gronau, Betty Anne Hackenburg, Paul Hackenburg, and Donald Perera; (back row) Dan Rossi, Fred Schaan, George Lund, Michael Harman, John Faye, Steve Bylick, John D'Agostino, Joe Finnigan, and Nick Nalisnik. (Inge Rist Lincoln.)

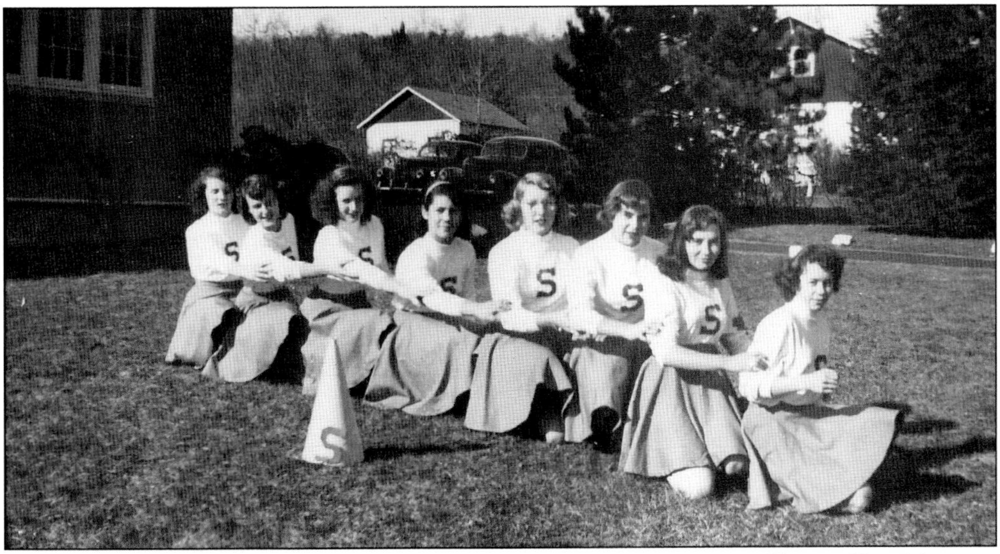

Central School cheerleaders, 1950. From left to right are Laura Frommer, Sheena Hay, Margaret Leidenheimer, Sylvia La Coultre, Ann Coriell, Nancy Miller, Charolette Achille, and Mary Irwin. (Ann Coriell MacDougall.)

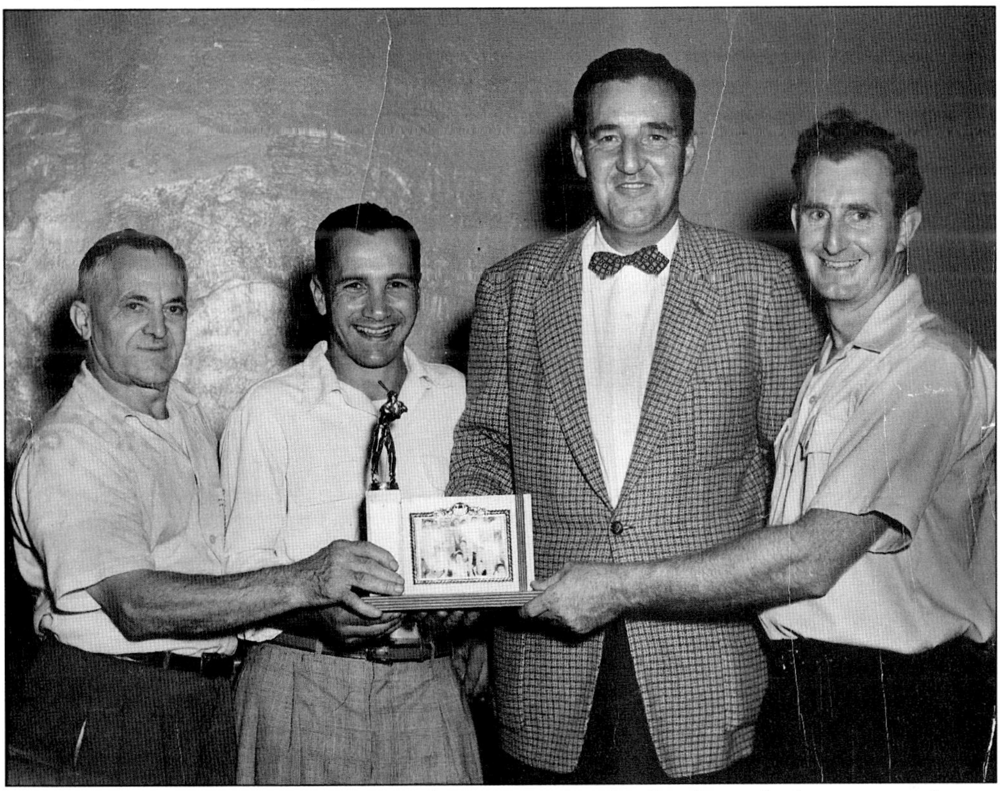

Awards Night at Central School in Stirling. Harry Hirsch, the physical education teacher, is shown receiving a trophy for the baseball team's winning season, c. 1956. From left to right are sponsor Dave Achille, coach Nunzio De Agostino, and coach Lou "Red" DeFilippis. (Jean DeFilippis Falzarano.)

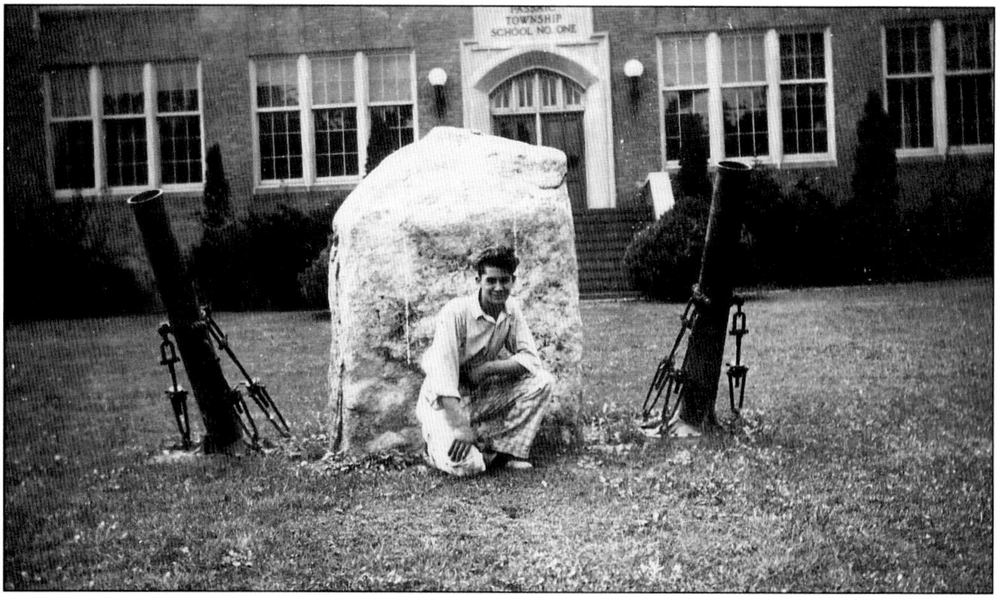

Joseph Truppi in front of the World War I war memorial on the Central School lawn in 1938. (Ralph Malfatone.)

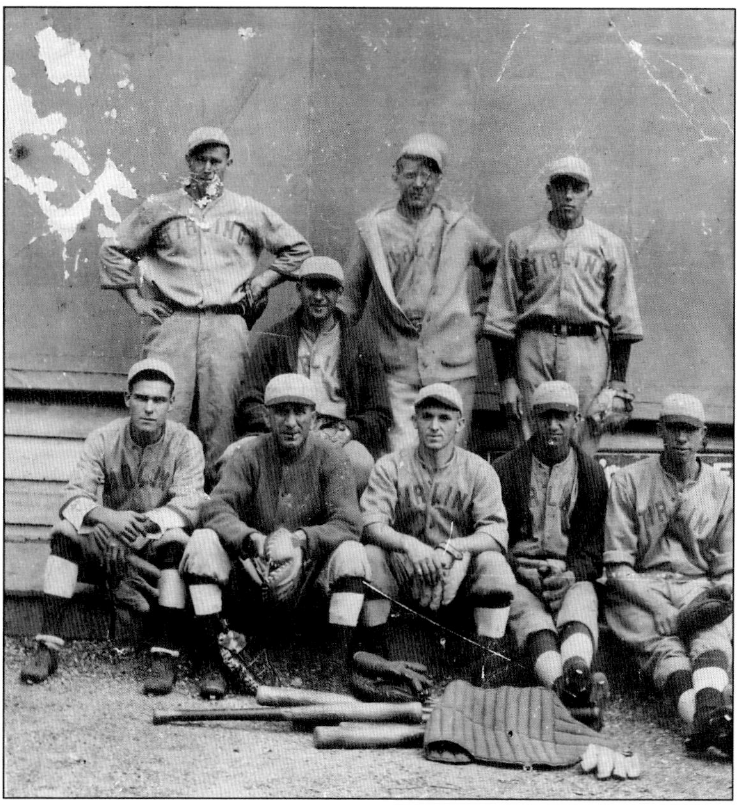

One of the oldest photographs of the baseball team from Stirling, c. 1897. There was also a football team in Stirling at this time. Team members played without any of the modern equipment players have today, but with the same earnest enthusiasm and will to win. (Ralph Malfatone.)

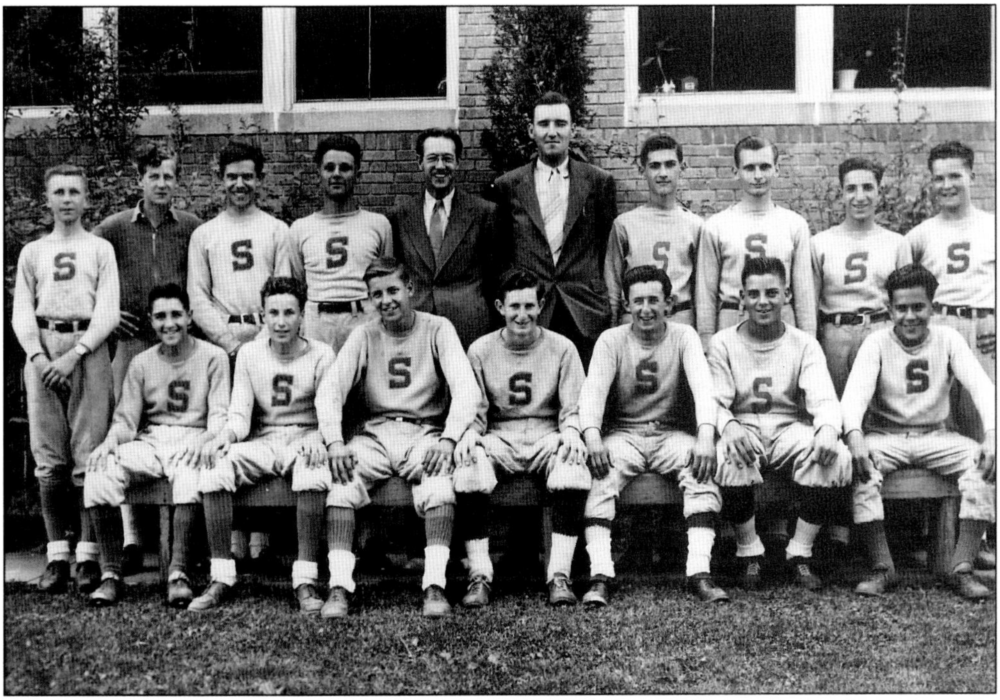

The baseball team of Central School in 1939. From left to right are: (seated) C. Gregory, P. Richter, H. Van Dine, L. DeFilippis, F. DeFilippis, F. Fennimore, and R. Truppi; (standing) L. Lillis, F. Richter, R. Turrin, J. Armenti, W. May, H. Hirsch, J.R. Falzarano, T. Ruggerio, D. Cortese, and B. Finn. (Marion McCollum Armstrong.)

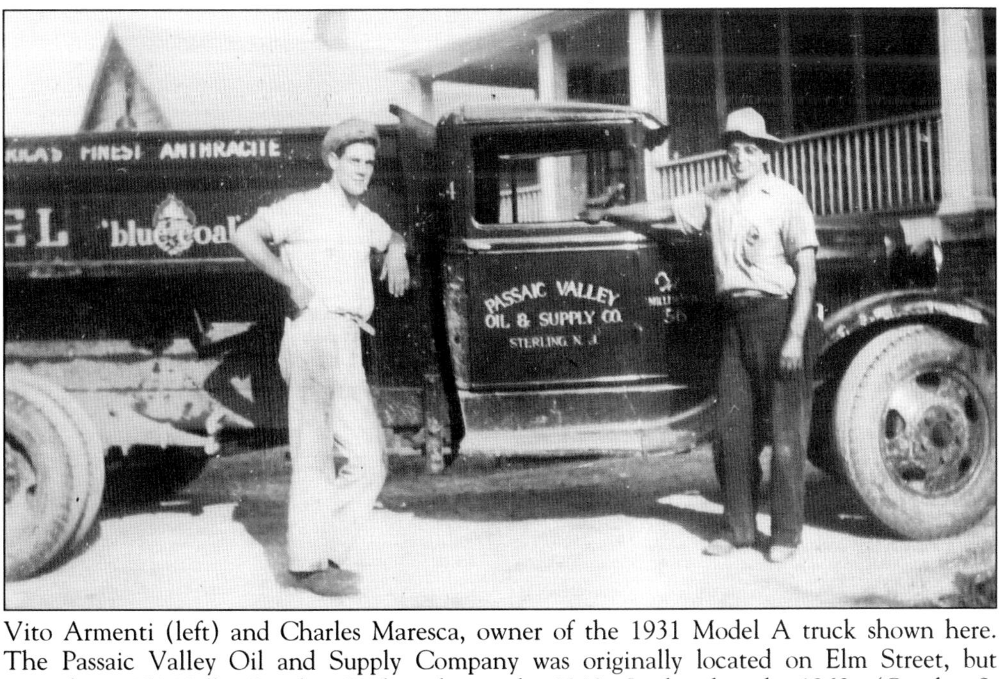

Vito Armenti (left) and Charles Maresca, owner of the 1931 Model A truck shown here. The Passaic Valley Oil and Supply Company was originally located on Elm Street, but moved to 1050 Valley Road in Stirling during the 1940s. It closed in the 1960s. (Carolyn & Ralph Malfatone.)

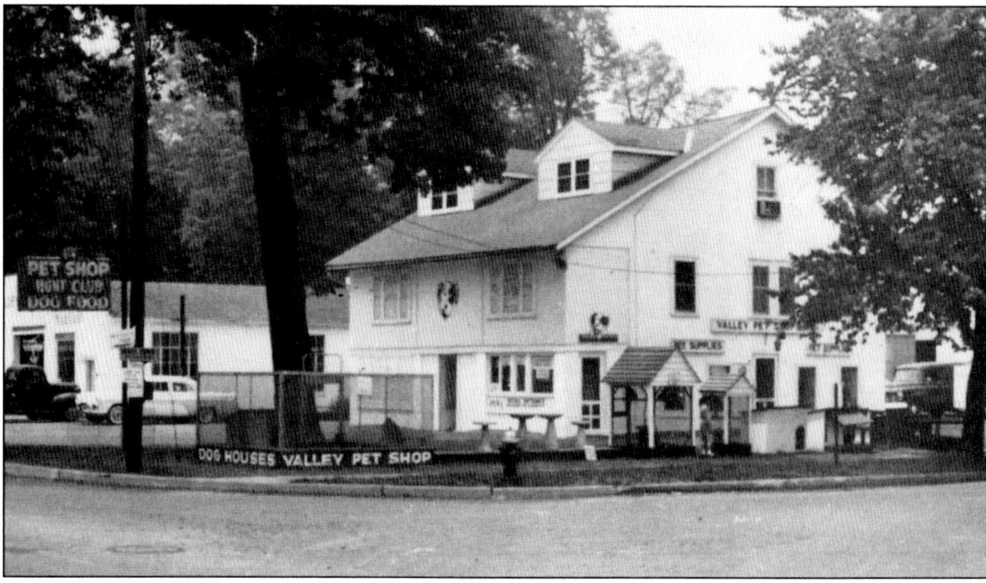

The Valley Pet Shop, *c. 1950*, located on the corner of Valley Road and Main Street in Stirling. Originally it was the private home of the Dewalder family. (Marion Harman Gehling.)

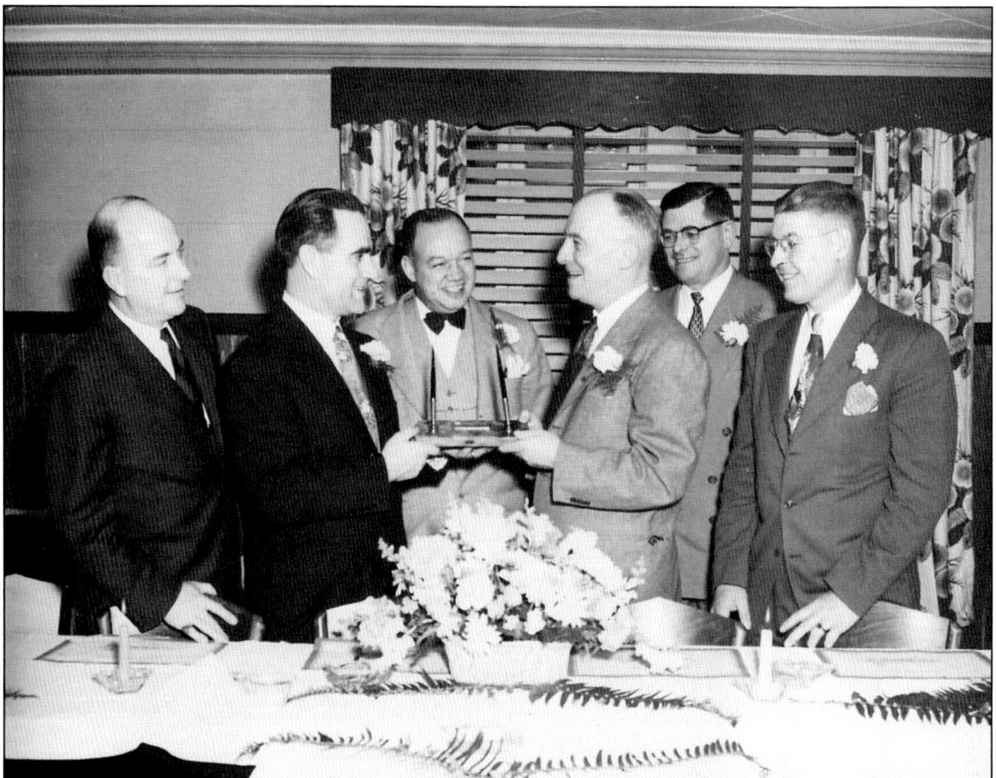

A dinner party given for Frank Rowe in 1952. For many years Mr. Rowe served on a township and county level. From left to right are Bob Jack, Armondo Rossi, Dr. Jim Beard, Frank Row, Irwin (Rudy) Rudolph, and Ernest (Mickey) McCollum. (Marion McCollum Armstrong.)

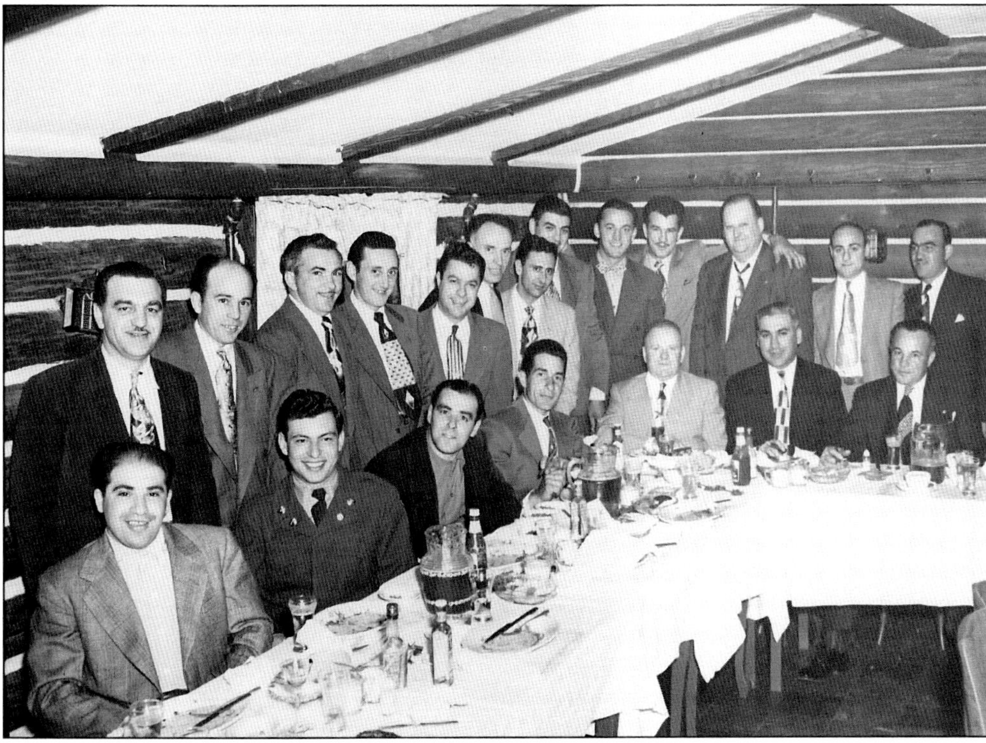

A special dinner at the Old Log Cabin Restaurant and Bar on Valley Road in Stirling. This event was held in honor of Leo Maren for his twenty-five years of service to the Stirling Volunteer Fire Company #1. The restaurant no longer stands today. Mr. Maren also worked as a superintendent at the silk mill in Stirling. From left to right are: (seated) Giacomo Massaro, Gene Piano, Ralph Maresca, Mario Dorsi, Leo Maren, John Falzarano, and Dan Cerulli; (standing) Tony Pepe, Joe Cerulli, Frank Cerulli, Jim San Giovanni, Tony DeFilippis, Bill Metzler, Vinnie Piano, Anthony Maldonato, John Dolan, Angelo Cerulli, Herbert Pattberg, George Armenti, and Al Pepe. (Leo Maren.)

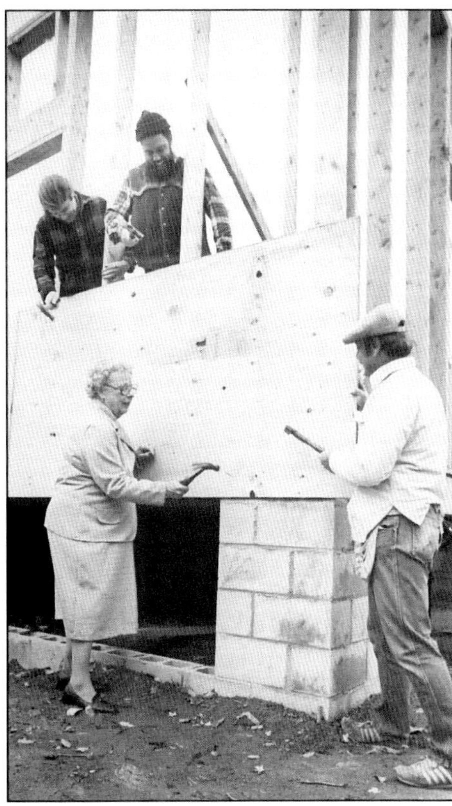

The building of the American Legion Hall on 234 Union Street, in Stirling, during the 1970s. Helen Clancy, who served in our community as police commissioner, member of the township committee, and deputy mayor, is shown hammering on the left. "Skeeter" Kielblock, wearing a cap, and Jack Brown are hammering above her, and John Rister is standing at the right. (Emma & Archibald Stiles.)

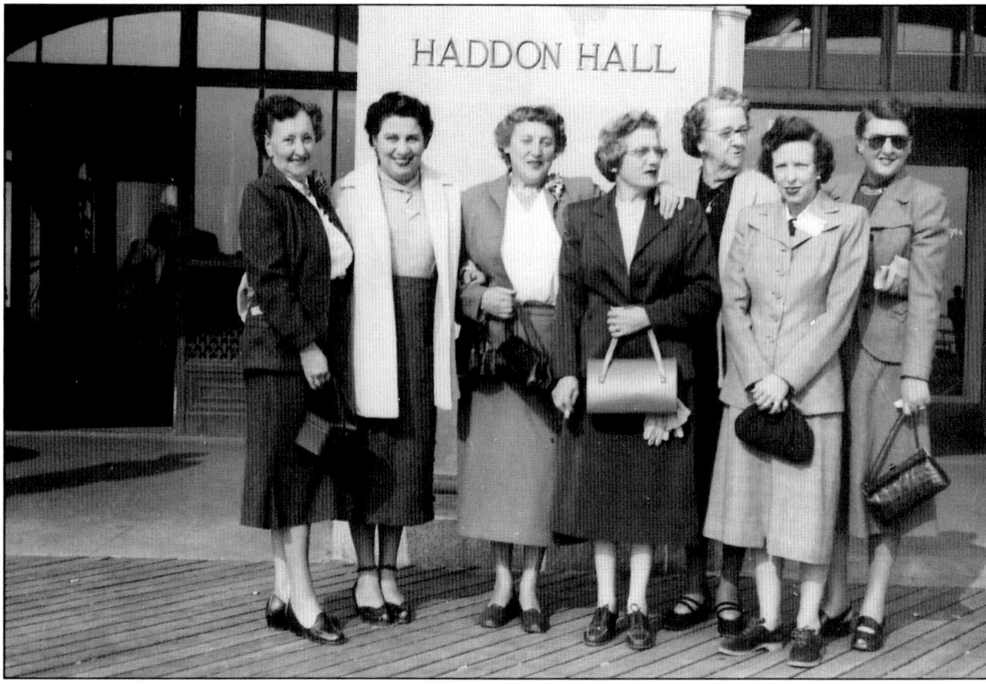

The Republican club of Long Hill Township, attending the annual convention in Atlantic City in 1953. From left to right are Marion Rowe, Fanny Rossi, Eve Rudolph, Grace McCollum, Ma Schmidt, Eunice Jack, and Edna Schaan. (Marion McCollum Armstrong.)

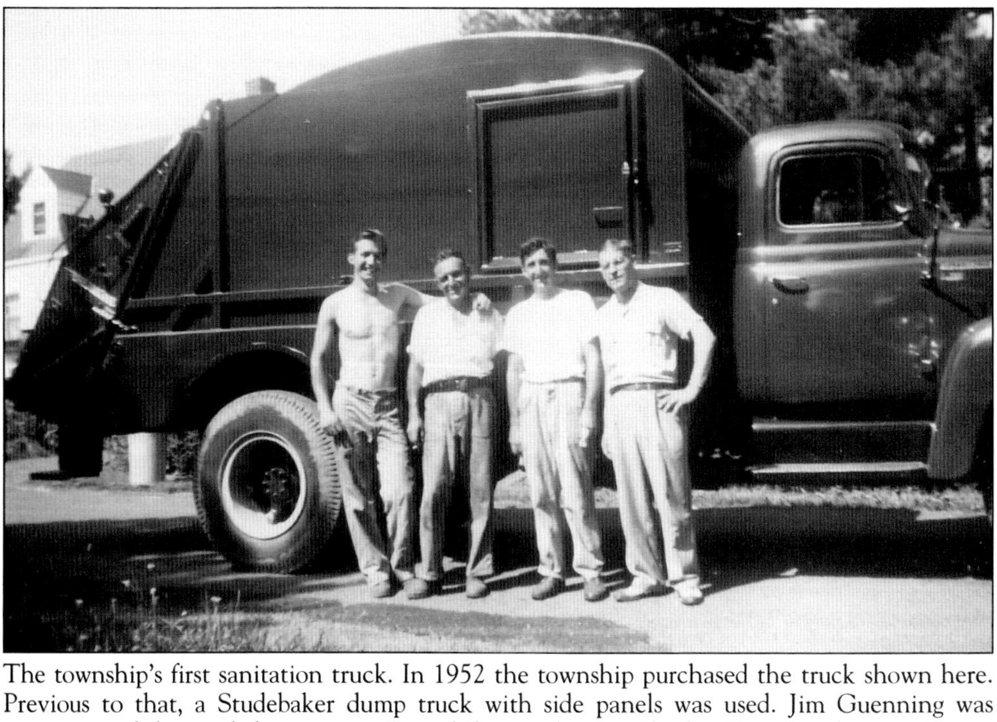

The township's first sanitation truck. In 1952 the township purchased the truck shown here. Previous to that, a Studebaker dump truck with side panels was used. Jim Guenning was supervisor of the road department. From left to right are Charles Dropp, unknown, Jimmy Sangavianni, and Micky McCollum. (Marion McCollum Armstrong.)

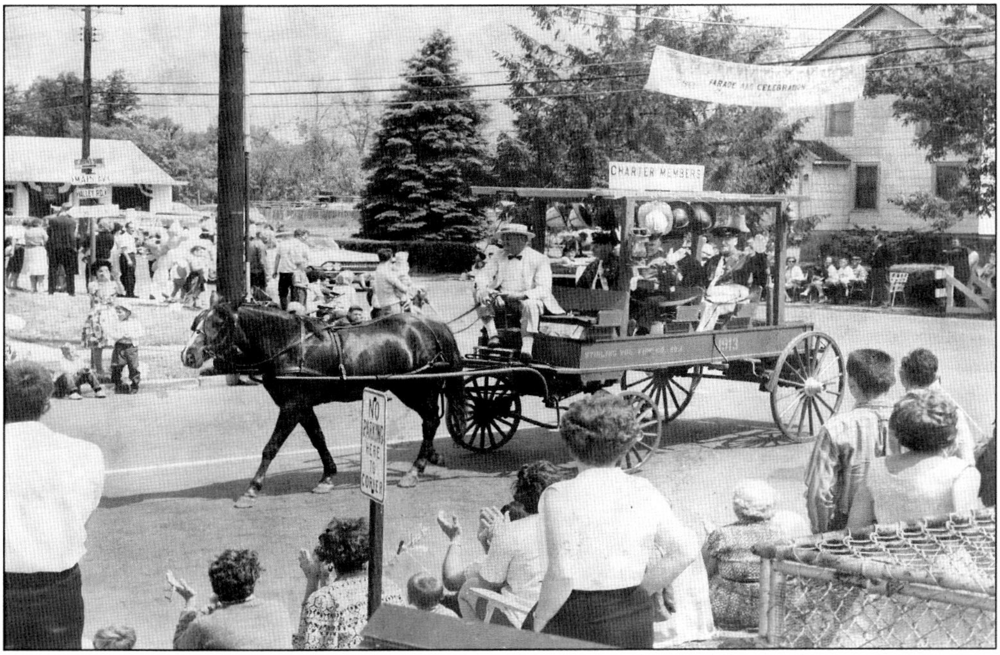

A parade on Main Street, *c.* 1953, to honor the charter members of the Stirling Volunteer Fire Company #1 for fifty years of committed service. Driving his horse and wagon is Archibald Stiles, and seated are Frank Murphy, Christof Lindenmeyer, and Dave Achille. (Emma & Archibald Stiles.)

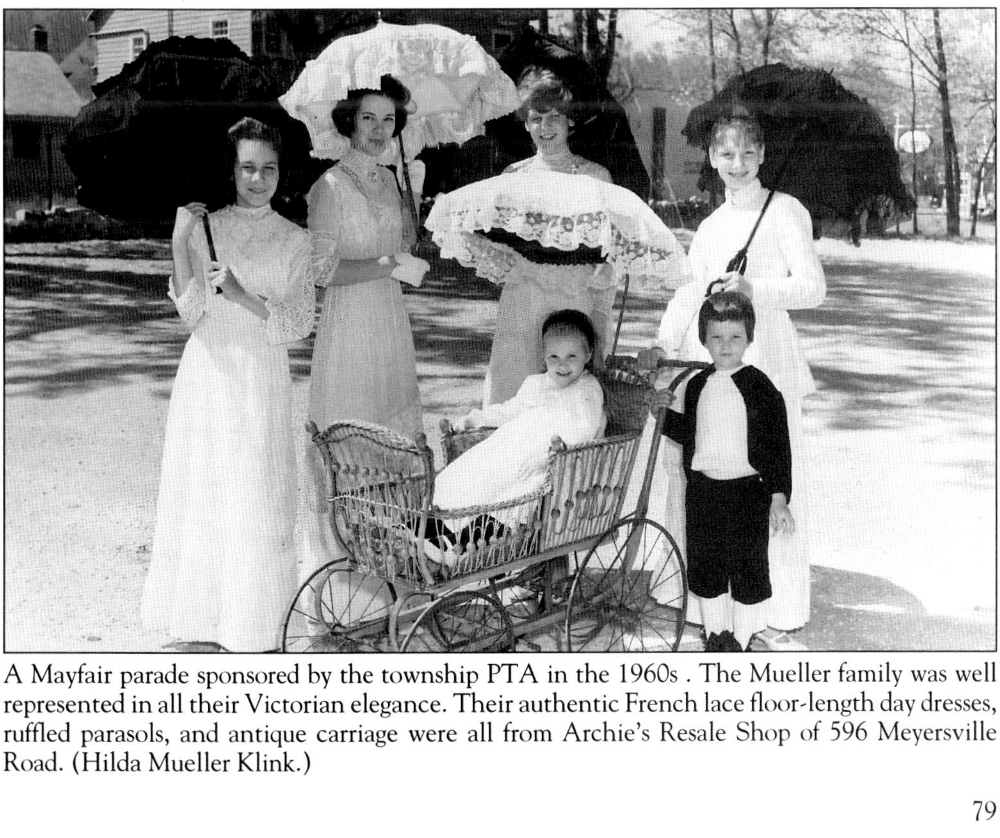

A Mayfair parade sponsored by the township PTA in the 1960s . The Mueller family was well represented in all their Victorian elegance. Their authentic French lace floor-length day dresses, ruffled parasols, and antique carriage were all from Archie's Resale Shop of 596 Meyersville Road. (Hilda Mueller Klink.)

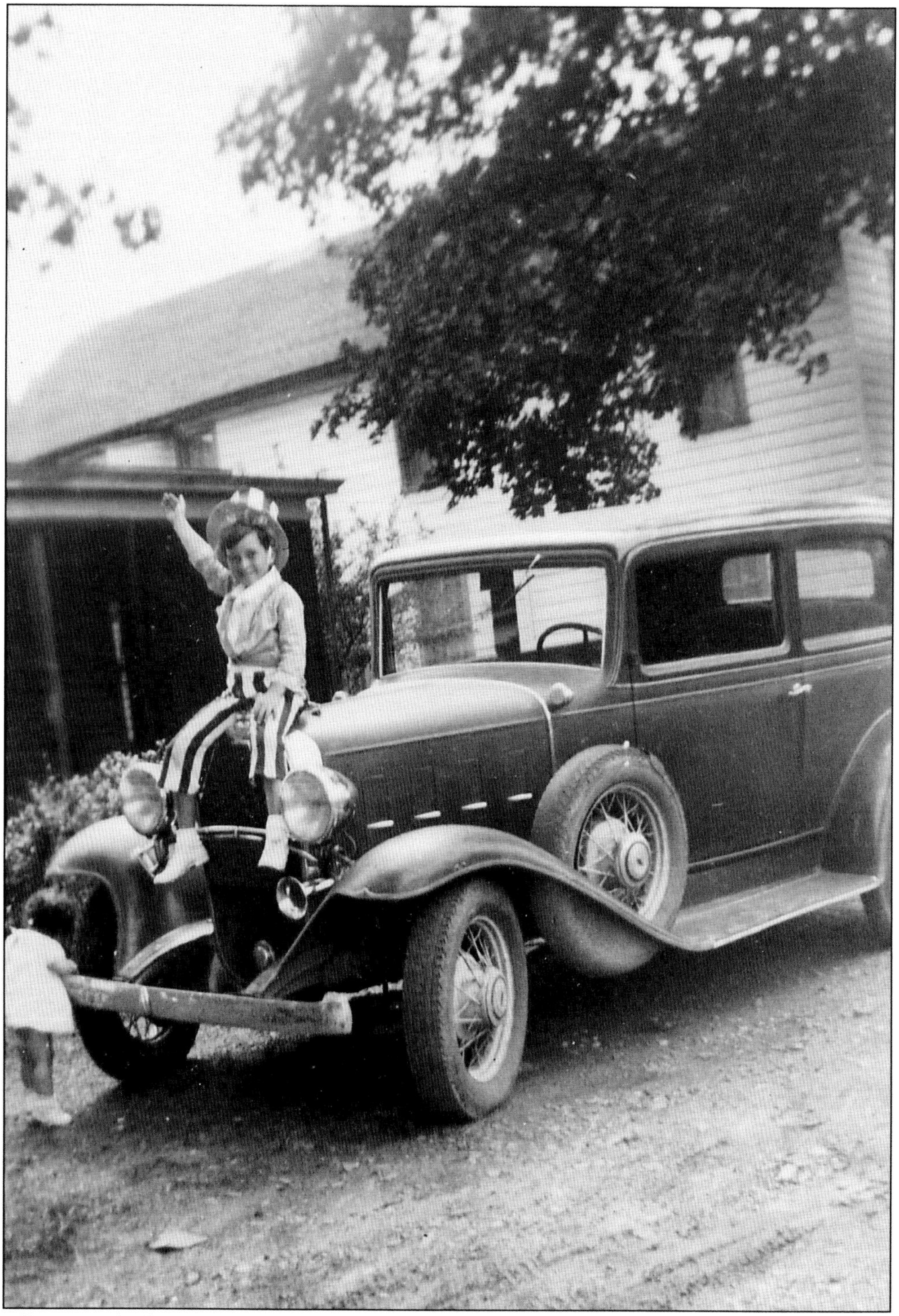

Albert Landwehr on the first Long Hill Township police car, a 1932 Chevrolet. Albert's sister, Mary Lou, awaits one of Stirling's parades on Main Street, c. 1938. (Mary Lou Landwehr Weller.)

Three

Gillette and Homestead Park

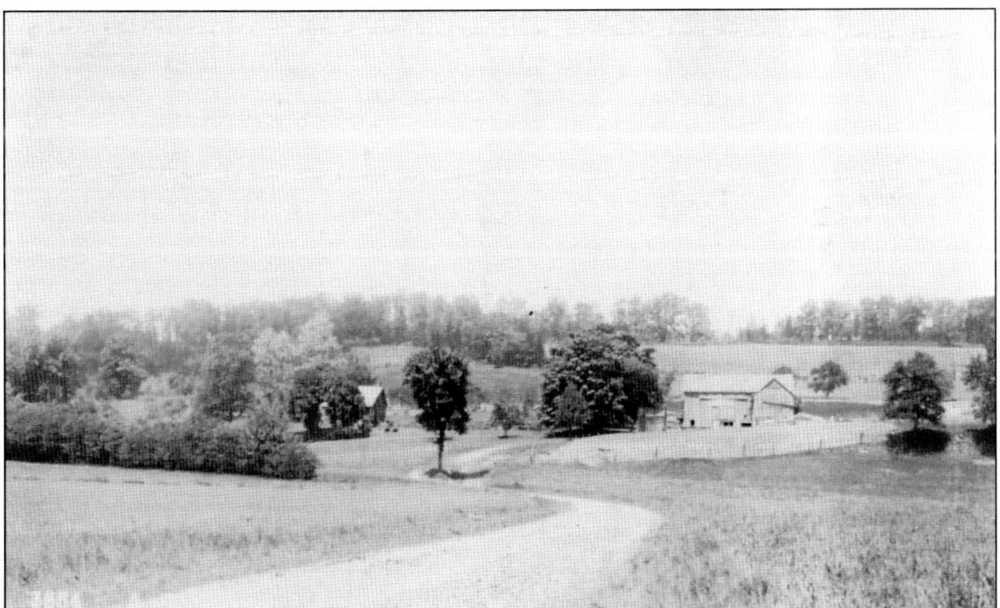

The Cornish farm, *c.* 1940, on 275 Mountain Avenue, Gillette. The farm was built in 1732 by James Caldwell, an Irish immigrant who was Gillette's first settler. Ancestors of the Cornish family purchased the farm in 1856. George Howell, a land surveyor, married Rachael Gillette Cornish in 1870 and named the area Gillette in appreciation of obtaining the right-of-way for the West Line Railroad to come through. There was a footpath from the Cornish homestead to Valley Road through their land before the advent of Mountain Avenue. (Mrs. J.B. Cornish.)

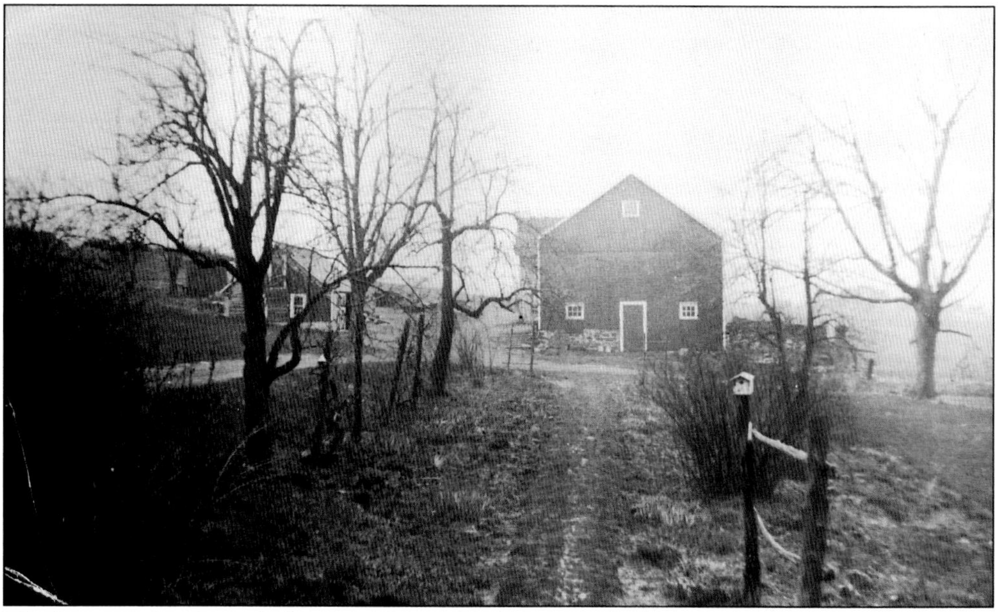

The barn on the Cornish farm, c. 1860. This barn was purchased from a farm on the site of what is now the St. Joseph Shrine, on Long Hill Road in Stirling. The building was taken apart and brought to the Cornish farm, where it was reconstructed by means of a turn-of-the-century instruction list. The list used Roman numerals, and called for hand-hewn beams and pegs to hold the barn together. It burned in 1957. (Mrs. J.B. Cornish.)

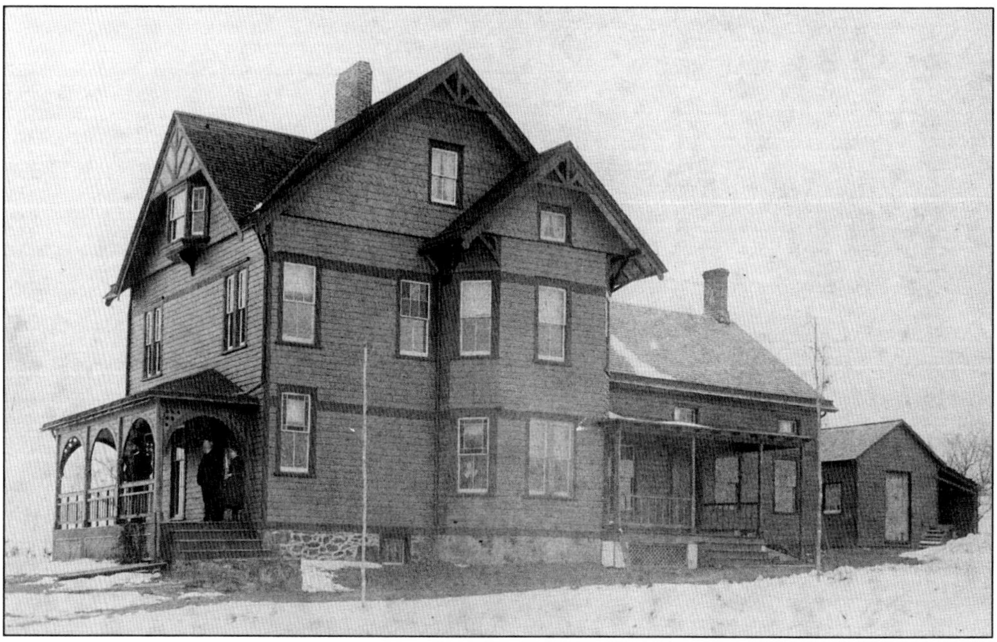

A Queen Ann-style nineteenth-century home owned by Robert Bates Cornish in the 1860s. He had a weather station and post office on the estate in the early 1900s. Mary Cornish established a small library on the east side of the house in 1937, to encourage the elementary students from Gillette School to stop by on their way home and pick up some extracurricular reading. (Cindi and Scott Heller.)

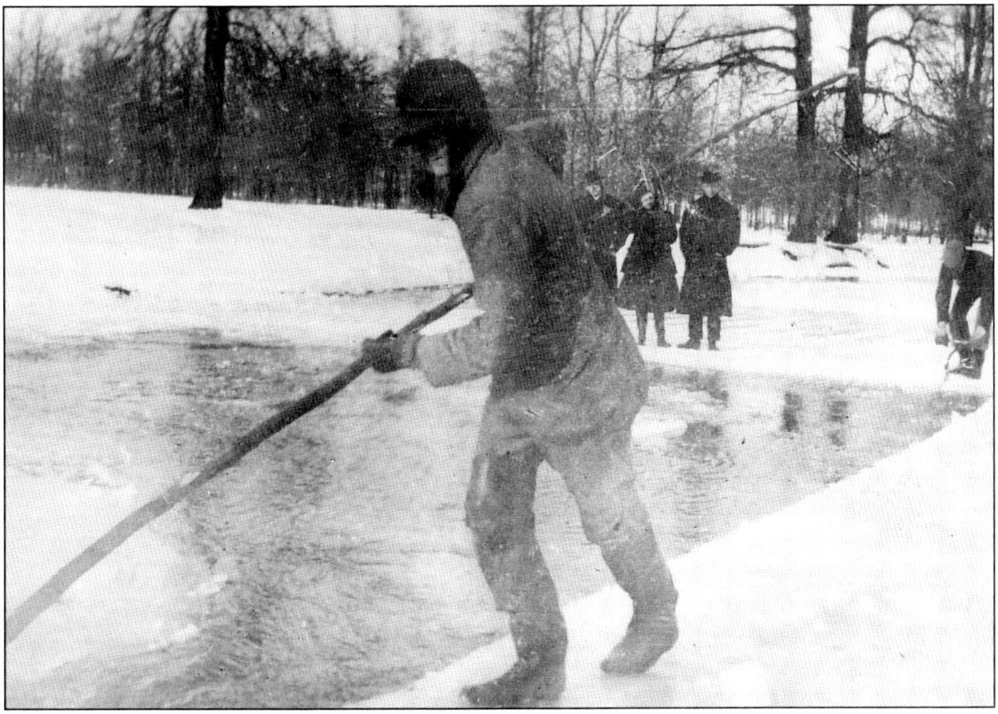

Charles A. Cornish cutting ice on the Passaic River in the early 1900s. The ice blocks were transported by horse and sleigh to the Cornish farm, and then stored in sawdust, where they would stay frozen until spring. (Mrs. J.B. Cornish.)

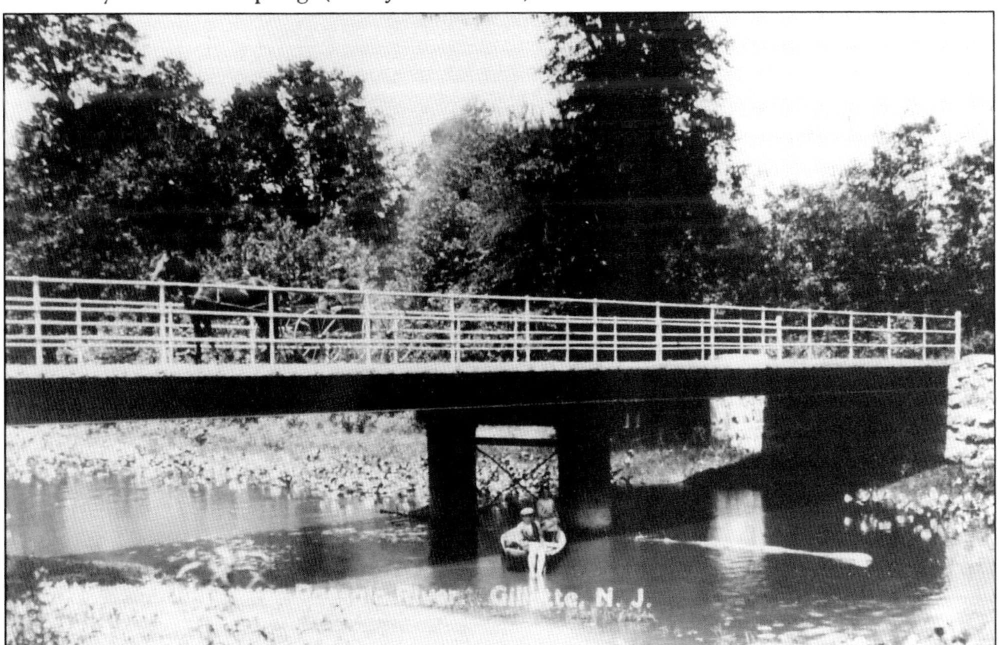

A horse-drawn buggy rolling over the Passaic River Bridge in Gillette in 1911. The river was considered an abundant fishing hole, and these children are shown trying their luck. (Ruth Castle Griffin.)

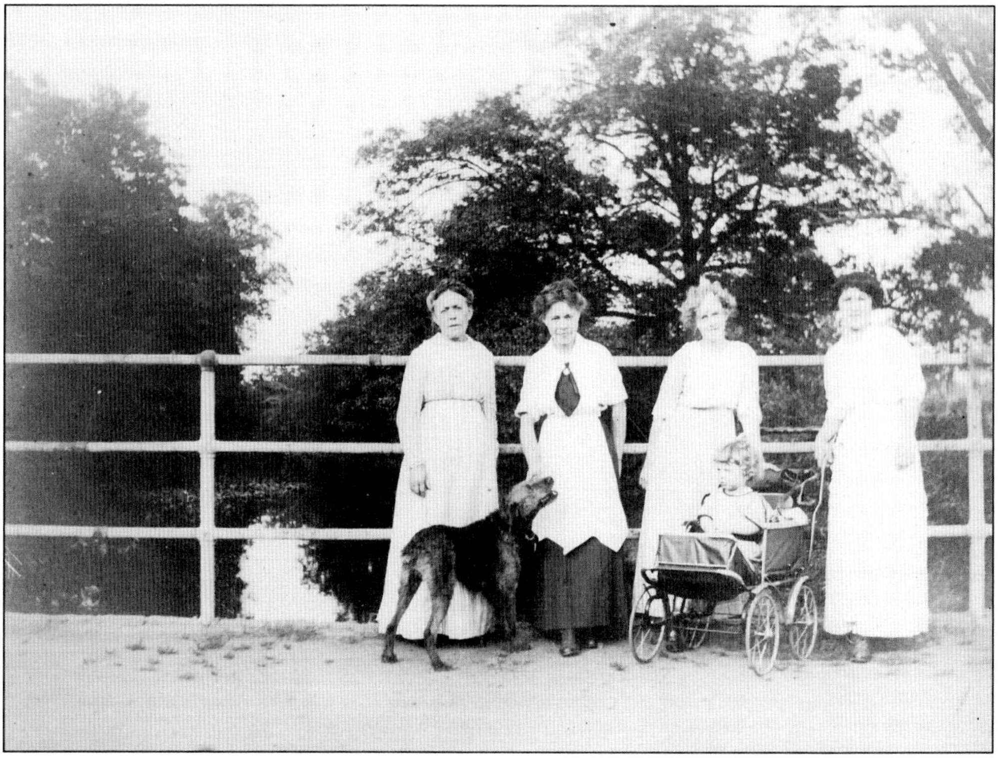

Longtime Gillette resident Freda Castle (second from left) and friends out in the midday sun on the Passaic River Bridge, *c.* 1919. They are the epitome of Victorian charm. (Ruth Castle Griffin.)

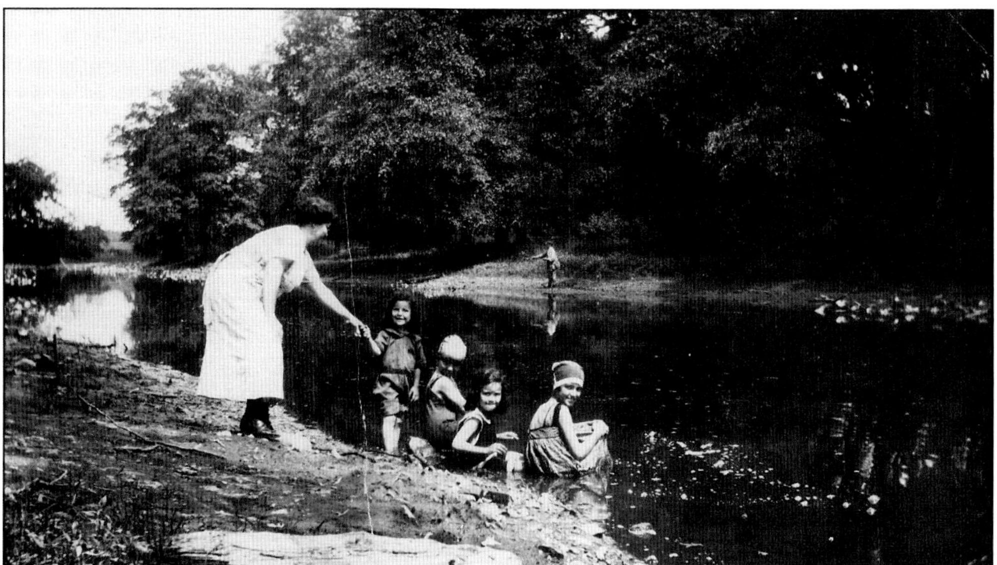

The Passaic River. The river was a treasured swimming hole in the early 1900s. Here we see Lydia Bogart watching over her daughter Dorothy and playmates as they wade at the river's edge. (Lynn Deveney Spurrier.)

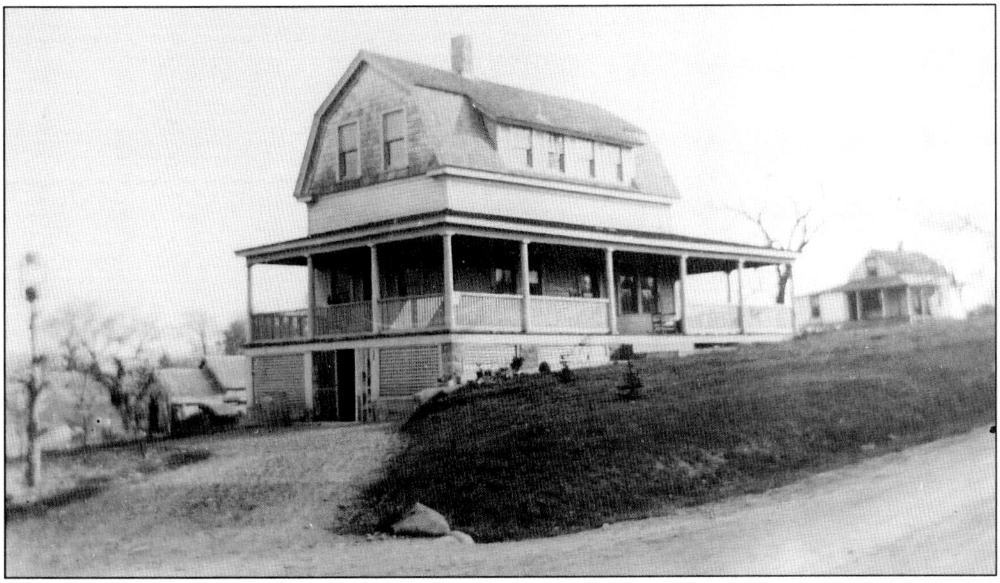

The Castle homestead. Built in the early 1900s on Valley Road, this is an accurate example of country colonial architecture. A street which ran behind the home was named Castle Place in behalf of the family. For fifty years the Castles ran and owned Castle Brothers Plumbing, one of the first and most prosperous businesses in Gillette, on Valley Road. The small bungalow to the right of the house was the home of Art and Mildred Welte. The building has since been taken down. (Eleanor Castle Groves.)

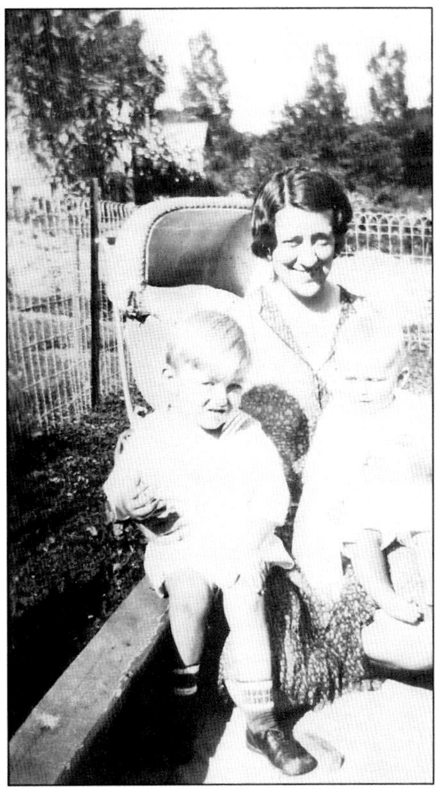

Mrs. Mildred Welte, neighbor Wesley Castle, and daughter Joan Welte at the Castle home on Valley Road in Gillette, c. 1930. Mildred's husband Arthur was township treasurer for many years. (Joan Welte Ogden.)

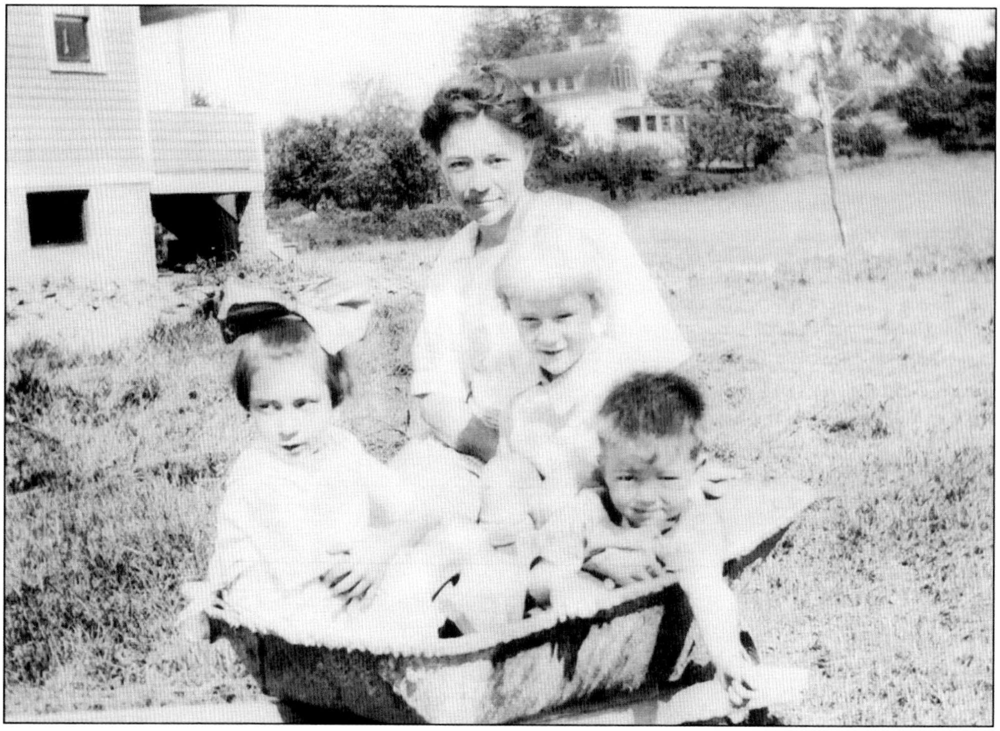

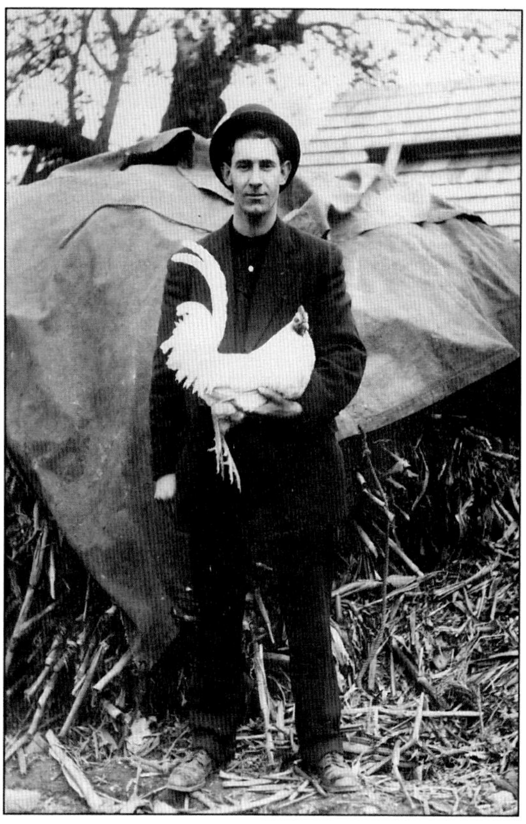

A family snapshot, *c.* 1928. John Castle doesn't appear here because he was out and about gathering up the supplies necessary to build their home on Castle Place. From left to right are daughter Ruth, wife Freda, young Walter Guy, and son John Castle Jr. (Ruth Castle Griffin.)

Charlie Castle, at home in the early 1920s, proudly displaying his prize rooster. The three Castle brothers raised chickens as a side business. (Eleanor Castle Groves.)

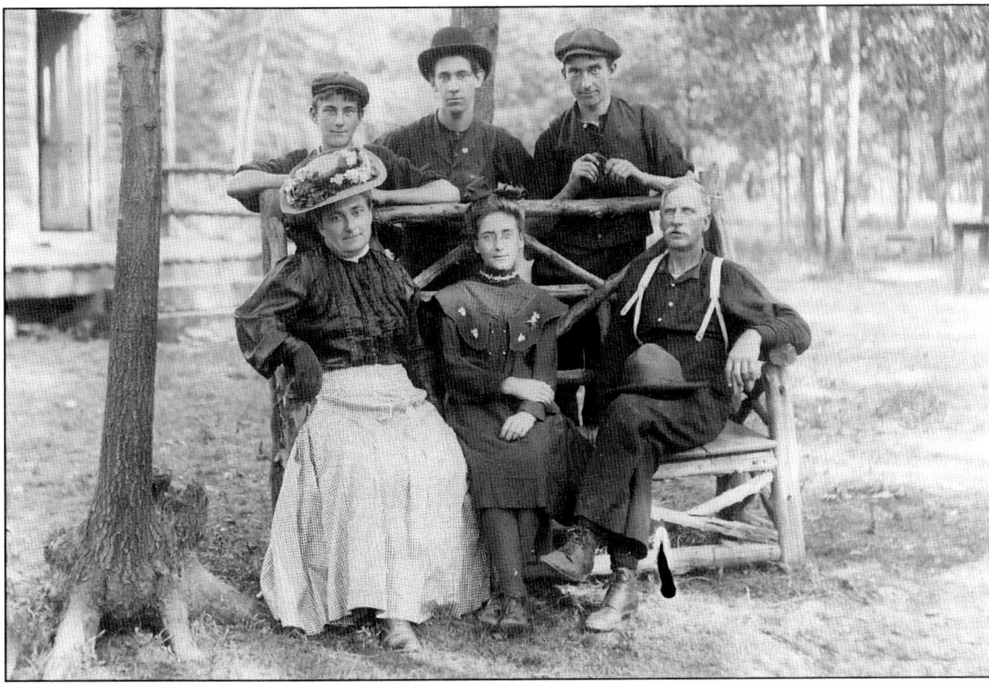

A Castle family portrait from the early 1900s. From left to right are as follows: (seated) wife Annie, daughter Edwina, and Charles Sr.; (standing) George Wesley, Charles Hamilton, and John Charles. The photograph was taken out on the side lawn on an Adirondack-style bench. The mode of dress depicted here—the straw bonnet adorned with posies, black ruffles, sweeping gingham, and workman's vests—typifies casual Victorian elegance. (Eleanor Castle Groves.)

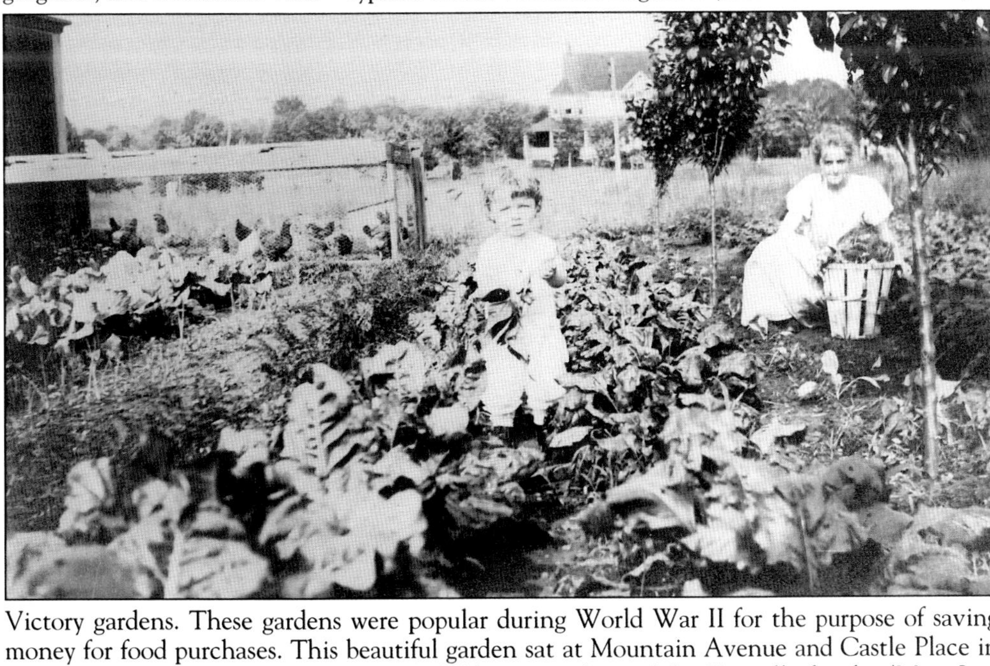

Victory gardens. These gardens were popular during World War II for the purpose of saving money for food purchases. This beautiful garden sat at Mountain Avenue and Castle Place in Gillette. It is believed the mother and child are members of the Hanville family. (Mary Lou Landwehr Weller.)

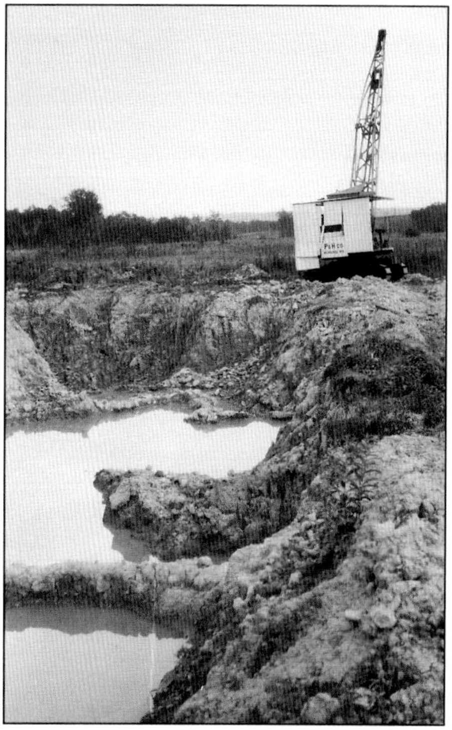

A gas-powered bucket loader, shown close to the Erie Lackawanna Railroad on Mountain Avenue, used to dig clay pits along the railroad in Gillette. The clay was sent to Newark by train, and flower pots were made by the William Ritger family of East Orange from 1878 through the early 1900s. (Craig R. Engesser.)

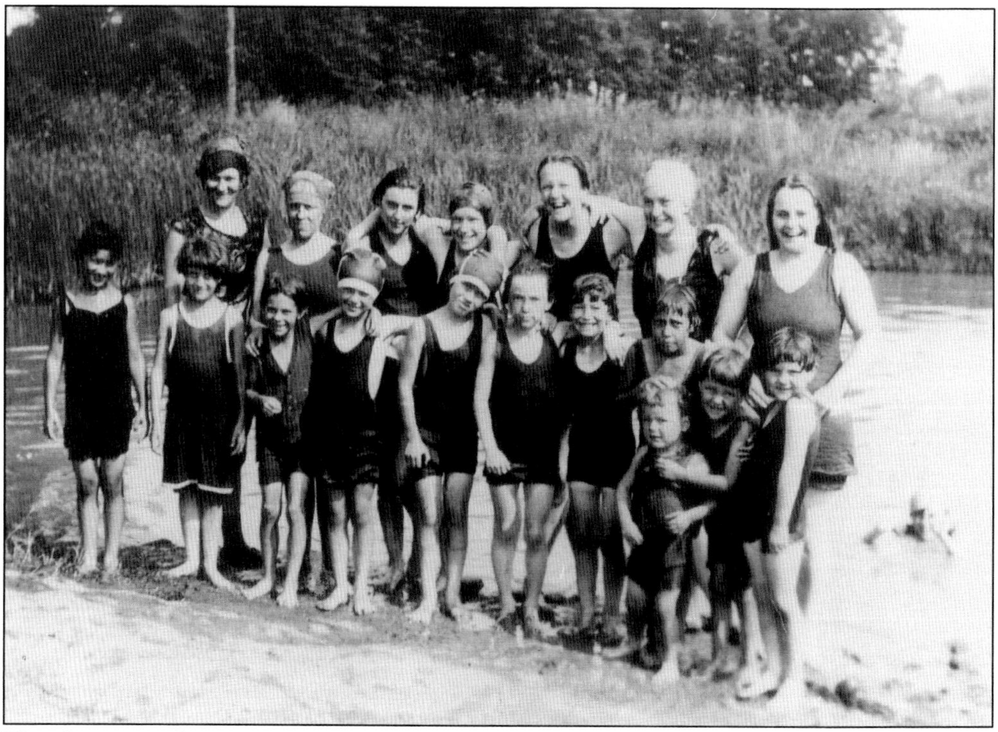

The clay pits, a favorite swimming hole for local children until the late 1950s. The pits were located just north of the railroad tracks. The clay was used by William Ritger to make flower pots. Catherine Cornish Thomas is fifth from the left in the top row. (Mrs. J.B. Cornish.)

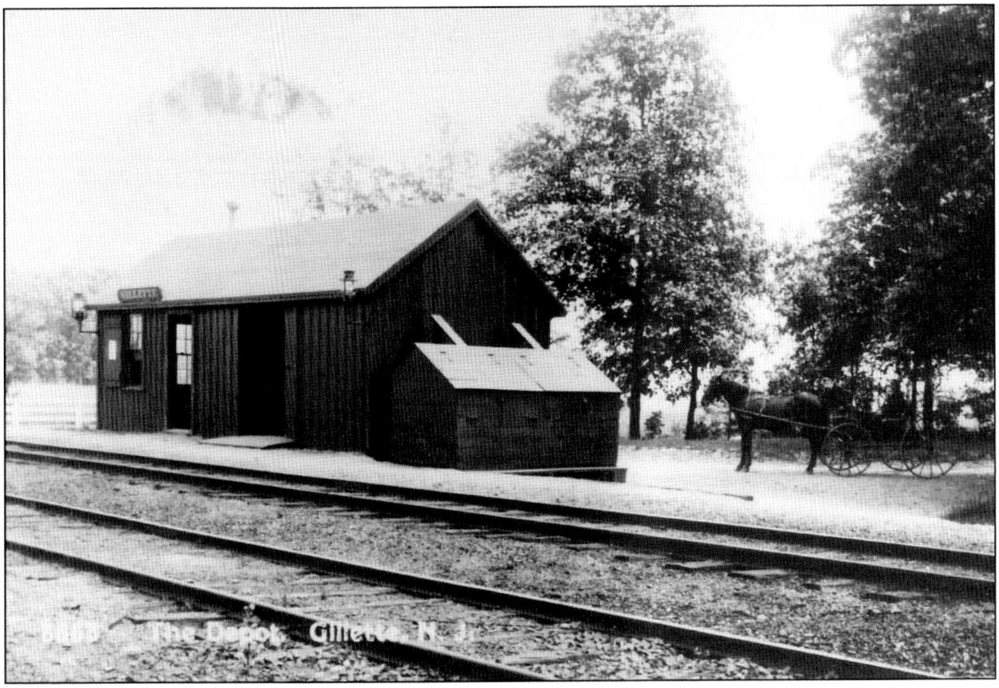

A 1912 postcard of the Gillette train station at the time of the Delaware Lackawanna Railroad. The taxi was the horse-drawn buggy. Inside, a pot belly stove kept commuters warm during the winter. (Ruth Castle Griffin.)

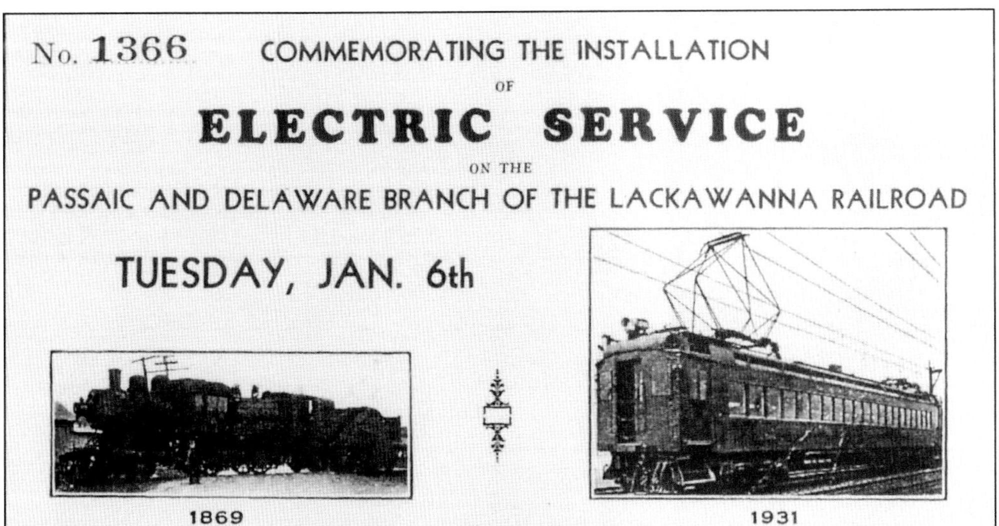
No. 1366 COMMEMORATING THE INSTALLATION

OF

ELECTRIC SERVICE

ON THE

PASSAIC AND DELAWARE BRANCH OF THE LACKAWANNA RAILROAD

TUESDAY, JAN. 6th

1869

1931

A ticket entitling the bearer to ride on the first official electric train of the Passaic and Delaware Branch of the Lackawanna Railroad. (John Castle.)

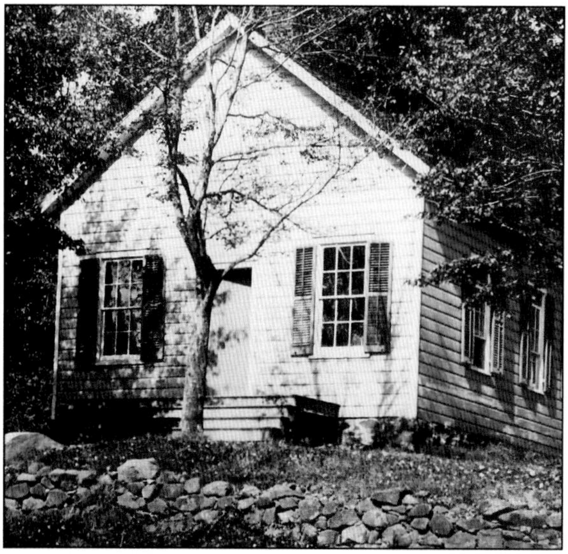

The Long Hill Schoolhouse, one of the first one-room schoolhouses in the area. Shown here *c.* 1890, it was built *c.* 1813 on part of the tract of Daniel Cory, an early settler, on the top of Long Hill Road in Gillette. The original foundation was built using huge logs with the bark left on, and the beams were connected by wooden pins. A horse and wagon transported the children up Long Hill Road to school each day. The school was also used for town meetings, church affairs, and Sunday school. It was sold in 1926, and is now a private residence. (Long Hill Township Historical Society.)

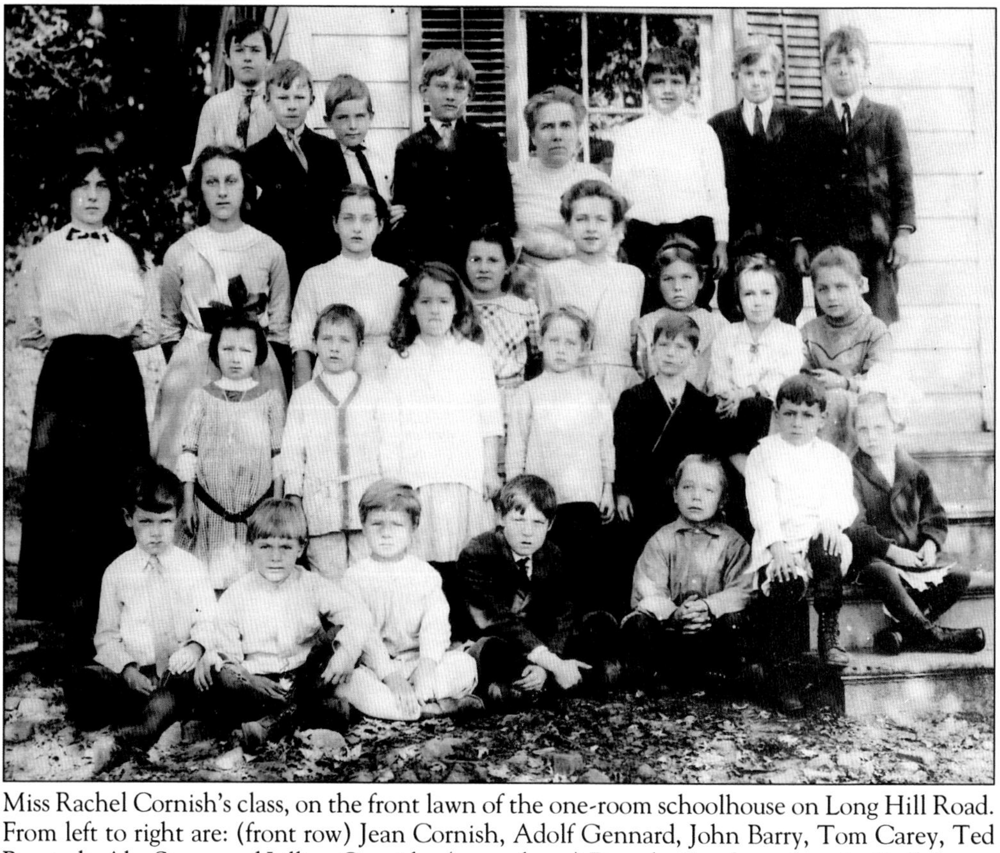

Miss Rachel Cornish's class, on the front lawn of the one-room schoolhouse on Long Hill Road. From left to right are: (front row) Jean Cornish, Adolf Gennard, John Barry, Tom Carey, Ted Reystedt, Abe Stern, and Lillian Cornish.; (second row) Dorothy Southern, Juanita Dull, James Burns, and Robert Weitzman; (third row) T.R. Weatherbee, Albertha Ortman, unknown, unknown, unknown, Anna Bebout, unknown, and Emma Rystedt; (back row) Brogley, Lloyd Ortman, unknown, Howard Ortman, Miss Rachel Cornish, Weatherbee, Allen Cornish, and Frank Nixdorff. (Mrs. J.B. Cornish.)

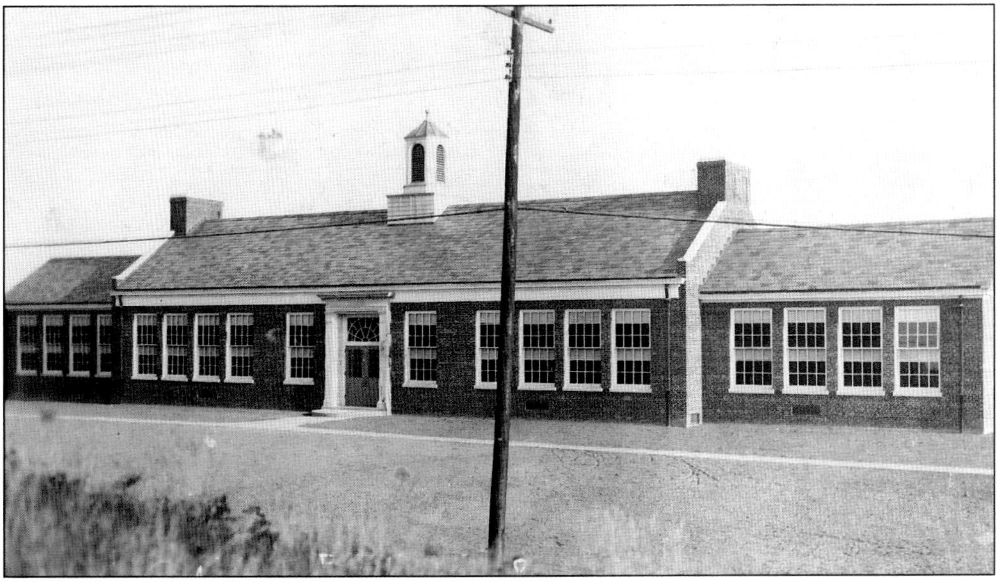

The Gillette Elementary School on Valley Road in Gillette, built by the Public Works Program in 1935. The Millington School was designed and built identically to that of Gillette's. Neither of the public schools had a library until Esther Cornish and Edna Adams Burback started one in the Gillette School with just a handful of books. At that time, grades were combined to conserve space. (Eleanor Castle Groves.)

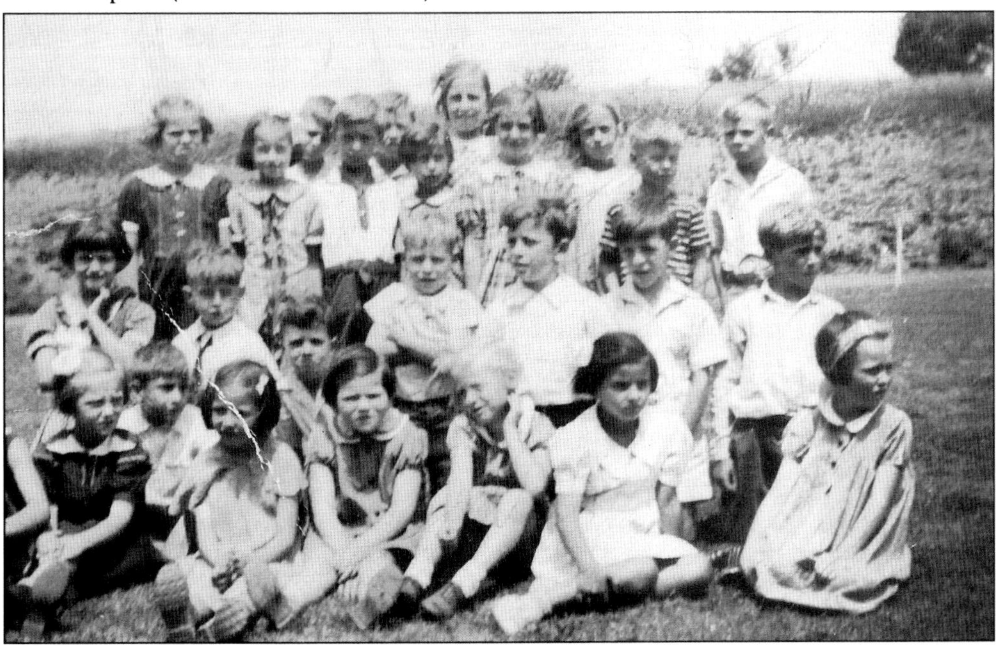

The Gillette Elementary School Class of 1936. Those that can be identified are, from left to right, as follows: (front row) four unidentified students, Marion McCollum, Clementine Malfatone or Romona Cortese, and Joan Welte; (second row, by himself) Herbert Litwin; (third row) Eileen Bray, Lorraine Patterson, Walter Ziegelmeier, Libby Litwin, Theresa Green, Mary Radder, Roger Meara, and Peter Wawzik; (back row) Peter Wawzik, Steve Schaffer, and Violet Green. (Joan Welte Ogden.)

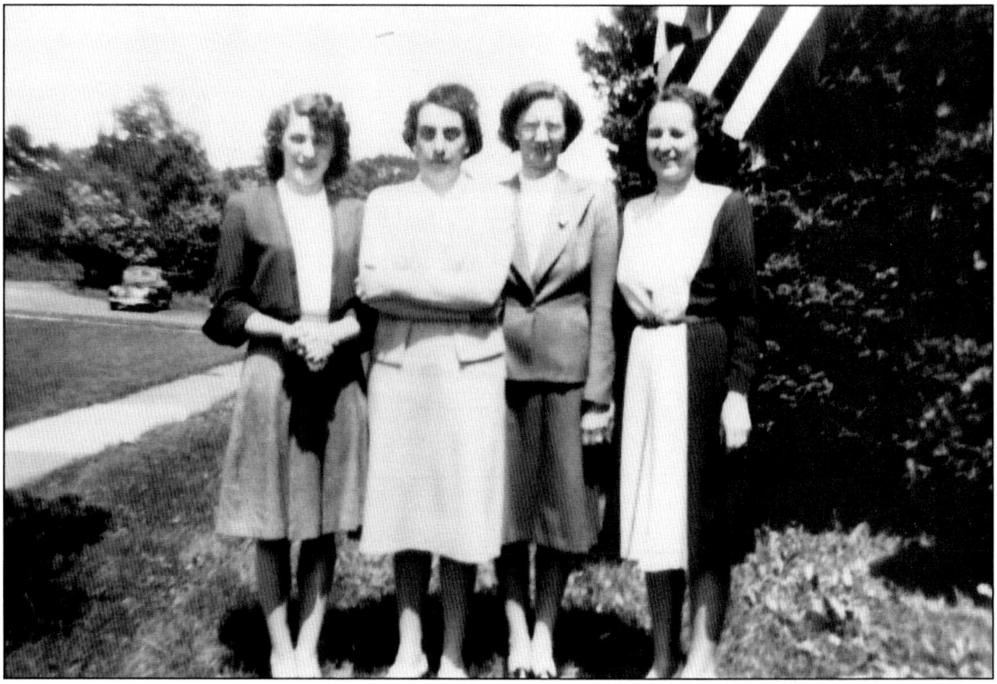

The Gillette Elementary School teachers in front of the school. In this June 3, 1946 photograph are, from left to right, Hazel Davis, Mrs. Edna Burbach, Sybill Davis, and Matilda Sage. (Mary Falyarono Thoms.)

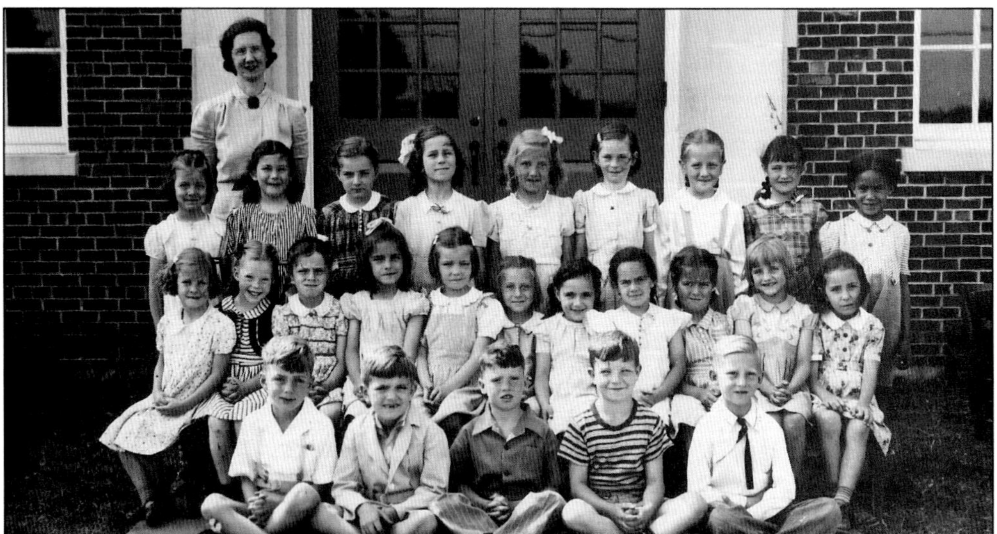

The Gillette Elementary School Class of 1940, grades three and four. The teacher is Mrs. Sybil Davis. From left to right are as follows: (front row) Burton Sharpe, James Frey, unknown, Donald Swertsfeger, and Tommy Ackerman; (middle row) Ruth McMane, Barbara Hansen, Pat Spaulding, Lois Patterson, unknown, Adele Housecamp, unknown, Mary Lou Landwehr, Katherine Crysler, Lois Page, and Ruth Daniels; (back row) Virginia Meyers, unknown, Margaret Leidenheimer, Vera Karg, Rose Marie Zander, Joan Stewer, Gladys Jansen, Nancy Reynolds, and Lavina Hilbert. (Mary Lou Landwehr Weller.)

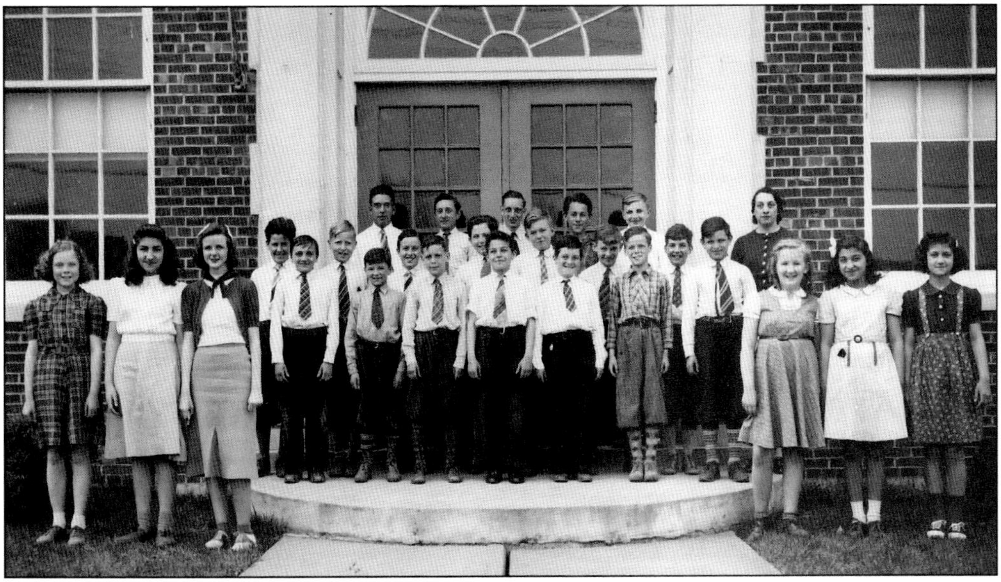

The Gillette Elementary School Class of 1939–40. The teacher is Mrs. Burbach. The girls, moving from left to right, are as follows: unknown, Dorothy Cortese, Helen Rist, Katherine Kutcher, Freda Fucci, and Mary Rademacher. The boys, from left to right, are as follows: (front row) Anthony Falzarano, three unknown students, Albert Landwehr, Irving Meara, and Eugene Piano; (middle row) Carl Torsilere, George Riesz, unknown, Anthony DeSiena, Wesley Castle, William Thievon, and Albert Zander; (back row) Sal LoPresti, James Sangievanni, Edwin Bianco, Elmer Wolfe, and John Skrobacz. (Eleanor Castle Groves.)

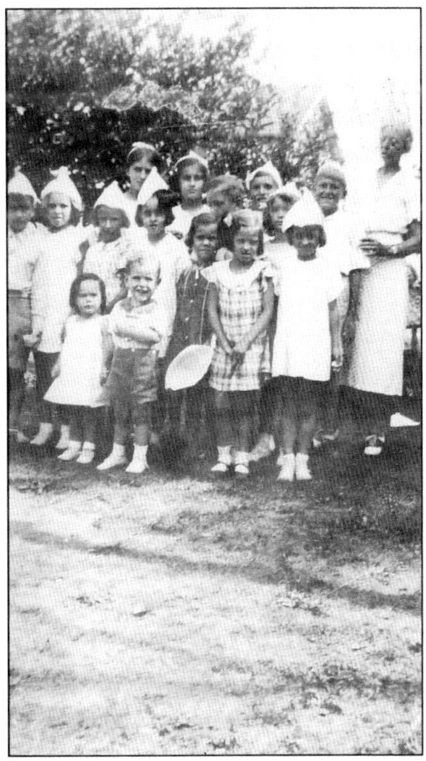

A 1937 birthday party at the home of Mrs. Keim, on Castle Place in Gillette. Local children pose in their party hats and finest dress. (Mary Lou Landwehr Weller.)

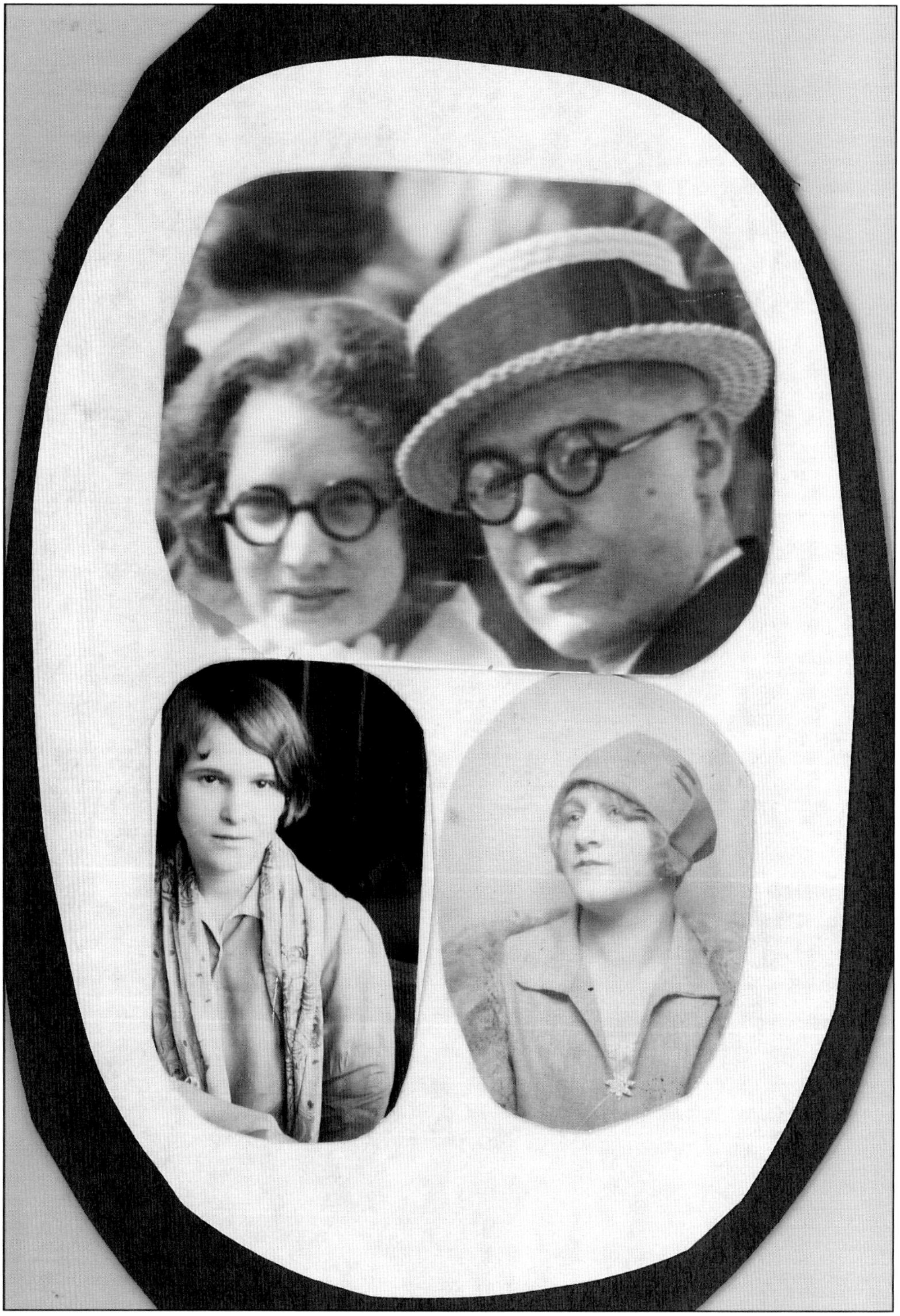

A collage of "The Roaring Twenties," gracefully represented by Grace and Micky McCollum, Helen Jacenty, and Margaret Landwehr in all their Great Gatsby-style charm. (Marion McCullom Armstrong, Joe Jacenty, and Mary Lou Landwehr Weller.)

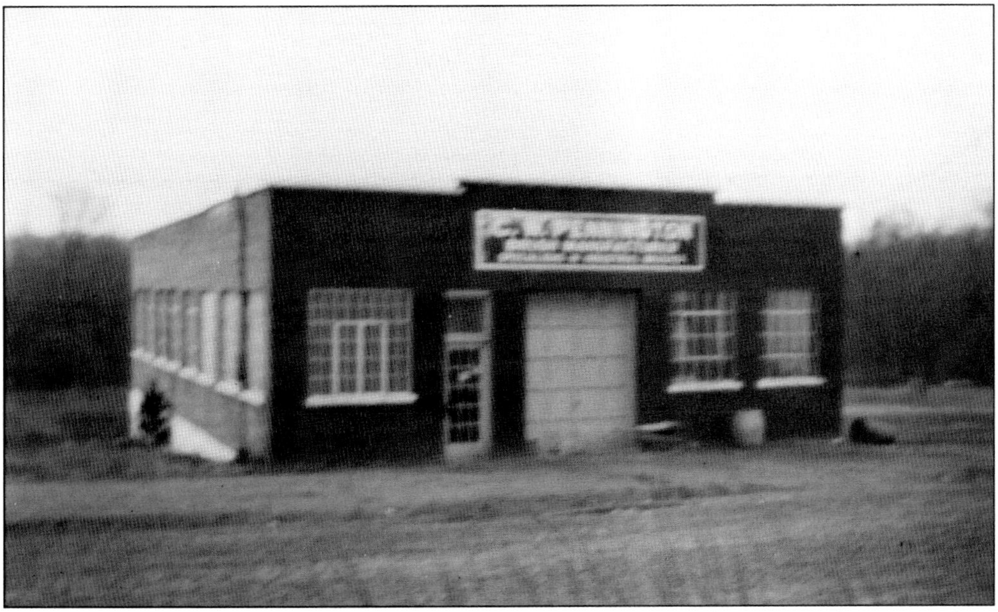

The Pennington Brush Factory, one of the few industries in Gillette, *c.* 1940. Located on Riverside Avenue, the company made varnished wooden brushes of all kinds and was active from the 1940s through the late 1960s. Many Gillette residents still recall working here. Today, the building is vacant but still standing. (Lynn Bogart Spurrier.)

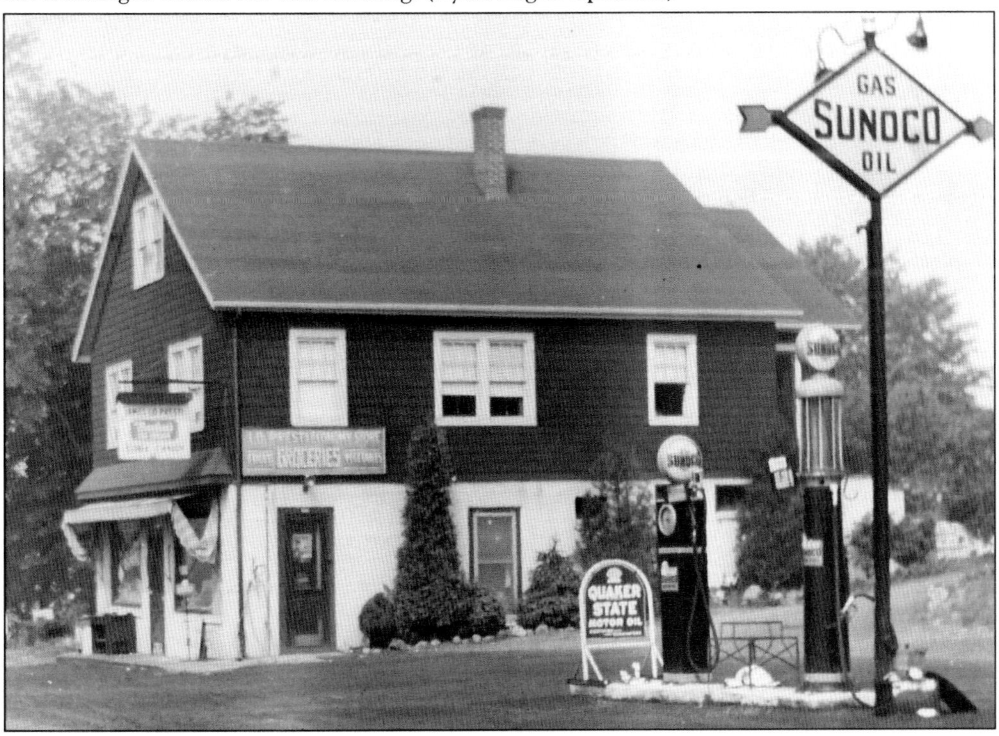

LoPresti's General Store, owned and operated by James and Rose LoPresti. Shown here *c.* 1950, this authentic country "Mom and Pop" business flourished from the 1920s through the 1960s. Liquor, gas, and fresh home-grown fruit and vegetables were sold here. (Lynn Bogart Spurrier.)

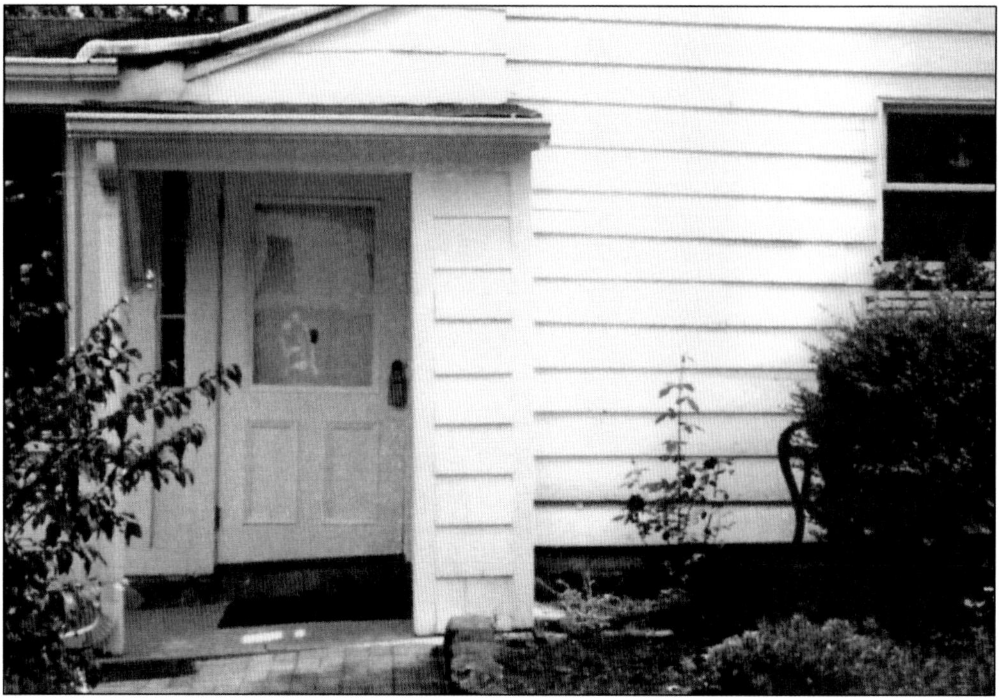

The first site of A.W. Nixdorff's general store. In the *Atlas of Morris County, New Jersey* (1868), this house is identified as being owned by J. Mathews. It was originally reached by a small dirt road off of Valley Road and Mountain Avenue (which was not created until 1870). A.W. Nixdorff operated his general store, one of the first businesses in Gillette, from this house in the 1800s. The water pump and stone steps are still intact. The house has been remodeled and redesigned, and is now a private residence. (Mary Lou Landwehr Weller.)

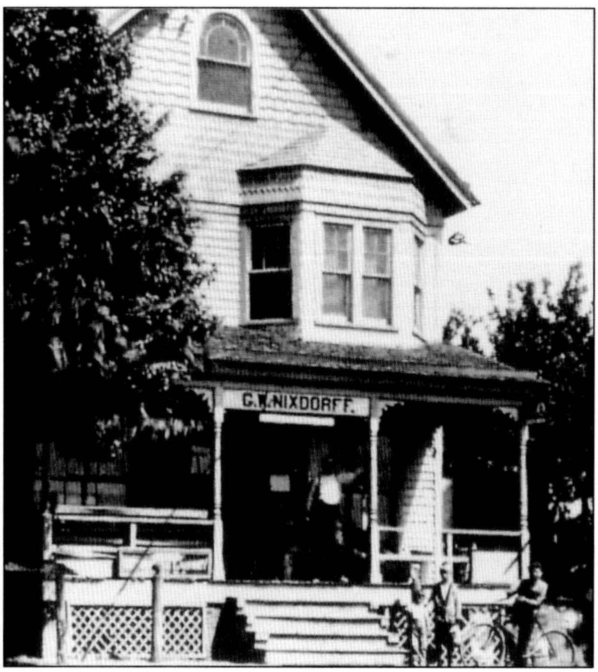

The second location of A.W. Nixdorff's general store. Nixdorff moved his general store to this building on the corner of Valley Road and Mountain Avenue. Shown here c. 1912, it was later to hold a post office. During the 1930s, owner William Musson took telephone orders and delivered groceries throughout the town. (Long Hill Township Historical Society.)

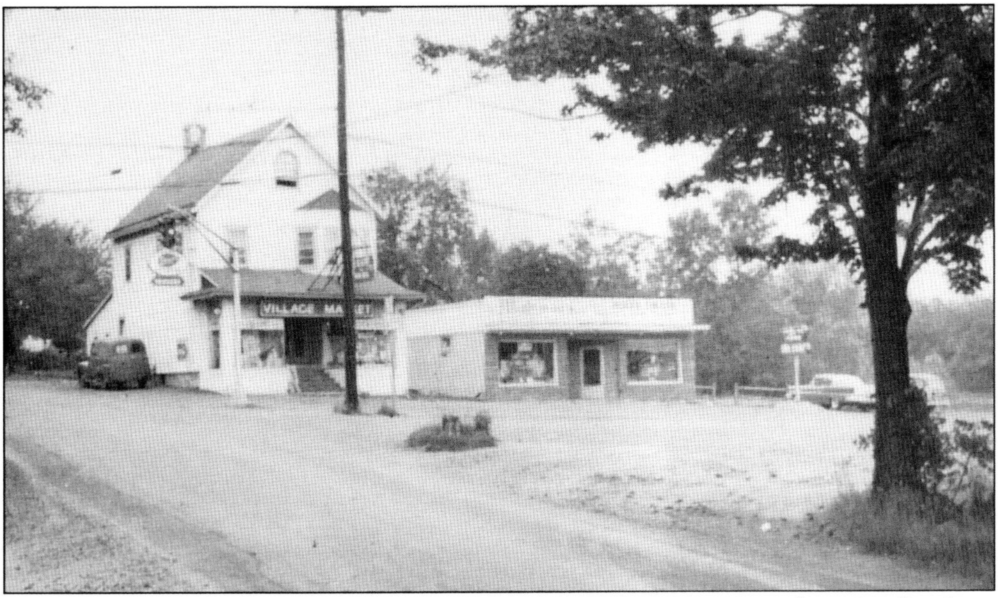

The center of Gillette, looking north from the Passaic River, *c.* 1950. William Brodhead ran the general store, which was owned at the time by the Joseph Tokash family. Wightmann's Variety and Gift Shop and a real estate office can be seen to the right of the store. (Mary Lou Landwehr Weller.)

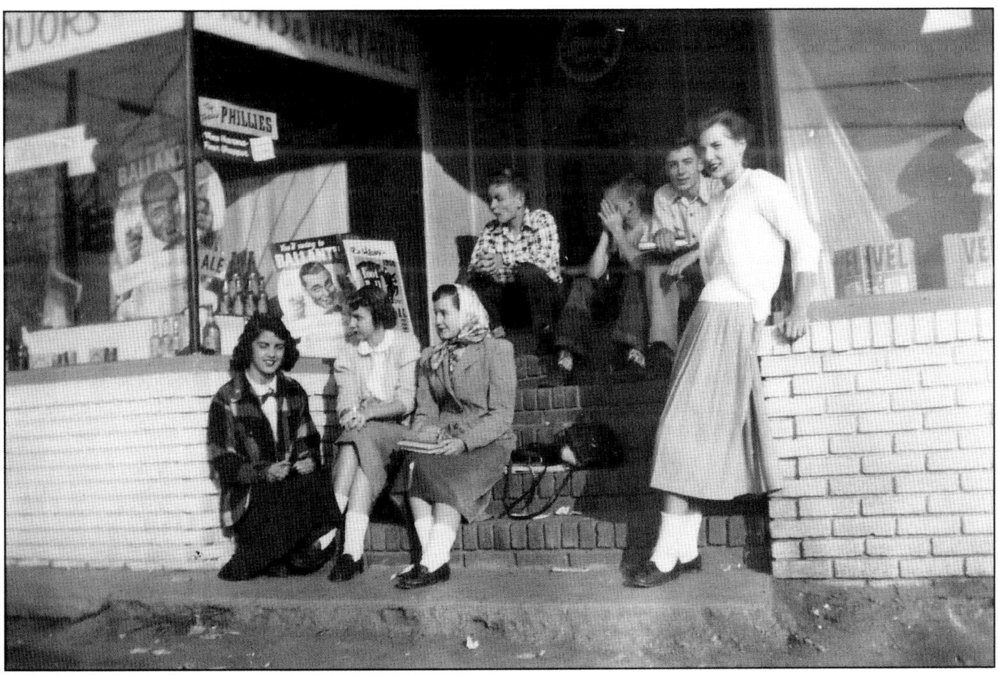

Awaiting the school bus on the front steps of the general store in Gillette, 1950. From left to right are Lois Patterson, Adele Housecamp, Mary Lou Landwehr, Joseph Tokash Jr., Fred Tokash, Burton Sharpe, and Margaret Leidenheimer. An ice cream parlor in the back of the store was an after school hangout for high school students seeking malted milk shakes and conversation. (Mary Lou Landwehr Weller.)

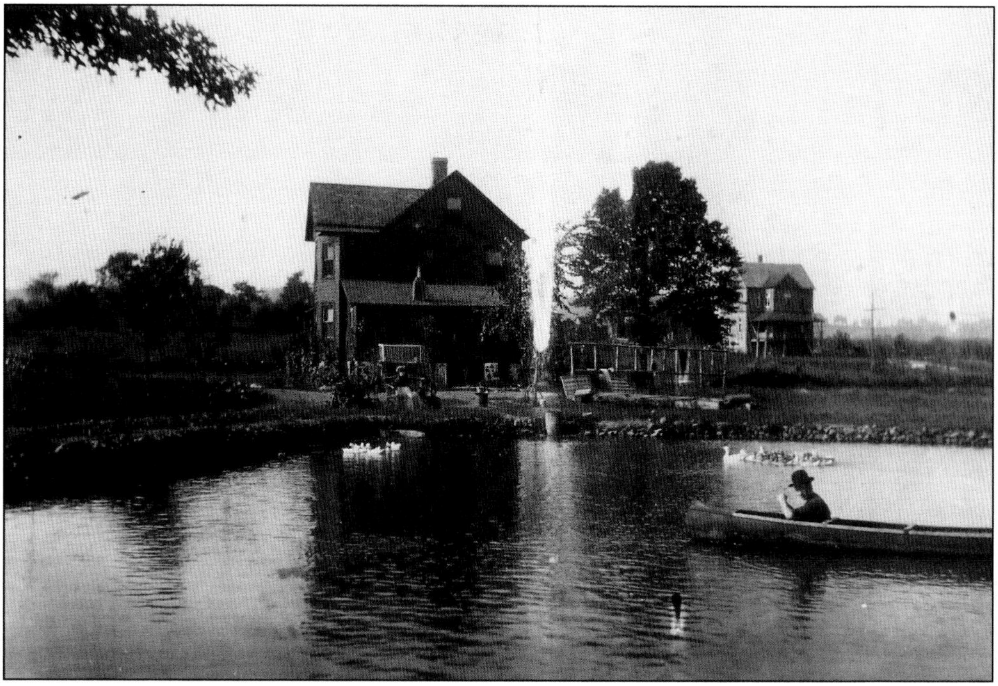

The Bogart homestead at 587 Valley Road in Gillette, heading east to Berkeley Heights. Edward Bogart is shown here in 1901 while in his wood canvas canoe. During the winter local children came to this pond to skate. The house visible on the opposite side of the dirt road (now known as Valley Road) belonged to the Rystedts, who owned the first automobile in Gillette, a 1915 Ford. (Lynn Bogart Spurrier.)

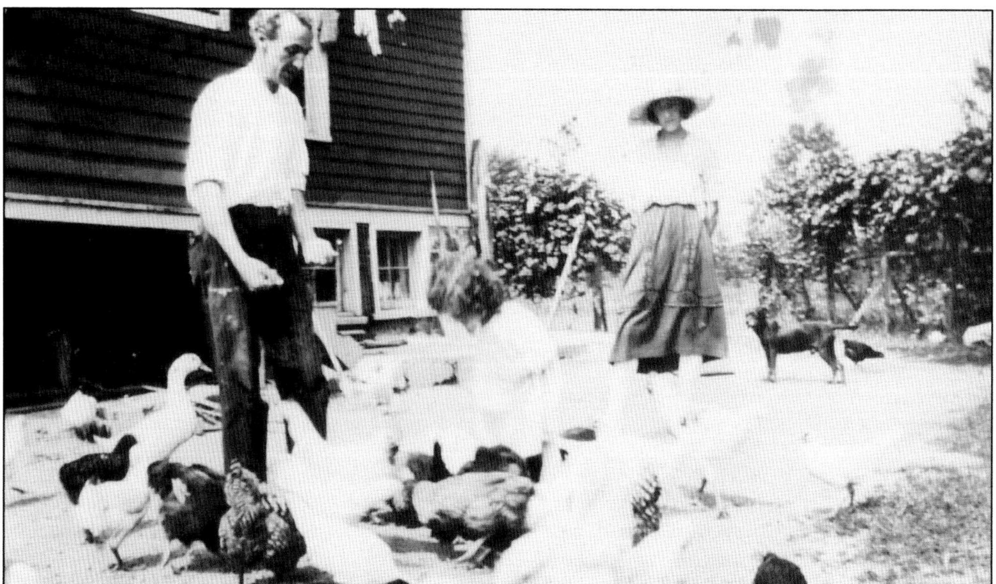

Gladys and Mortimer McHugh in 1917, feeding their chickens at their home on Valley Road in Gillette. The child's name is unknown. (Lynn Bogart Spurrier.)

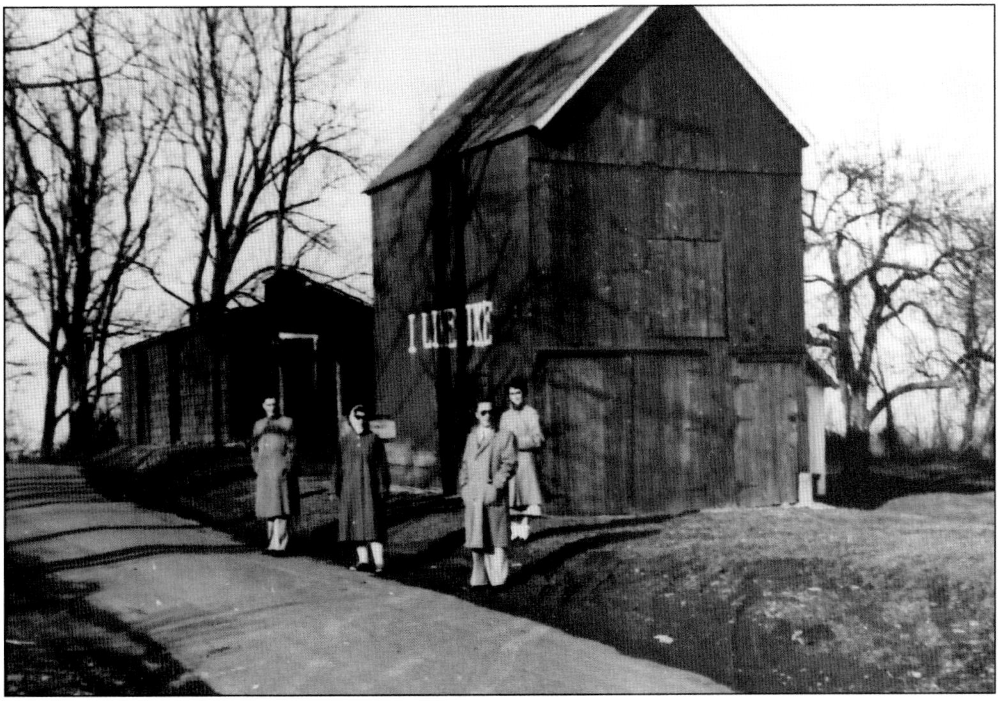

A c. 1957 photograph of the barn that sits behind one of Gillette's oldest homes, on 438 Hickory Tavern Road. "I Like Ike" was the trendy slogan during the Stevenson-Eisenhower campaign in the 1950s. Pictured, from left to right, are Reinhard Rist, Joey Ackerman, Marisa Navarro, and Inge Rist. (Inge Rist Lincoln.)

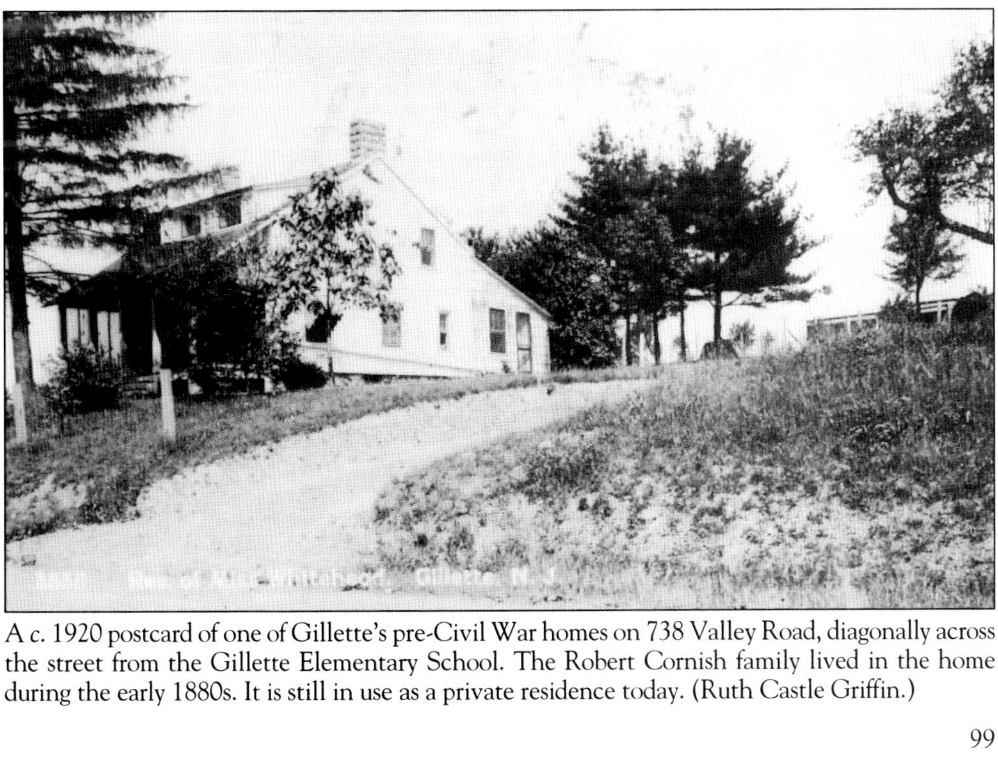

A c. 1920 postcard of one of Gillette's pre-Civil War homes on 738 Valley Road, diagonally across the street from the Gillette Elementary School. The Robert Cornish family lived in the home during the early 1880s. It is still in use as a private residence today. (Ruth Castle Griffin.)

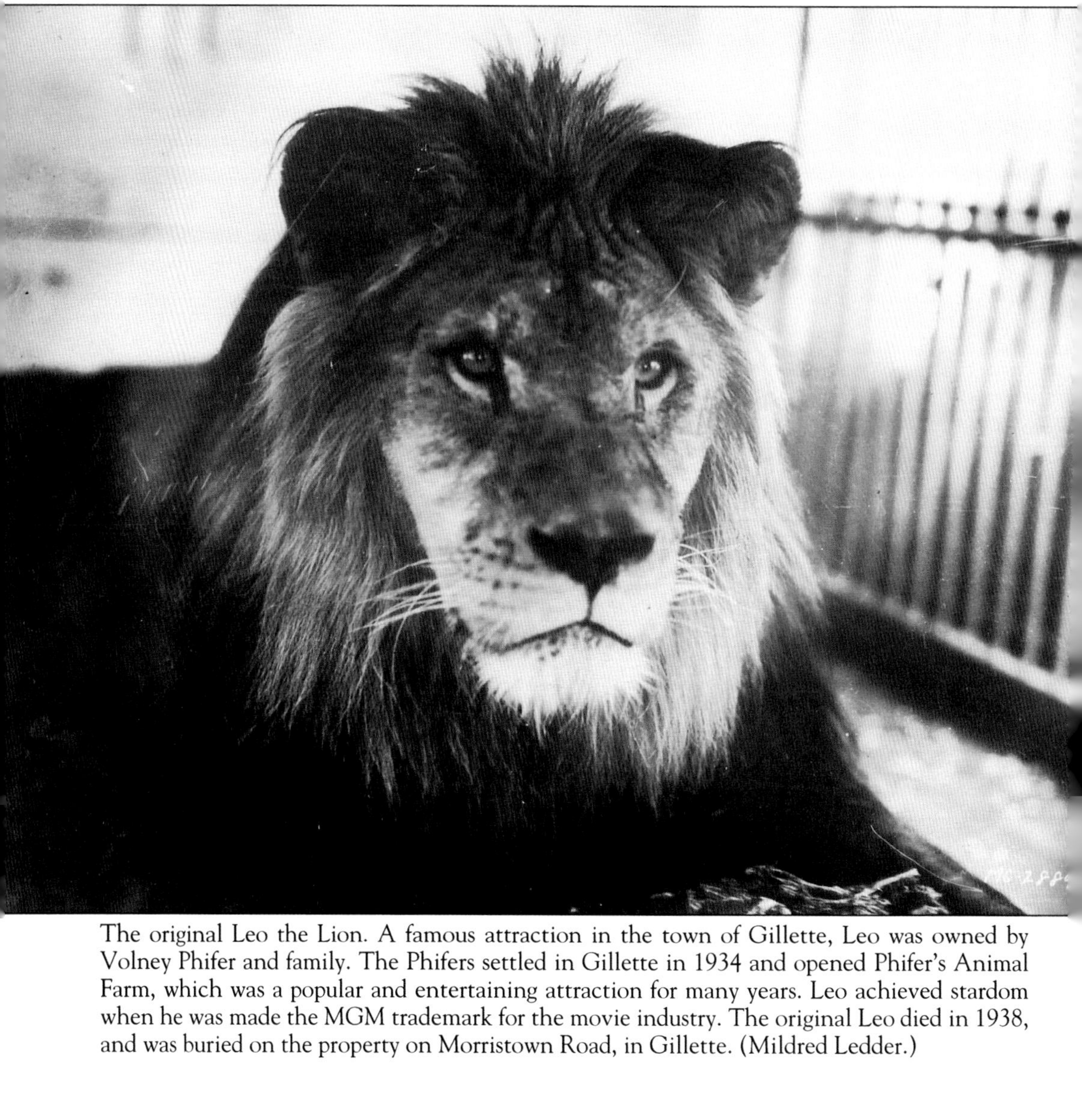

The original Leo the Lion. A famous attraction in the town of Gillette, Leo was owned by Volney Phifer and family. The Phifers settled in Gillette in 1934 and opened Phifer's Animal Farm, which was a popular and entertaining attraction for many years. Leo achieved stardom when he was made the MGM trademark for the movie industry. The original Leo died in 1938, and was buried on the property on Morristown Road, in Gillette. (Mildred Ledder.)

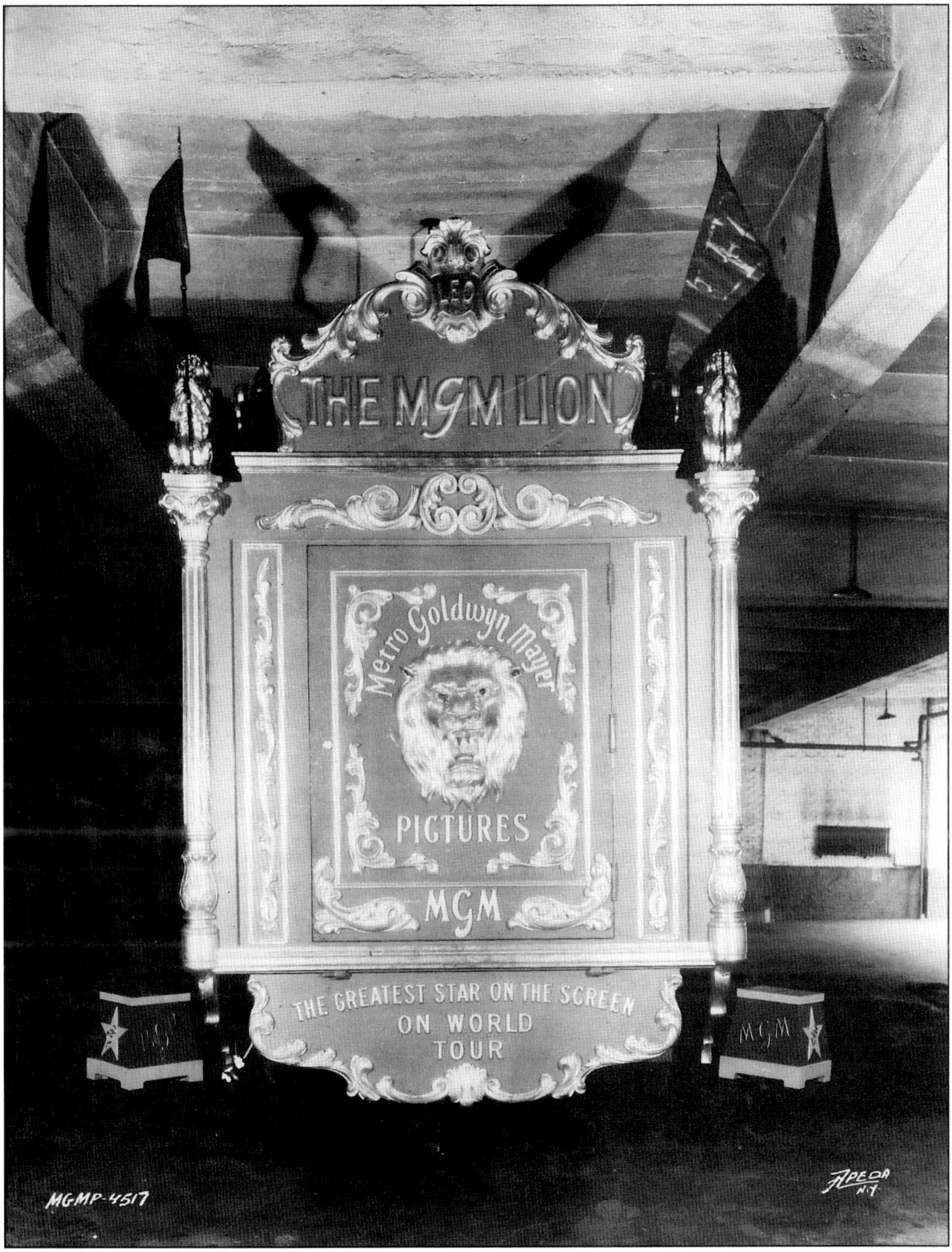

The original logo on the back of the traveling van used to transport Leo the Lion during the Phifers' journeys throughout the U.S. (Mildred Ledder.)

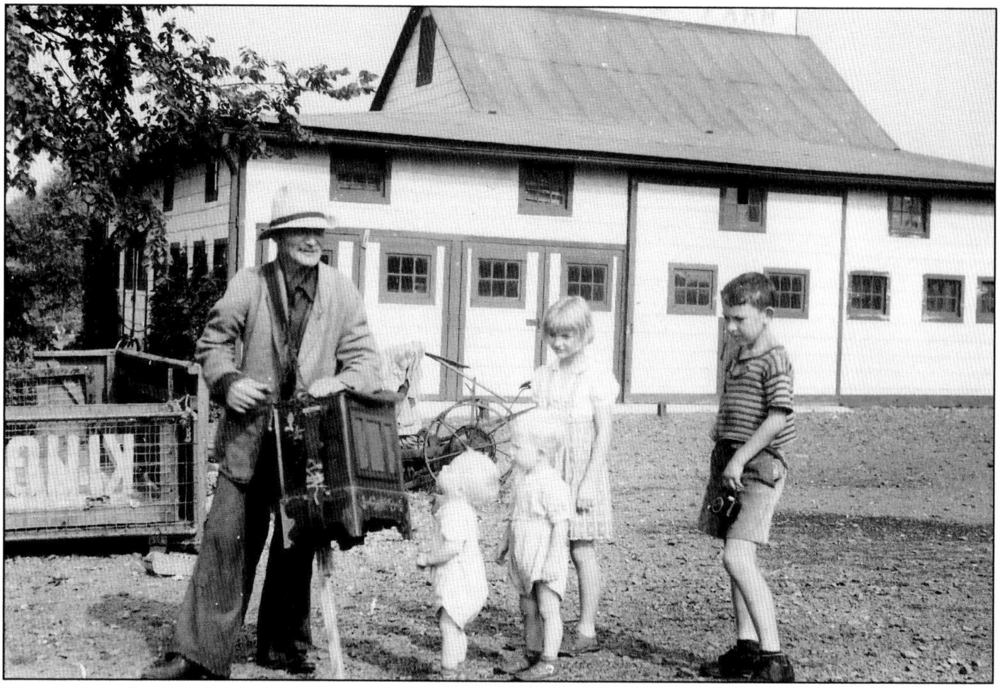

Remember the hurdy-gurdy organ grinder? He used to walk all over the area, playing music and entertaining children. He is pictured here with Wayne McCutchen, Bernard McCutchen, Lois Page, and Ellis Phifer, at Phifer's Animal Farm in the early 1940s. (Mildred Ledder.)

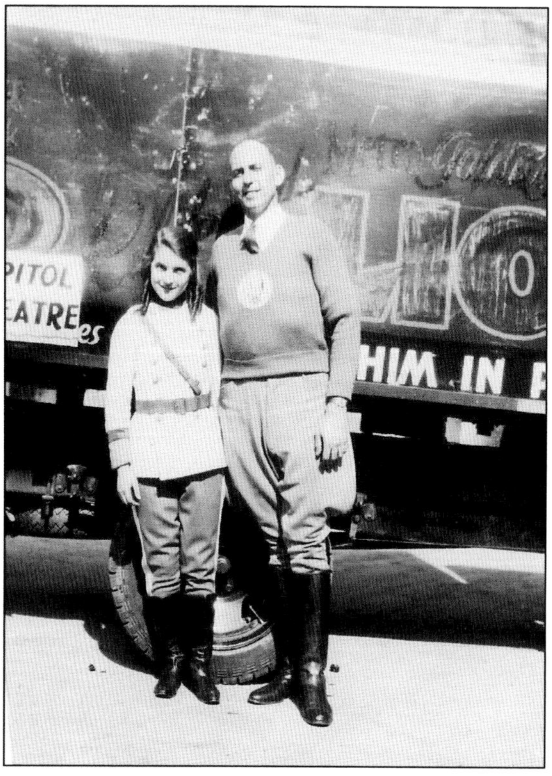

Volney Phifer and his wife Eloise. The couple is shown here in the 1930s, in front of one of their several touring trucks, at the farm where they worked together training animals. They had two children, Carole and Ellis. (Mildred Ledder.)

A Christmas card from 1950 of Ellis and Carole, sent out by Phifer's Animal Farm. (Mildred Ledder.)

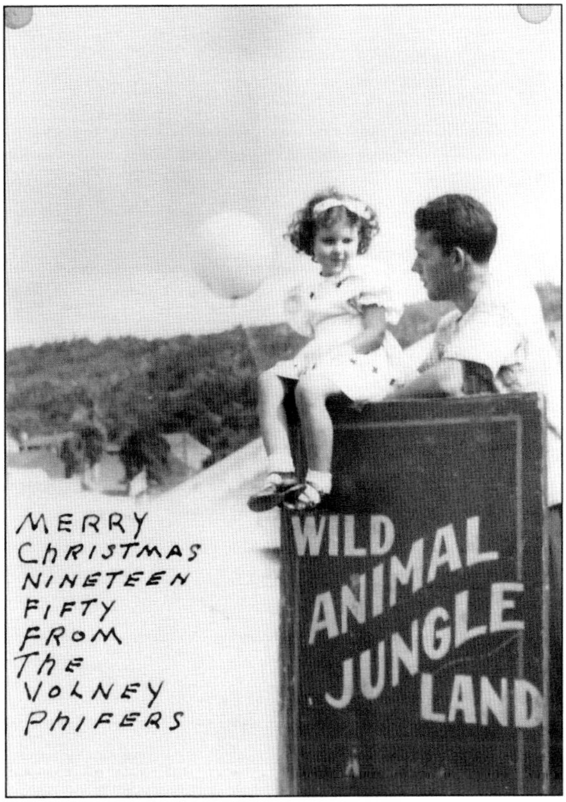

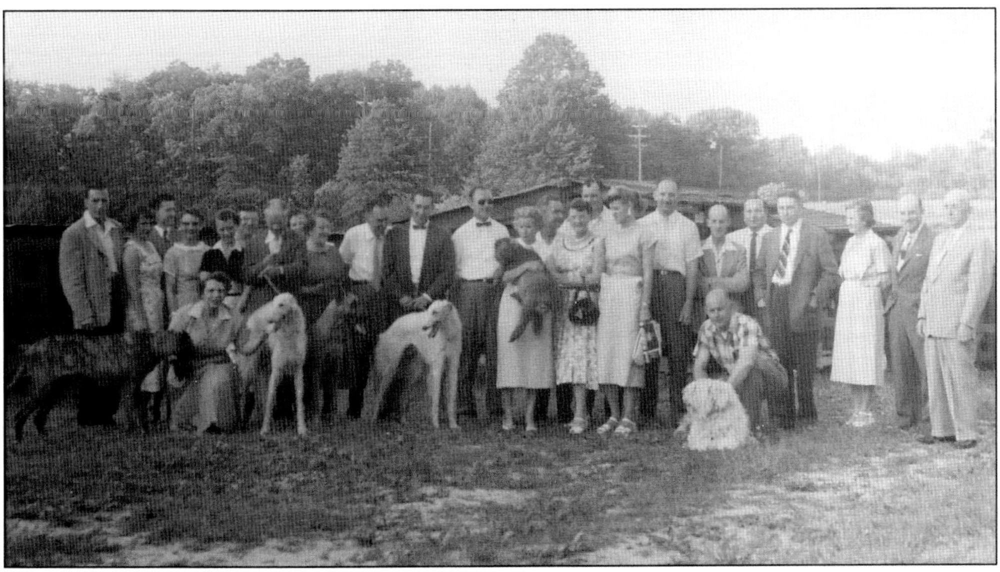

The Chamber of Commerce of Long Hill Township, one of many organizations through the years that picnicked at Phifer's Animal Farm on Morristown Road in Gillette. Included in this photograph are Tony Mishuk, Dot Mishuk, Walter McCutchen, Alma McCutchen, Mildred Ledder, Lorraine Diessen (kneeling), Mr. Diessen, Mr. and Mrs. Fred Schaan, Ted Ledder (kneeling), Russel Thomas, Kenny Hamler, and Sheena Hay, c. 1953. (Mildred and Ted Ledder.)

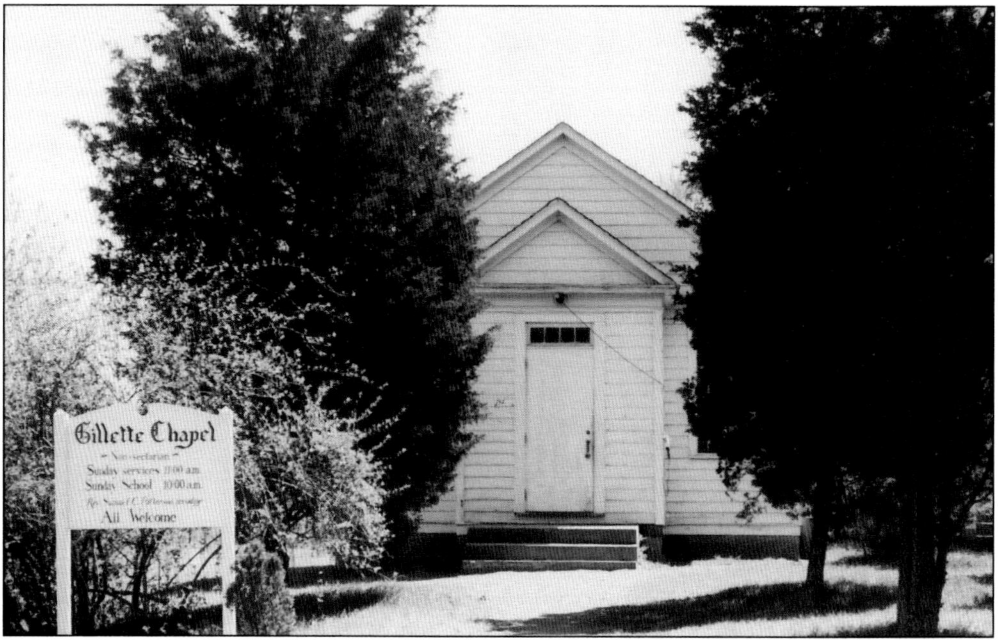

The Gillette Chapel, *c.* 1947. This chapel was founded by Reverend Samuel C. Patterson in 1947, in a small building on Lackawanna Boulevard in Gillette. The building was originally intended for Sunday school, but served various other purposes as well. It was known as the Gillette Community House, and was used for Girl Scouts, art clubs, and the like. (Lois Patterson Stortz.)

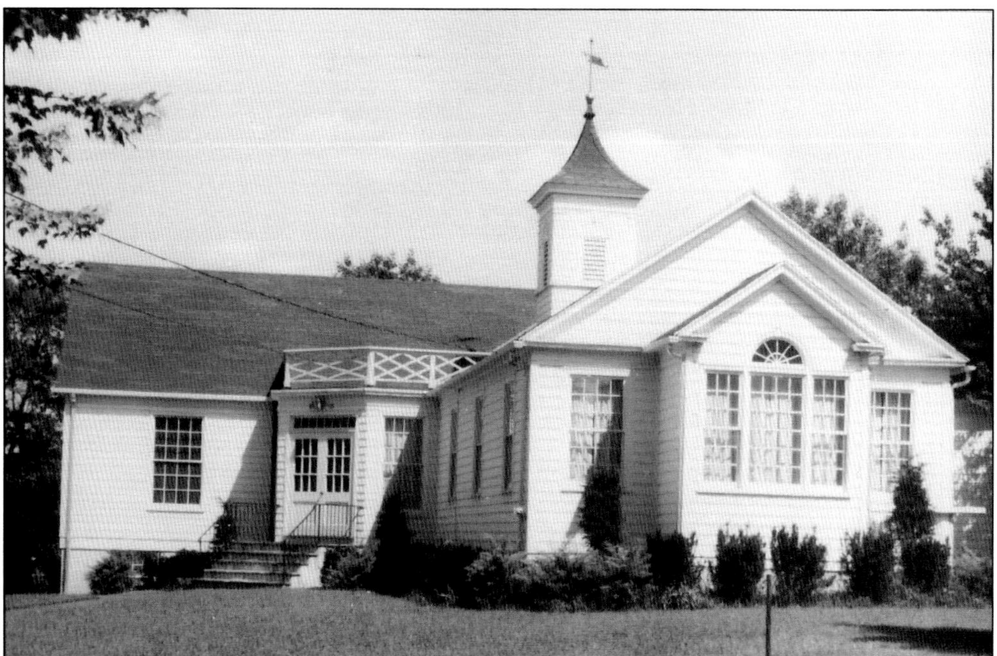

The new Gillette Chapel, upon its completion in 1958. There was a ground-breaking ceremony in 1957 for the renovation and enlargement of the church. (Lois Patterson Stortz.)

Reverend Samuel C. Patterson, who founded the Gillette Chapel in 1947. (Lois Patterson Stortz.)

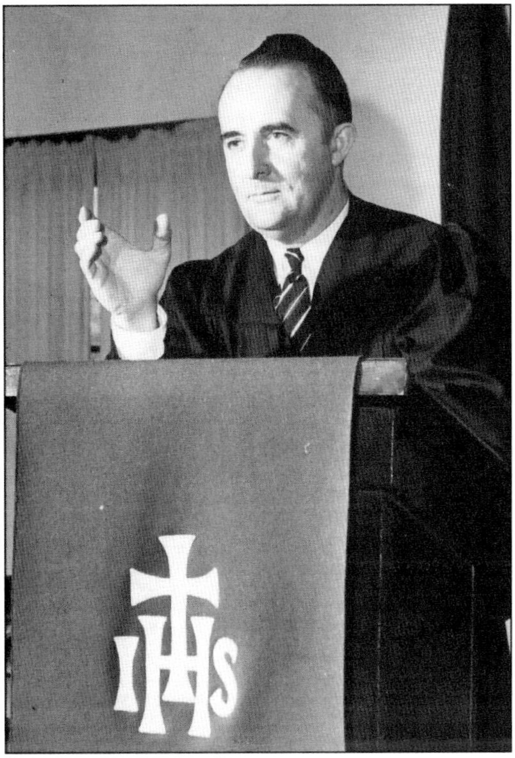

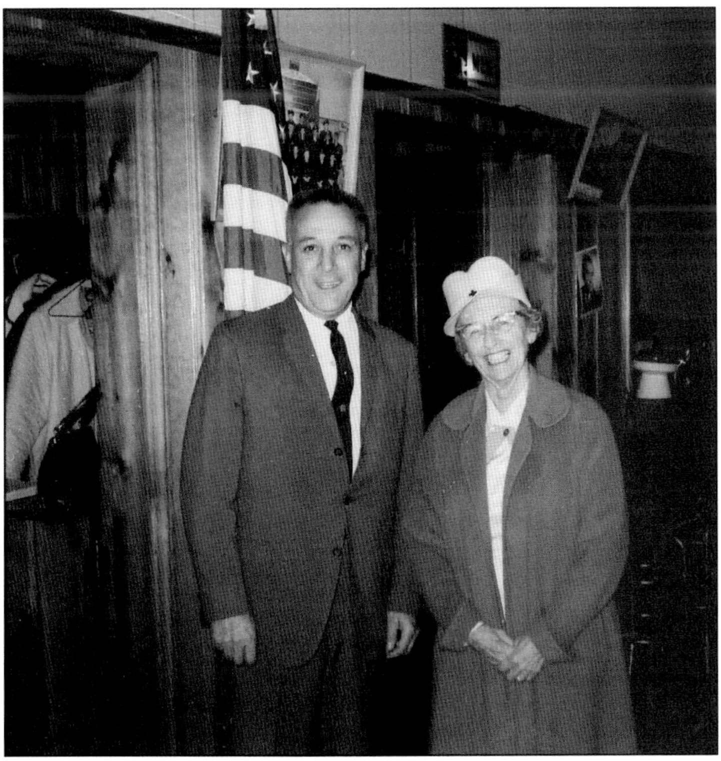

George Wrigley and Harriet Roy, shown in the 1960s during a fund drive for the American Red Cross. Mrs. Roy headed the organization and remained an active member in Long Hill Township for many years. Mr. Wrigley was the mayor of Long Hill Township in 1968, and was on the township committee from 1966 to 1969. (Harriet Roy Holland.)

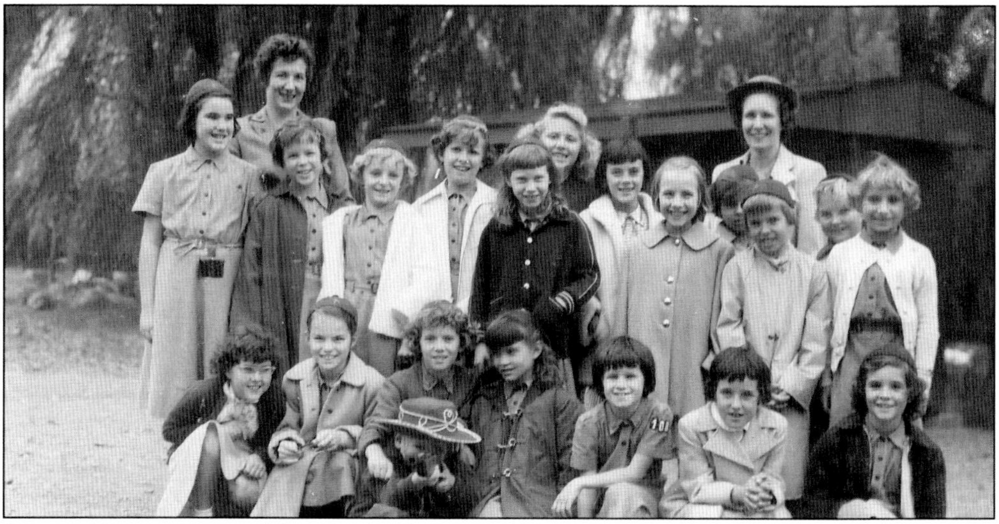

Brownie Troop 108 in 1955, under the direction of Mrs. R.L. Headley, Mrs. E. Bay, and Madeline Schott. From left to right are: (front row) Carol Phifer, Robin Gegauff, Elena Bay, Sandra Bartell, Peggy Beatty, Gail Giacobbe, and Karen Patterson; (back row) Andrea Snyder, Janice Ballenger, Nancy Mishuk, Barbara Headley, Susan Stahl, Sandy Sayre, Susan Hildebrant, Mary Jane Wolff, Marilyn Carlson, and Betty Mishuk. (Evelyn Headley.)

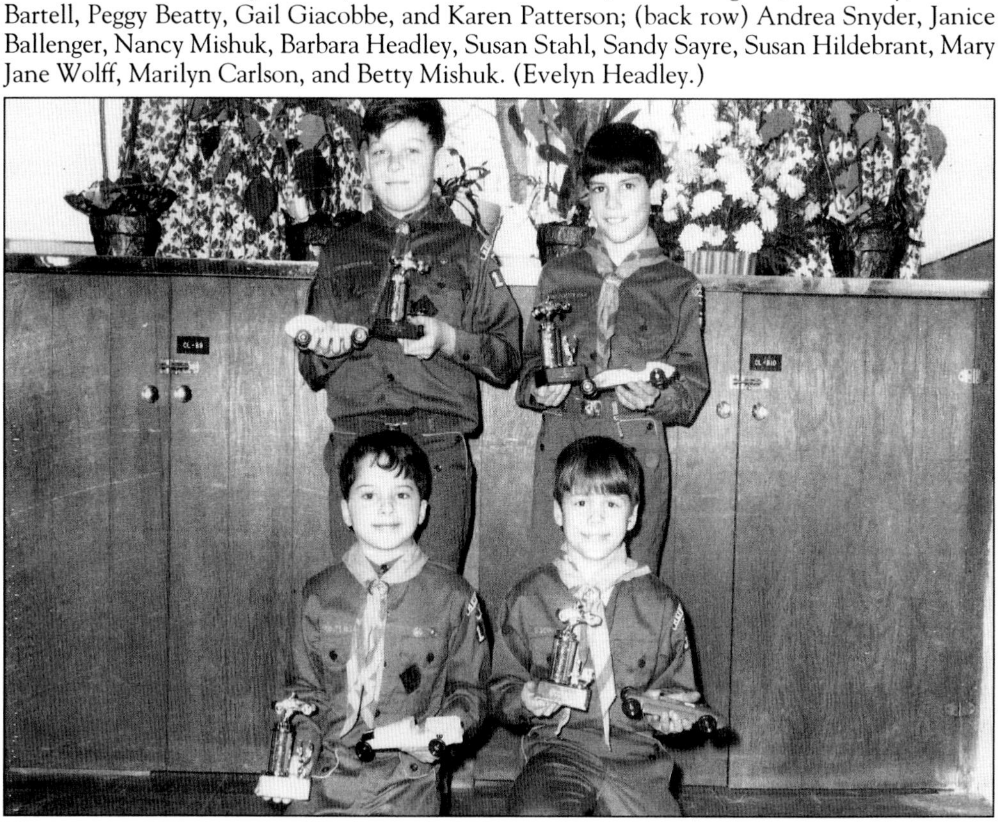

The winners of the Pinewood Derby sponsored by Cub Scout Pack 156 with their trophies and cars. Kneeling, from left to right, are David Shand (best looking car) and Douglas Weller (first place B.). Standing, from left to right, are Craig Engesser (first place A) and David McIntire (most original car). The group met in Meyersville in 1971, but all winners in the picture were from Gillette. (Mary Lou Landwehr Weller.)

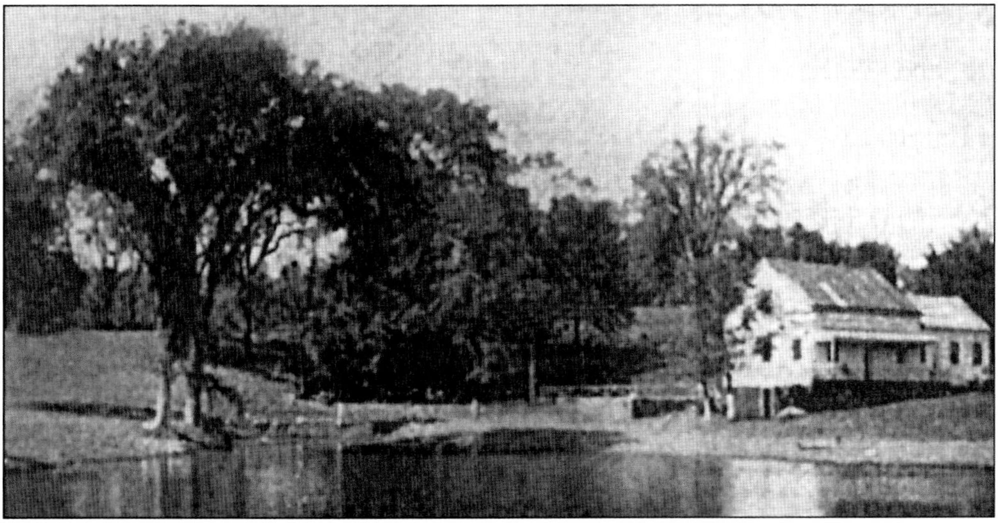

The Cammeyer estate. This was quite a lavish establishment, encompassing all of 270 acres in the eastern corner of Long Hill in the nineteenth century. It was sold and developed as Homestead Park by the "Own-Your-Home" Association. The park was built and operated by L. Preston Gates and Mitchell Kaplan. A spring fed water to all the homes. A small wooden building was used as a gas station and store for the community. The wooden building stands today, on the left side of the road heading north on Long Hill. Homes were built there until the 1960s. (Ruth Buehrman McMane.)

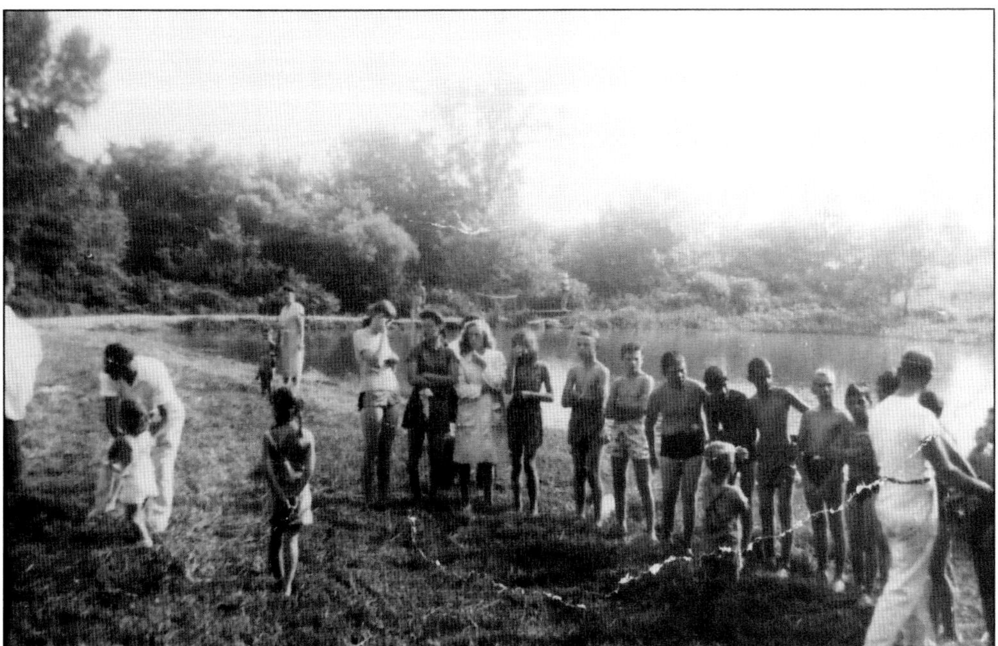

A 1940s photograph of a Sunday school class of the Meyersville Presbyterian Church at the Homestead Park pond. Billy and Eddie Meeker are among the class members. (Inge Rist Lincoln.)

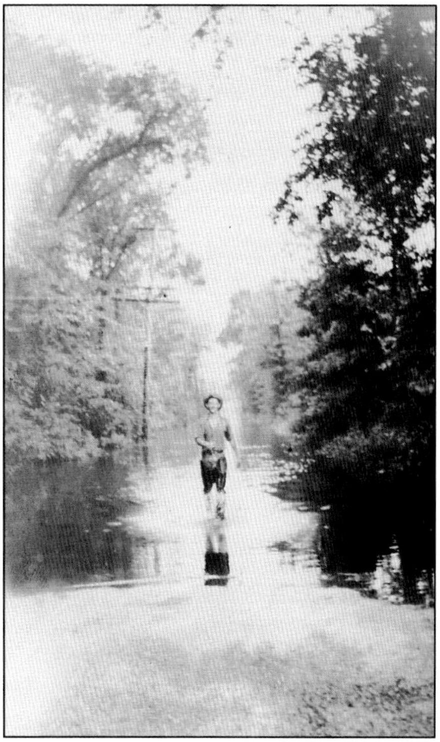

Harold Deveney. Mr. Deveney lived in the Warren and Gillette area all of his life. He married Dorothy Bogart, and they lived in the Bogart homestead, where they raised two daughters. Mr. Deveney was an artist, a writer, and an avid fly-fisherman. He is seen here wading through the overflow after a heavy rain at the Passaic River in Gillette. The poem below is just a sampling of his talent, capturing the natural wonder of one of his passions: the Passaic River. (Lynne Deveney Spurrier.)

Let us wander to the river
Where the fragrant lilies grow
and the egrets wade the shallows
with their feathers white as snow . . .

Where great patches of pink mallow
crowd the low banks of the stream
and the baby raccoons wallow
where the brook comes flowing in . . .

And theres wonder by the river
on a pleasant summer day
where the shining riffles quiver
as the little zephyrs play
and the swallows all are gliding
just above the pleasant stream
where the towering pin oaks rise
like a mansion in a dream . . .

I was always in a hurry
to get home from work each day
for the river flowed behind the house
and there big pickerel lay . . .

I wouldn't even wait for dinner
I would change clothes right away
tie on a streamer fly and spinner
and I'd be on my merry way
and the air would be so fragrant
as I walked across the lawn
though the lilacs all had faded
and the apple blossoms gone

The path through the backfield
would pass by summer flowers
and bright butterflies would dance there
and through the day-light hours.

The slow river would be lying
like a ribbon silver blue
a great blue heron would be flying
and sometime there would be two.

I would hurry to the woodland
to fish along the Lily-pads
for the pickerel in this section
were as big as could be had.

—Harold Deveney

THE RIVER

Let us wander to the river
Where the fragrant lillies grow
and the egrets wade the shallows
with their feathers white as snow...

Where great patches of pink mallow
crowd the low banks of the stream
and the baby racoons wallow
where the brook comes flowing in...

And theres wonder by the river
on a pleasant summer day
where the shining riffles quiver
as the little zephyrs play
and the swallows allare gliding
just above the pleasant stream
where the towering pin oaks rise
like a mansion in a dream...

I was always in a hurry
to get home from work each day
for the river flowed behind the house
and there big pickerel lay...

I wouldn't even wait for dinner
I would change clothes right away
tie on a streamer fly and spinner
and I'd be on my merry way
and the air would be so fragrant
as I walked across the lawn

though the lilacs all had faded
and the apple blossoms gone
The path through the backfield
would pass by summer flowers
and bright butterflies would dance the
and through the day-light hours

The slow river would be lying
like a ribbon silver blue
a great blue heron would be flying
and sometimes there would be two

I would hurry to the woodland
to fish along the lily-pads
for the pickerel in this section
were as big as could be had.

Four

Millington

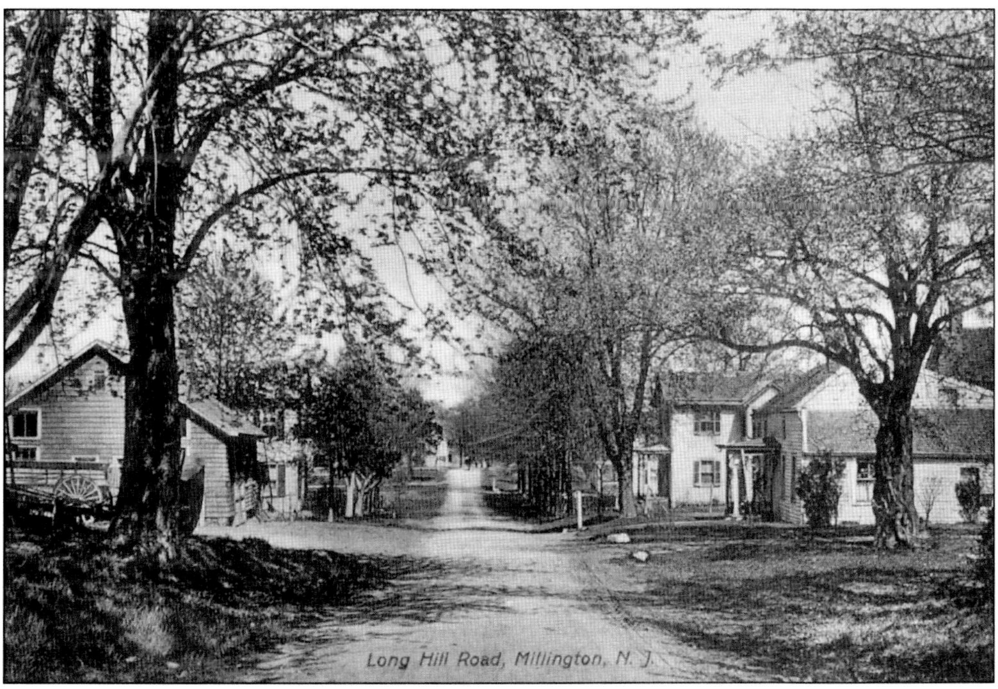

Long Hill Road, *c.* 1920s. Millington saw early settlers in the 1700s. Soloman Boyle, who owned vast amounts of land, built a gristmill, sawmill, and forge on the Passaic River, as well as a home on 42 Old Mill Road. It was because of these first mills that Millington got its name. The foundations of the mill can still be seen across the Passaic River. For some time, Boyle's home was used as a general store and post office. (Dale Monetti.)

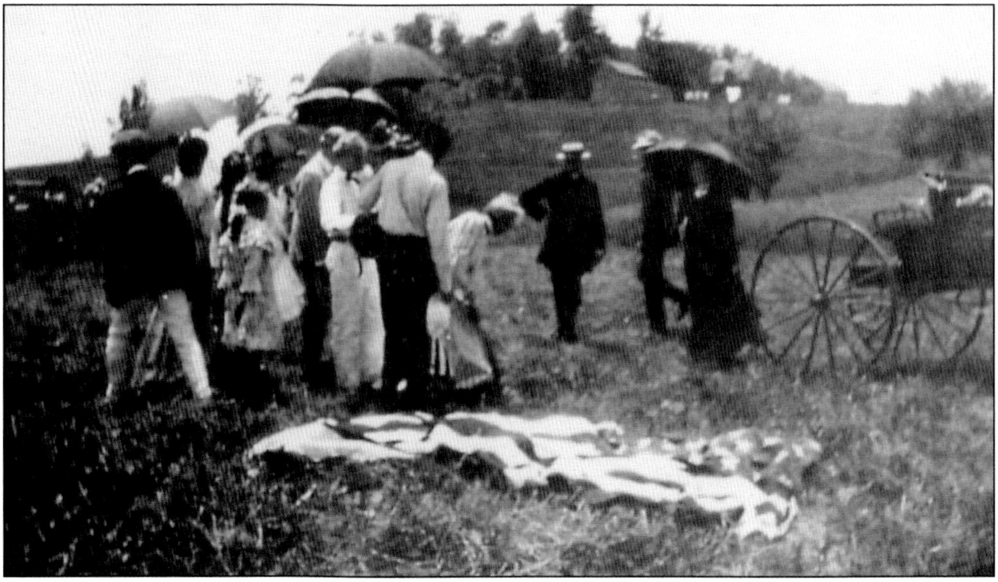

A picnic lunch on a social afternoon, possibly featuring architectural discussions revolving around the All Saints Mission Church. In 1904, N. Taff of Millington donated land for a church on Long Hill in Millington. A very civic-minded man, he was chairman of the finance committee, and president of the school board. The church was built and dedicated in 1906 and was called All Saints Mission Church. Bishop Lines requested that Mathilde Schumacher, the treasurer of the fund at the time, dig up the first spade of earth for the building. (All Saints Episcopal Church of Millington.)

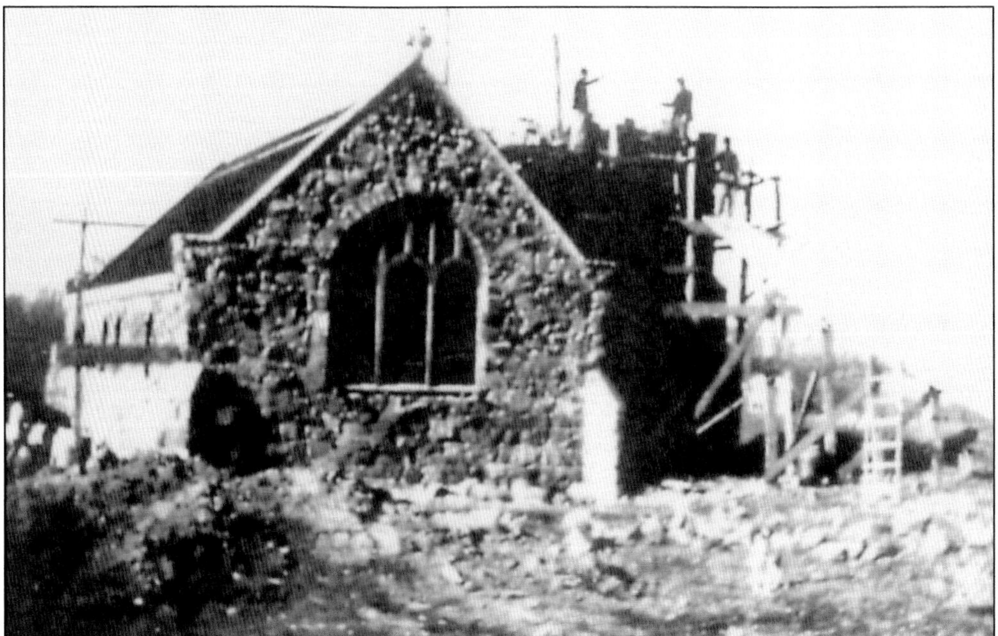

Determined workers and the beautiful partially completed All Saints Mission Church in 1905. The church was constructed to resemble an English country stone church. (All Saints Episcopal Church of Millington.)

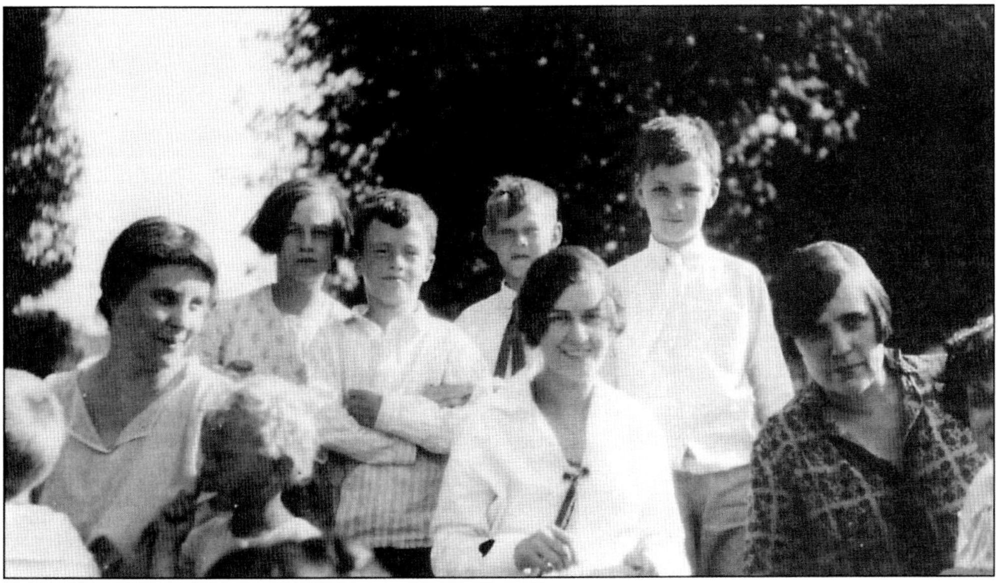

A picnic for the All Saints Church Sunday School, on June 15, 1922, on the hill in Millington. From left to right are David Wyatt, Mrs. Wyatt, Ruth Wyatt, Martha Compton, William Boucher, John Wyatt, Margaret Moody, Herbert Compton, Mrs. Maynard Brown, and Jane Beatty. (All Saints Episcopal Church of Millington.)

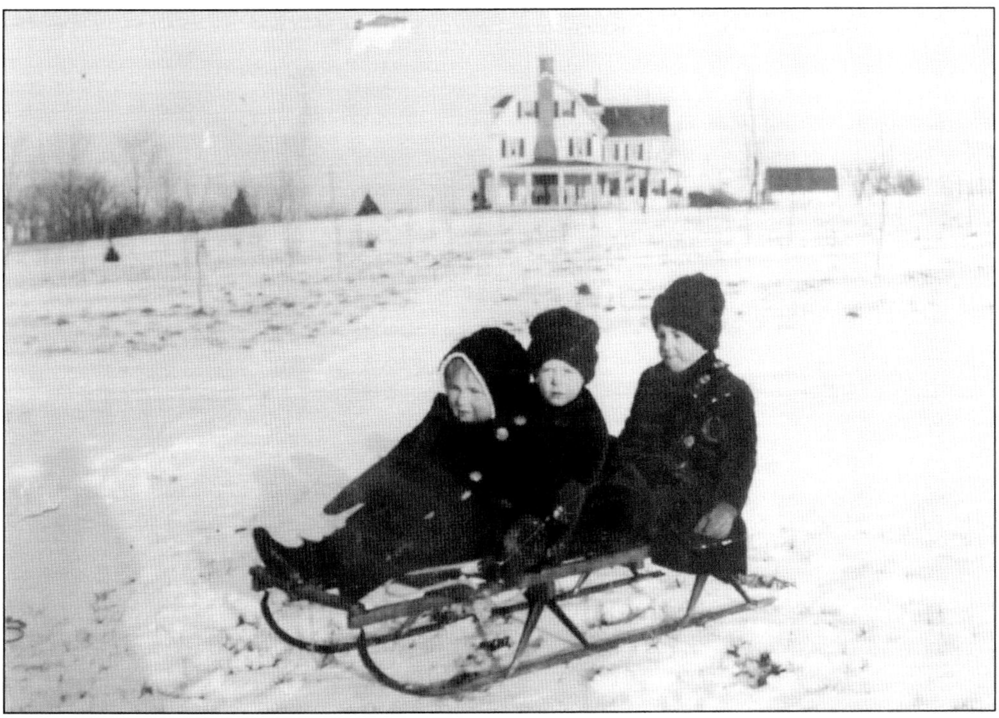

Frederick Taff's estate in Millington, c. 1914. Taff donated the land for the All Saints Episcopal Church. The three children bundled and ready for a sleigh ride are Duane III, Robert, and Barbara Nash. (Mr. & Mrs. Donald Kuhn.)

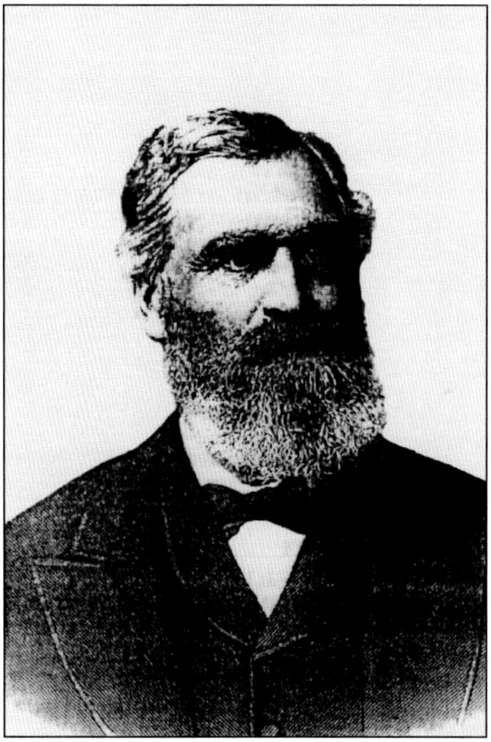

Frederick Nishwitz, of New York, *c.* 1880. Frederick came to settle in Millington, where he purchased Soloman Boyle's land for the purpose of his future endeavor—the Acme Harrow Company. In 1879 he invented and manufactured the Acme Harrow from his factory on River Road, employing 125 men. The harrow was a cultivating implement used for agricultural purposes, and was sold throughout the U.S. and Europe. His friend and neighbor, Duane H. Nash, was later to become his partner as a sales representative. (Long Hill Township Historical Society.)

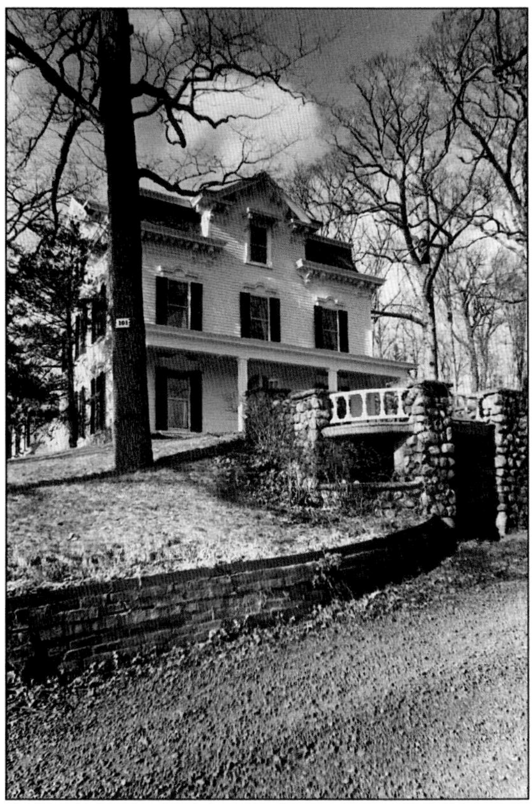

The summer home of Frederick Nishwitz. This home, built in 1870, is located on Oaks Road in Millington. It is still used as a private residence. (Long Hill Township Historical Society.)

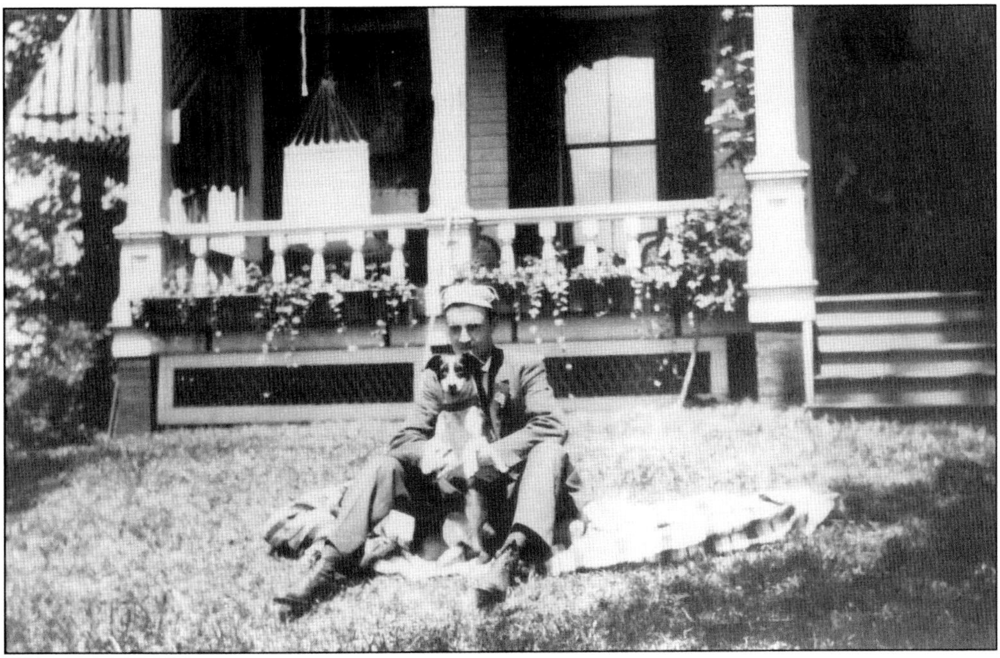

Duane H. Nash, on his front lawn at 123 Cross Hill Road in Millington, with his favorite dog Peggy, c. 1910. Duane was the sales manager for Frederick Nishwitz's Acme Harrow Company, the editor of an agricultural newspaper, and an avid breeder of Shetland Ponies. (Long Hill Township Historical Society.)

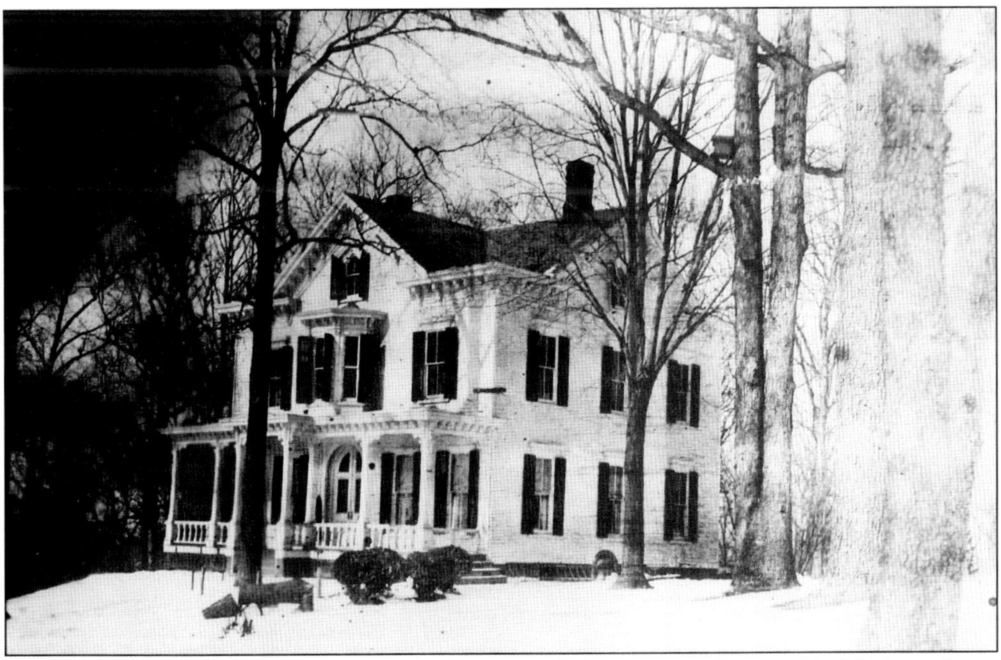

The home on Cross Hill Road in Millington belonging to Duane H. Nash and his family. Duane III, Robert, and Barbara Nash were raised here. (Long Hill Township Historical Society.)

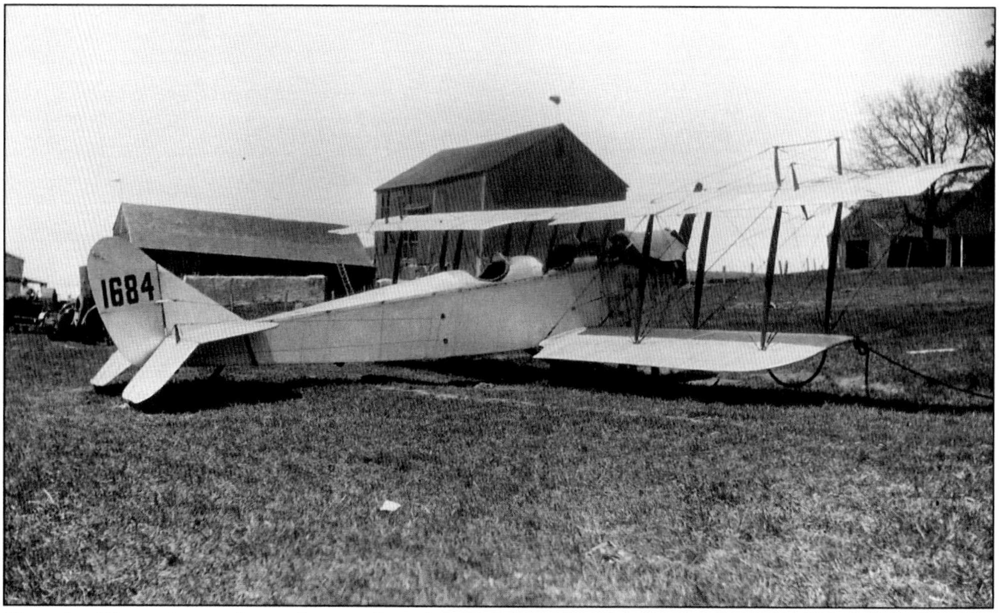

Rhoedes Farm, located on the south side of Valley Road between Northfield and Old Farm House Road. In the 1920s the farm was used as a landing strip for recreational flying. Here, we see an original Curtis Jenny, which was used as a trainer in World War I as well as for barn storming. "Red" Rhoedes was an avid pilot and teacher, and would offer rides to local residents for one dollar. (Winifred Shimol.)

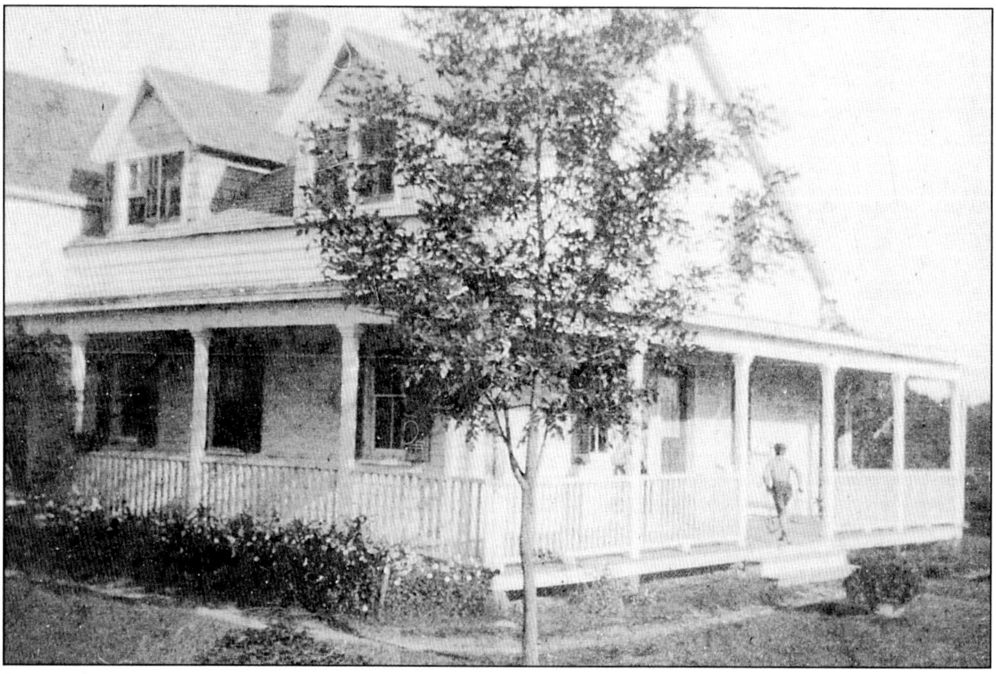

Riverside Farm, at 508 Carlton Road in Millington. Built in 1803 by John Carle, the farm included 108 acres along the Passaic River. Anna and Fred Ortman owned the farm from 1899 to 1922. Fred's brother Henry owned a blacksmith shop in the center of Meyersville. (Marion McCollum Armstrong.)

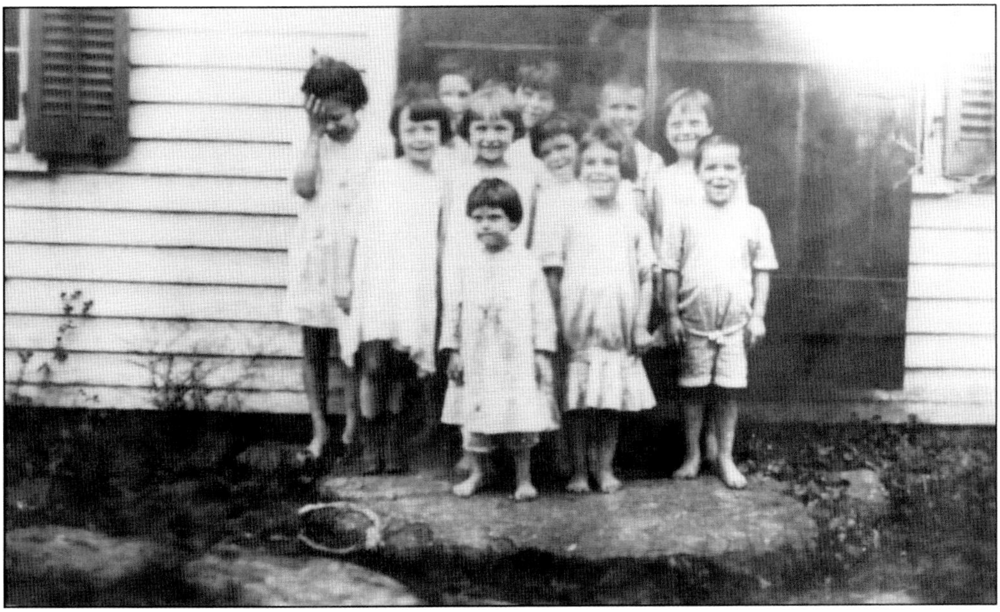

"Fresh air kids" on the spacious Riverside Farm in 1909. Summers in the country were a wonderful experience for the children. Some of these state children were permanently placed in the community and attended public schools. (Marion McCollum Armstrong.)

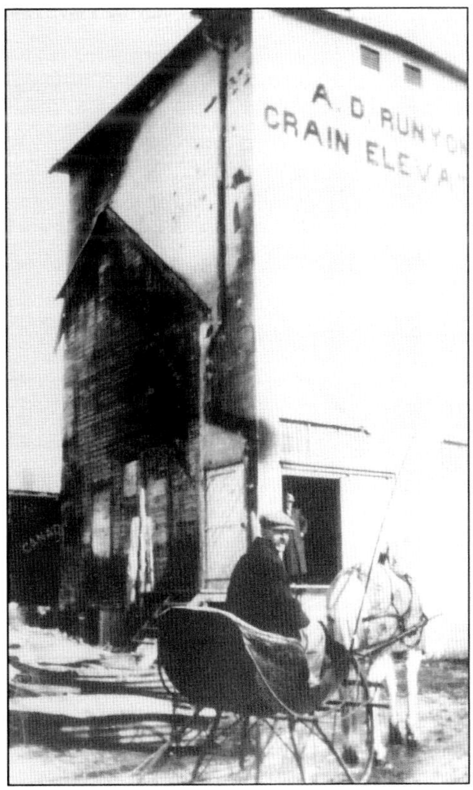

The A.D. Runyon feed mill. A.D. Runyon and his family were some of the township's earliest settlers. Miss Lettie Runyon taught local children in the All Saints Church in Millington, and also at their Runyon farmhouse. A.D. Runyon started a feed mill in the early 1900s. The mill burned but the silo survived, and a new building went up in 1917. Runyon started selling oil in 1937. The building is now owned by the Moore family. (Millington Volunteer Fire Company #1.)

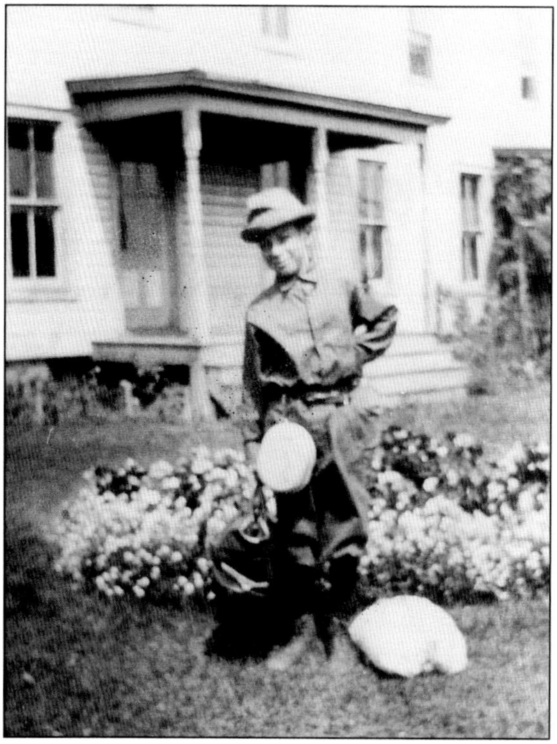

Nine-year-old John Kocisko in his Boy Scout uniform in front of the Kocisko home on River Road, in 1919. The home was built by Frederick Nishwitz as worker's housing for the Acme Harrow Company. Grandfather Kocisko worked in the factory for twenty years. (Winifred Shimol.)

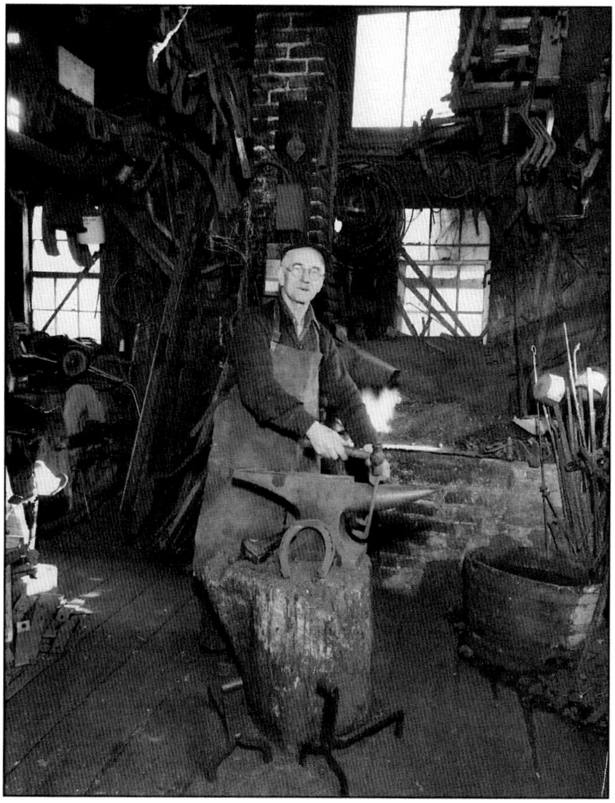

Compton's Blacksmith Shop. Located on Long Hill Road in Millington, this shop has been a landmark since 1866. Arthur Compton was regarded as a highly skilled craftsman for fifty years. For one of his most frequent customers, the Morris County Crushed Stone Company, he serviced twenty-two horse carts a day! The Compton ancestors settled in Liberty Corner prior to the Revolution, but later settled in Millington. (Carolyn & Ralph Malfatone.)

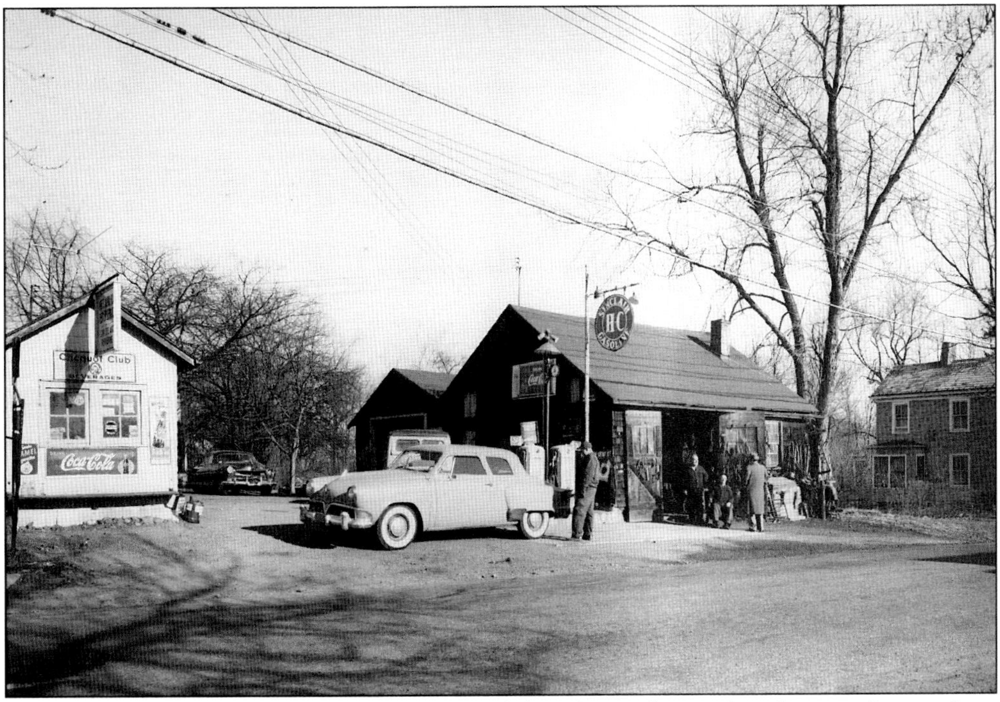

Compton's Blacksmith Shop, *c.* 1950s. Not much has changed since this photograph was taken, except for the present absence of the small convenience store to the left. Gas is being pumped into a classic 1953 Studebaker, while a 1951 Hudson Hornet sits parked beside the general store. (Carolyn & Ralph Malfatone.)

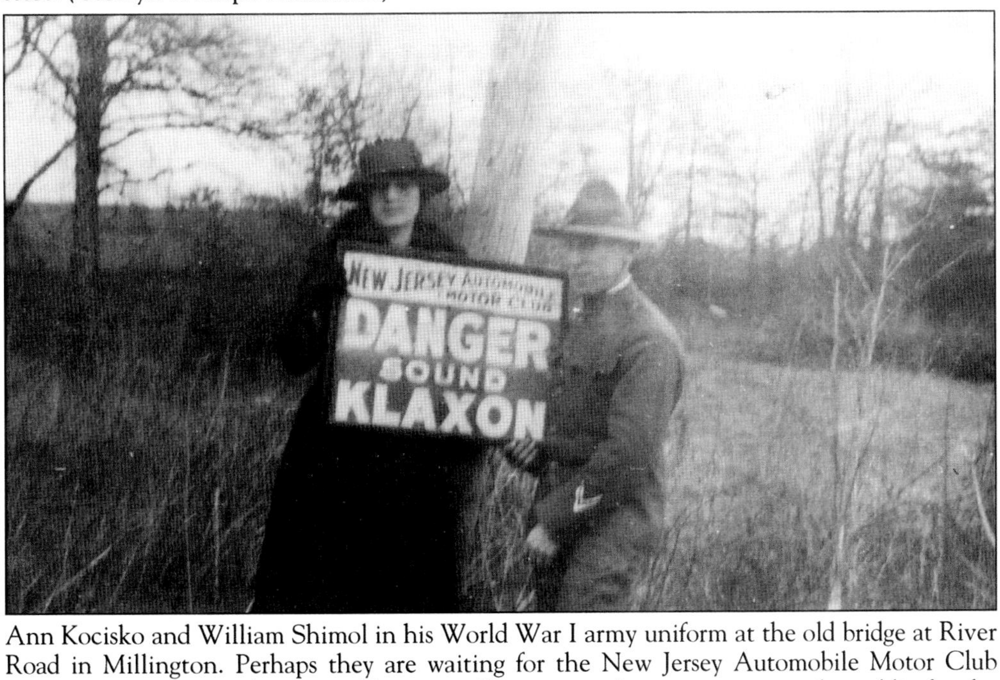

Ann Kocisko and William Shimol in his World War I army uniform at the old bridge at River Road in Millington. Perhaps they are waiting for the New Jersey Automobile Motor Club to drive past in a parade or possibly a race. We assume they are preparing the public for the oncoming choir of horns. (Winifred Shimol.)

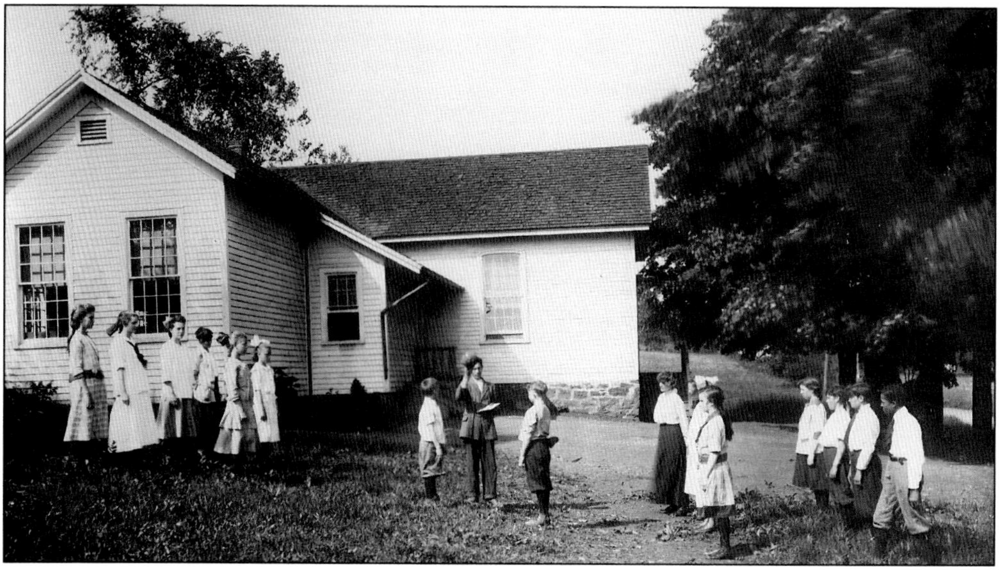

A physical education class in session, c. 1913, in front of the one-room schoolhouse in Millington, which presently serves as our municipal building. The building was used as a school for a century, from the early 1800s to its closing in 1926. This photograph was donated to the Historical Society of Long Hill by George Henry Osborn Sr., superintendent of schools at that time. (Long Hill Township Historical Society.)

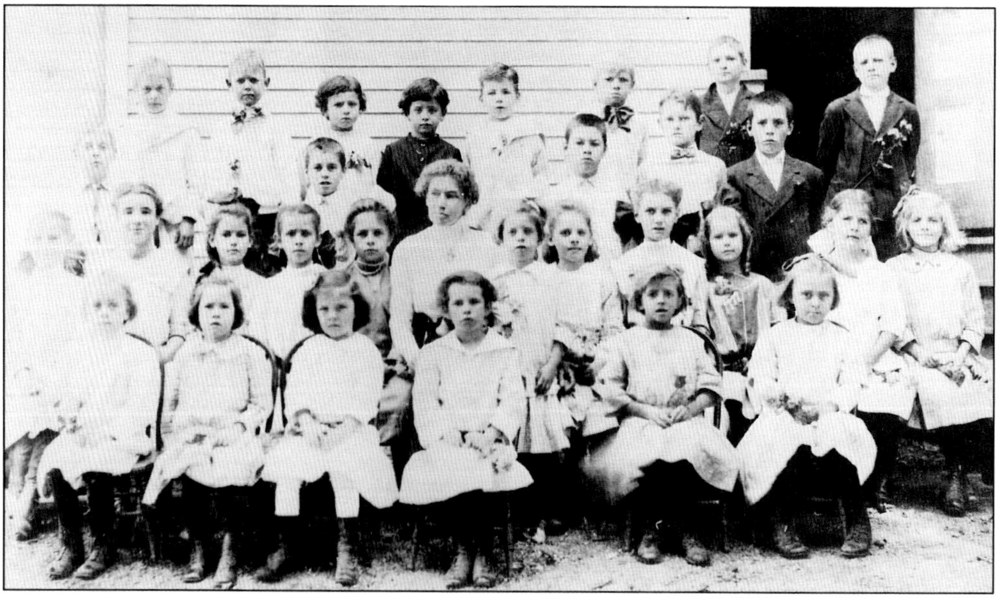

A class picture from the spring of 1914. From left to right are as follows: (front row) Anna Harwith, Myrtle Compton, Margaret Bailey, Margaret Fay, Rose Guldensheimer, and Margaret Horwith; (second row) Elizabeth Kocisko, Madelaine Ward, Amy Hedden, Elsie Beresh, unknown, teacher Miss Bloom, Anna Fay, Grace Ortman, Agnes Hedden, Elizabeth Hedden, Marion Bailey, and Margaret Guldensheimer; (third row) Fred Crane, Clifford Compton, Harry Compton, Edward Hedden, and Ray Compton; (back row) Herman Boss, George Hand, August Cavanato, Joseph Cavanato, Johnny Burns, Henry Beresh, Joe McDonald, and ? McDonald. (Winifred Shimol.)

The Long Hill Township Municipal Building, at 1802 Long Hill Road in Millington. This was one of the first one-room schoolhouses. The original part of the structure was built in the early 1880s. An addition to the west side of the original part was built around 1911. The school closed in 1926. (Long Hill Township Historical Society.)

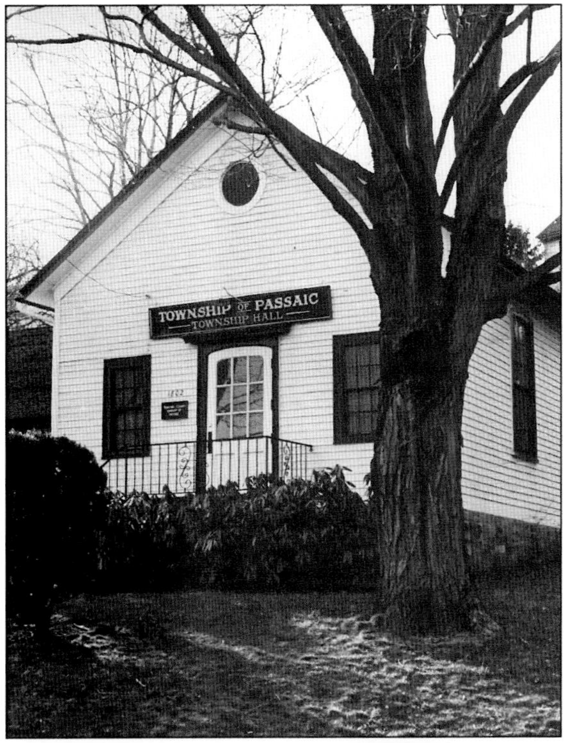

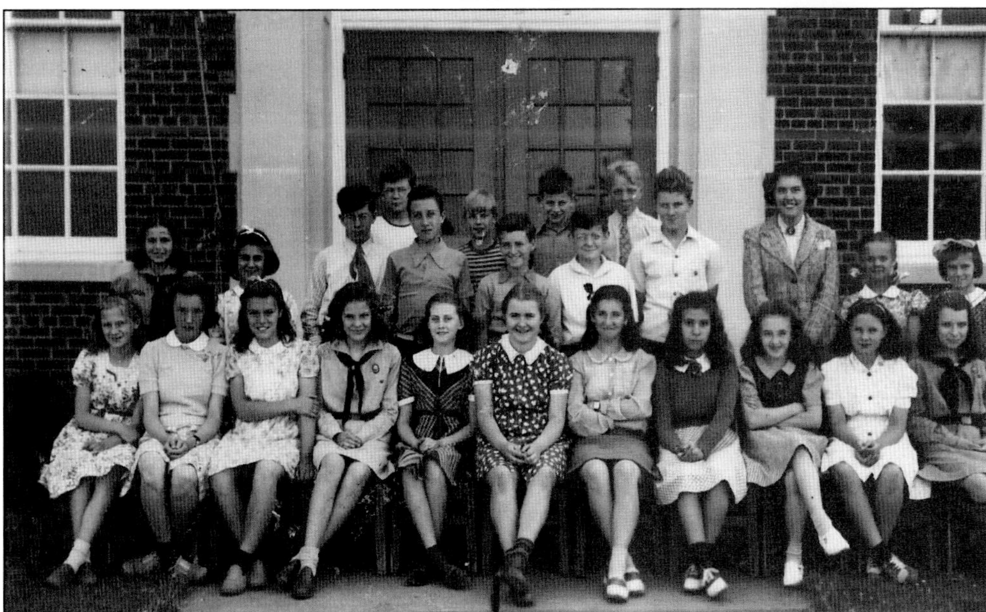

The Class of 1940–41 at the Millington Elementary School. The teacher, Mrs. Maines, is on the right. Included among the students are Bonnie Benson, Diane Denise, Barbara Compton, Phyllis Fennimore, Ann Runyon, Barbara Glieson, Millie Melise, Mary Russo, Judy Bromwell, Florence Dougerty, Claire Wesley-Gibon, Jean DeFilippis, Bob Hoagland, Ronald ?, Rudy Koch, Donald Scheler, Richard Grossman, Edna Lammie, Aneta Byllick, Donald Ralph, Kenneth Hedden, Frank Shanger, and Douglas Mertz. (Jean DeFilippis Falzarano.)

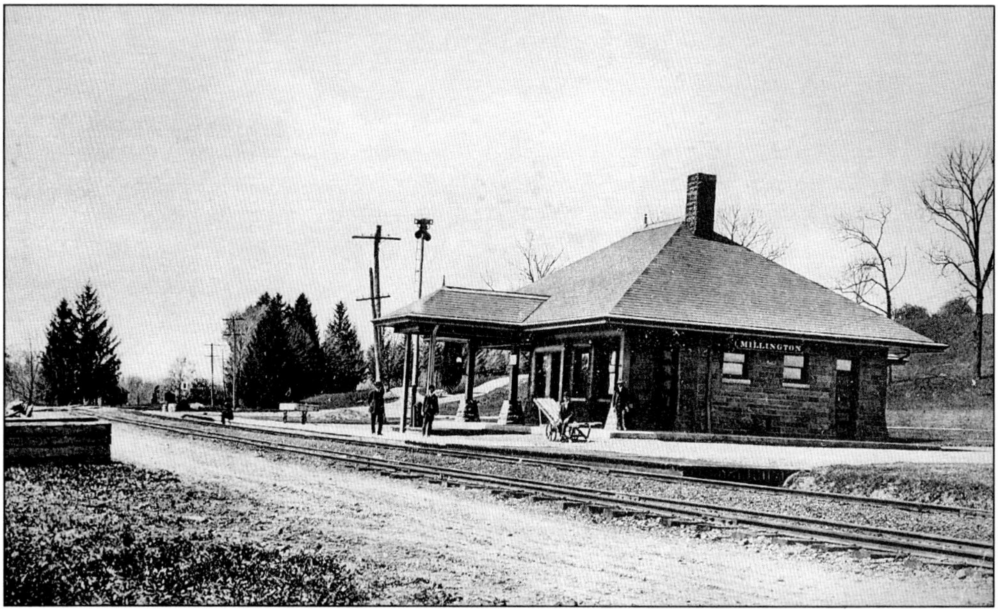

The first train station, a wooden structure, in Millington. The West-Line Railroad was extended from Summit to Bernardsville in 1870, and Duane H. Nash had a stone station built in 1901. This train station was placed on the National Register of Historic Places on June 22, 1984. (Ann Coriell MacDougall.)

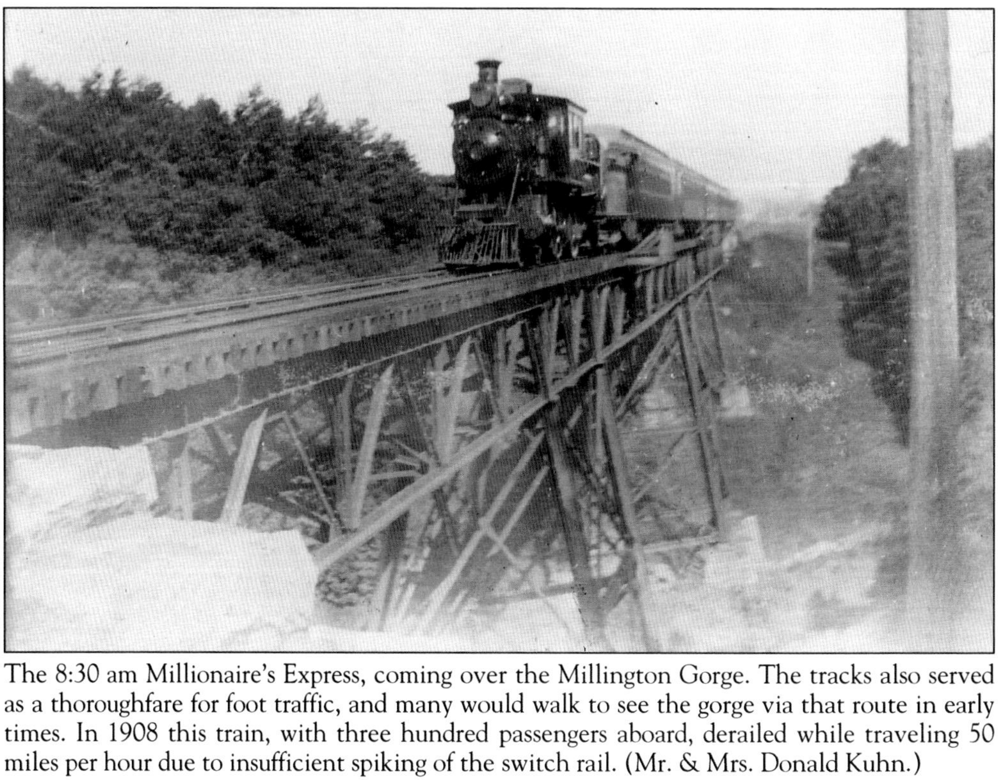

The 8:30 am Millionaire's Express, coming over the Millington Gorge. The tracks also served as a thoroughfare for foot traffic, and many would walk to see the gorge via that route in early times. In 1908 this train, with three hundred passengers aboard, derailed while traveling 50 miles per hour due to insufficient spiking of the switch rail. (Mr. & Mrs. Donald Kuhn.)

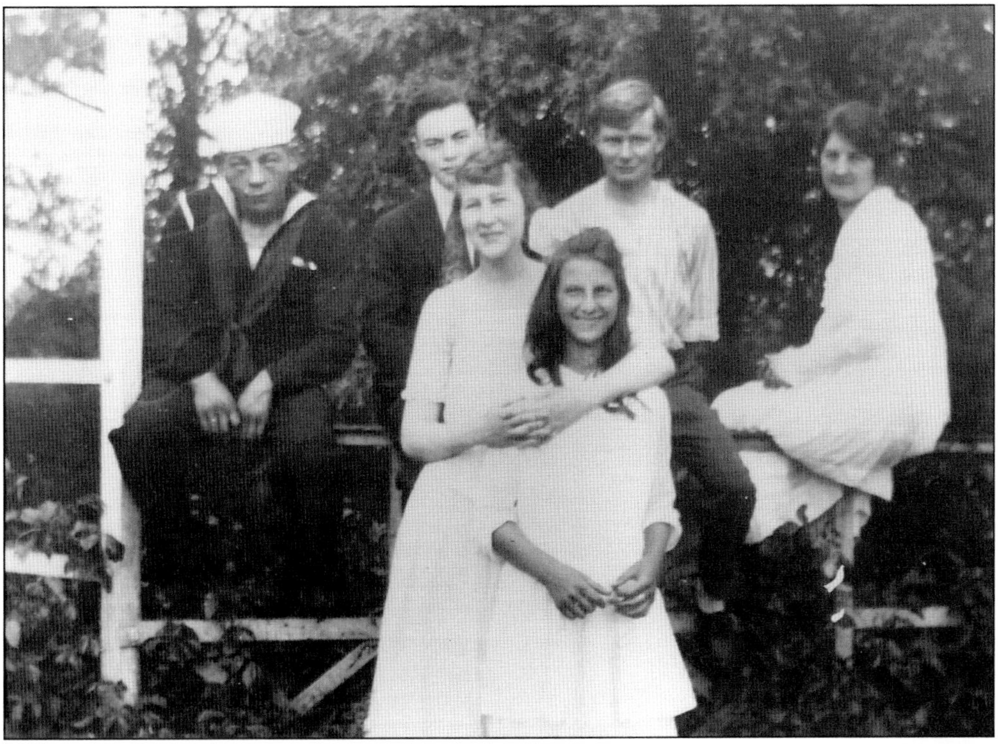

A snapshot taken on Memorial Day, c. 1919, at the Passaic River Bridge on River Road. George Kocisko is in the navy uniform; the others are Herbert Lockwood, Claude Harrison, Anna Kocisko (front), Ada Van Pelt, and Elizabeth Kocisko. (Winifred Shimol.)

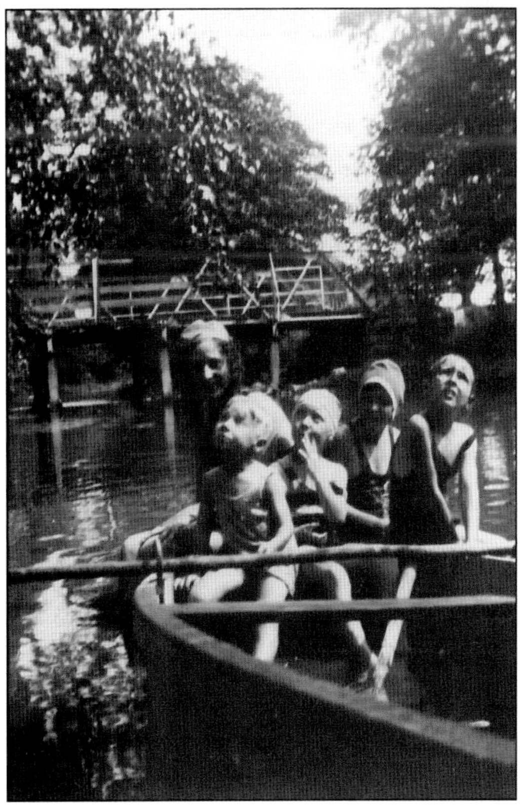

The simple things in life. In 1930, things such as rowing down the Passaic River brought much pleasure and discovery to children. This inquisitive bunch of bathers, bathing caps and all, are, from left to right, Elizabeth Kocisko, Willie Shimol, Winifred Shimol, and two girls from "across the river." (Winifred Shimol.)

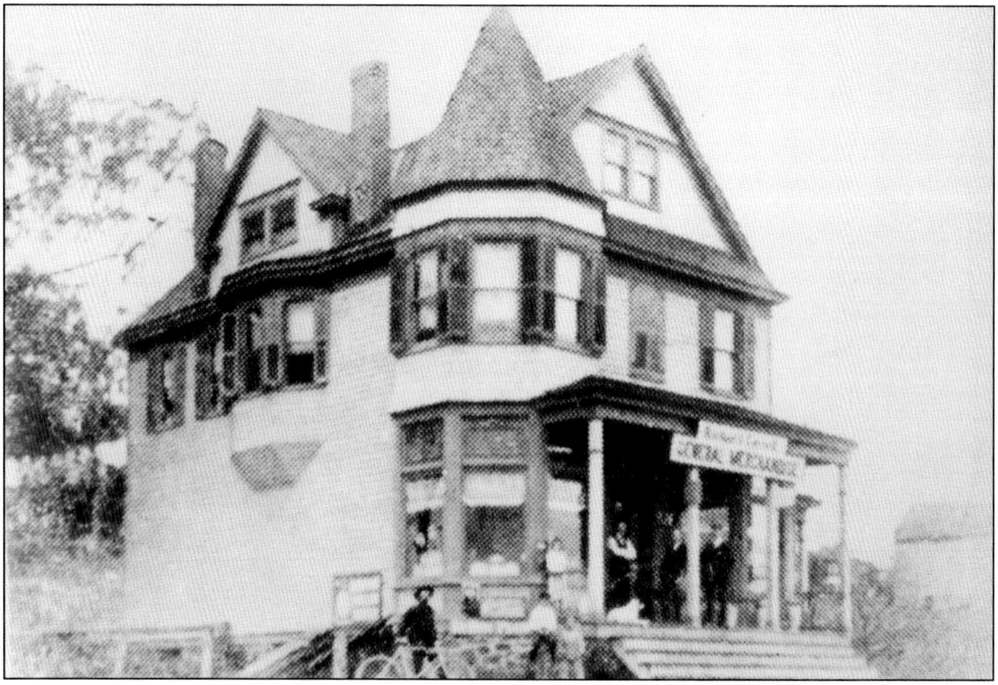

The Coriell house in the center of Millington. In 1901 Richard Coriell Sr. built this house. The family lived upstairs, and ran a general store downstairs. In 1920 the building was destroyed by fire, so the Coriells built a larger building across from the train station in the center of town. (Ann Coriell MacDougall.)

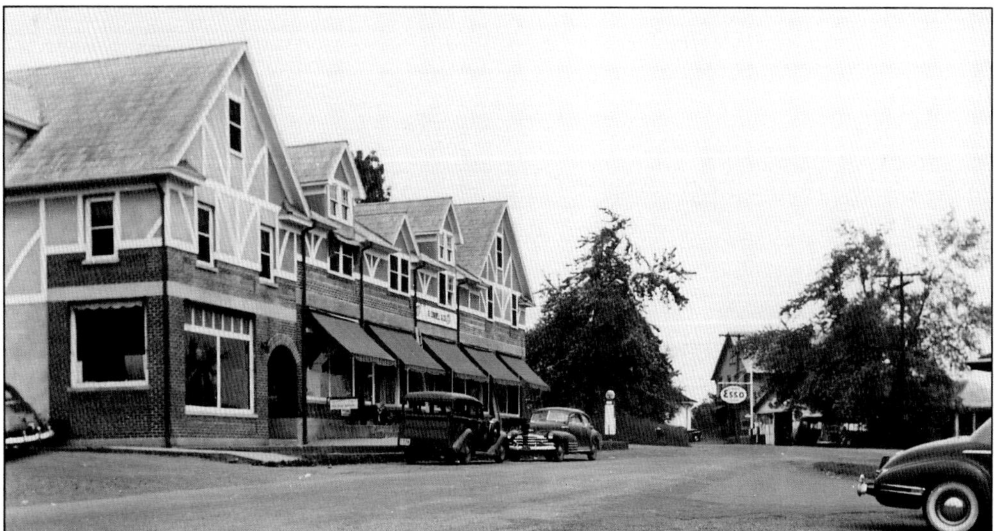

The Coriell building and post office. Because there was a need to finance homes in Long Hill Township, the Millington Building and Loan was incorporated in 1911. It met at various places in town. The Building and Loan grew and expanded, moved to the second floor of the Coriell building, and in 1957 became known as the Millington Savings and Loan. They bought the Coriell building in 1969. More recently, an even larger and more expansive Savings and Loan has been built. (Ann Coriell MacDougall.)

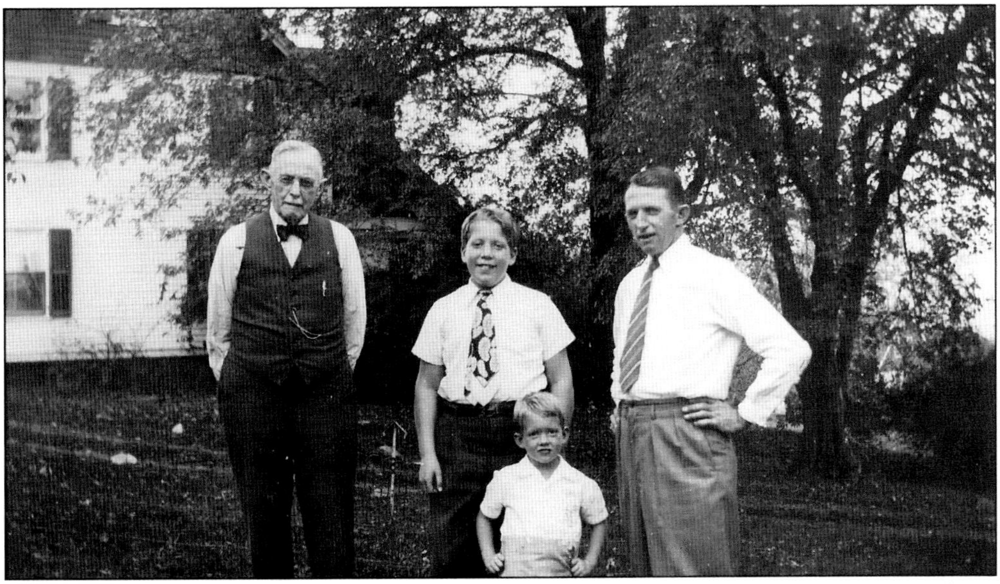

Four generations of Coriells. From left to right are Richard Coriell Sr., Richard Coriell III, R. Lawrence Coriell, and Robert Coriell (front). (Ann Coriell MacDougall.)

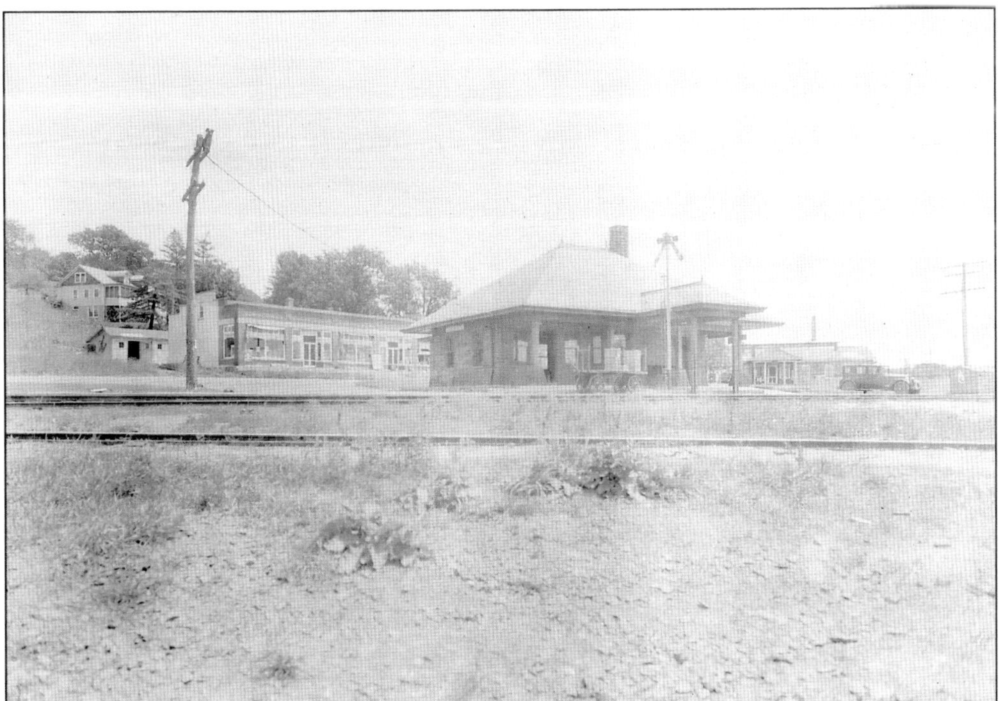

Another view of the train station in Millington, *c.* 1922. The Coriell's general store can be seen on the far left, before the addition of the post office. (Ann Coriell MacDougall.)

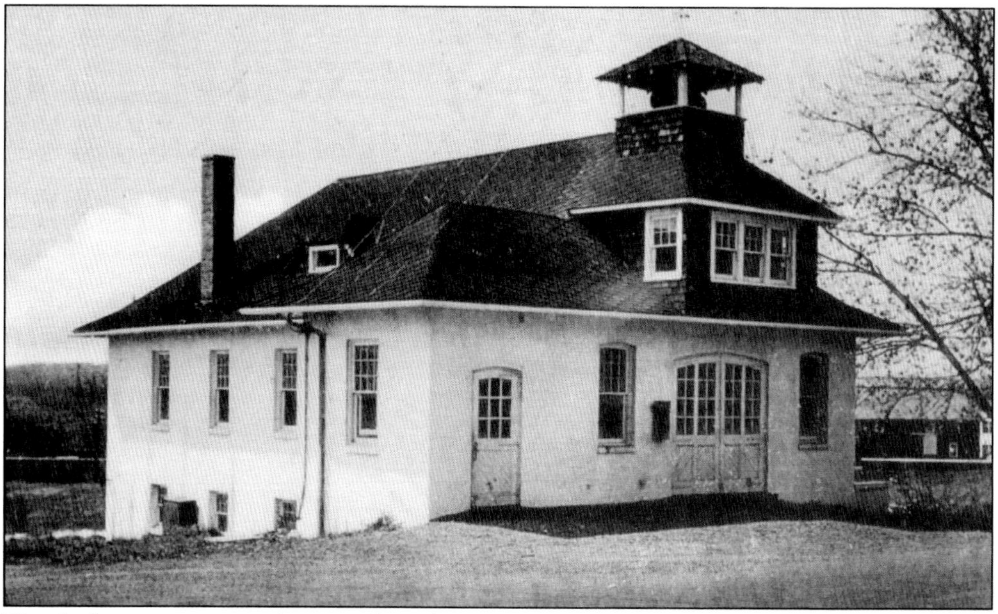

The firehouse constructed c. 1915–16 by Nicolas Thomas and his fellow firemen for the Millington Volunteer Fire Company #1. The company was organized in 1913, with one horse-drawn fire wagon. It has been said that Thomas housed horses for the fire company in the barn behind his home on Long Hill. Note the A.D. Runyon building on the right. (Millington Volunteer Fire Company # 1.)

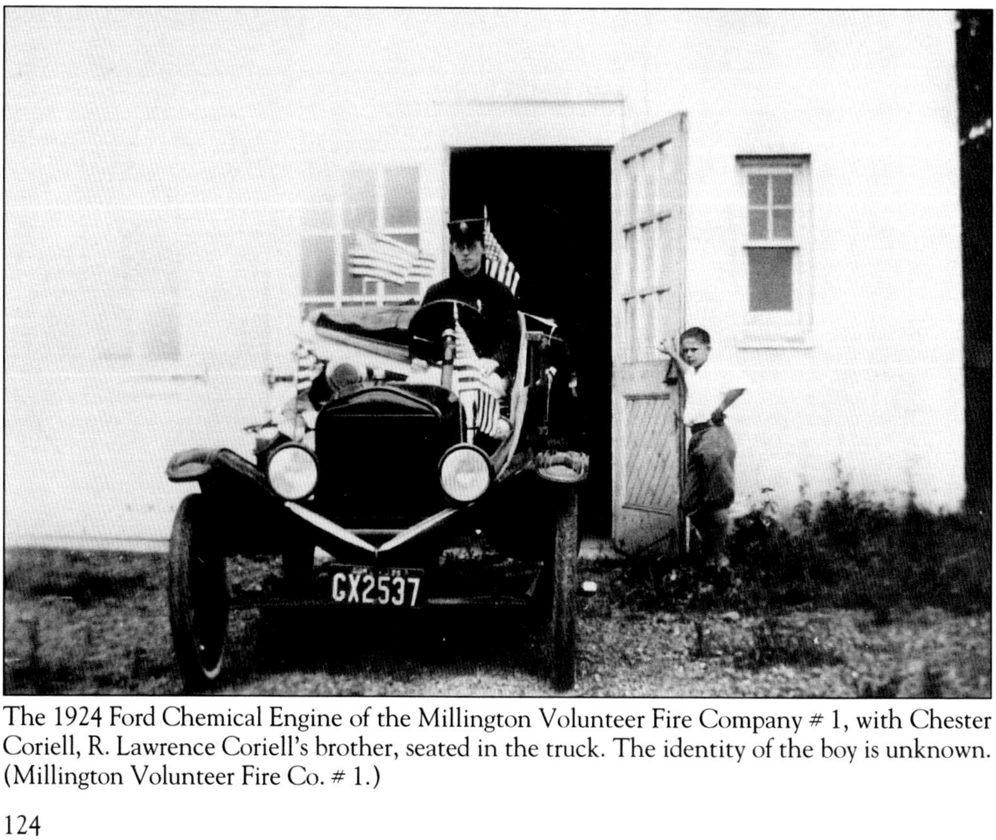

The 1924 Ford Chemical Engine of the Millington Volunteer Fire Company # 1, with Chester Coriell, R. Lawrence Coriell's brother, seated in the truck. The identity of the boy is unknown. (Millington Volunteer Fire Co. # 1.)

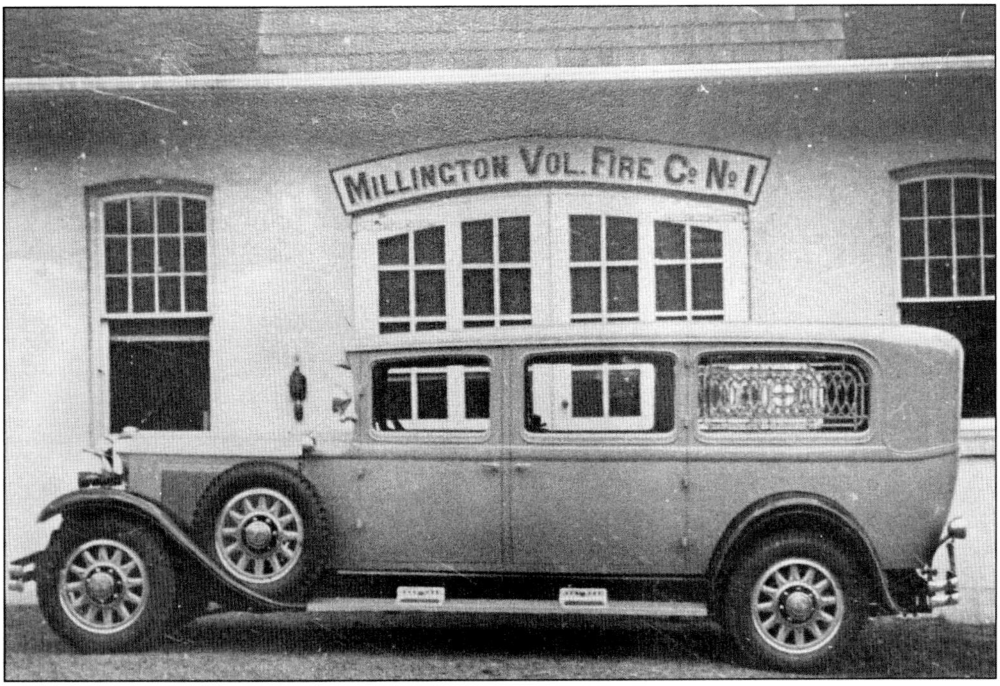

A 1928 Nash, the first rescue squad vehicle for the Millington Volunteer First Aid Squad, now the Long Hill First Aid Squad, in Gillette. The first squad operated under the Millington Volunteer Fire Company #1. The Passaic Township First Aid Squad was formed in 1973–74. When the township changed its name to Long Hill Township, so too, did the rescue squad. The squad is located at 949 Valley Road, in Gillette, and covers the entire township. (Millington Volunteer Fire Company #1.)

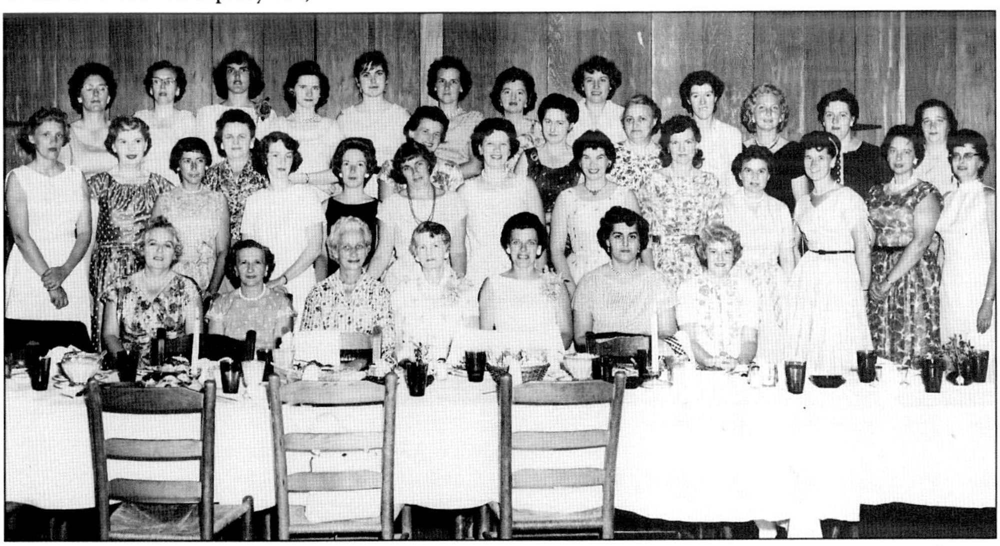

Telephone operators in 1953. When the first telephones were installed in 1902, an exchange was placed in a home at 42 Stonehouse Road in Millington. It was moved to Waverly Place, Millington, in 1912. In 1963, dial service was installed, and a new telephone building was constructed at the north corner of Division Avenue and Meadowview Road, in Millington. (Adele Arata Fellows.)

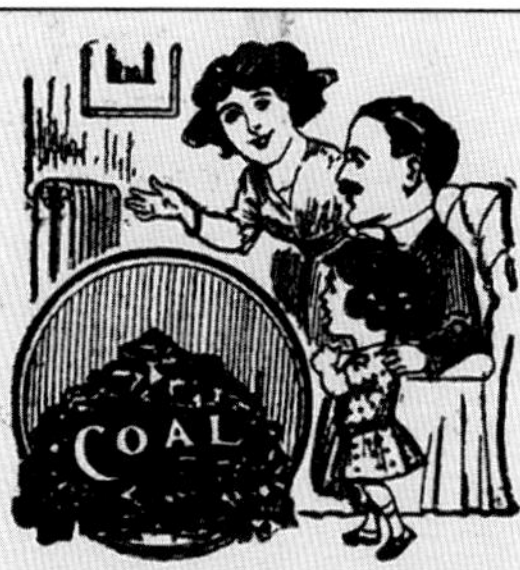

A COLD WAVE

This may mean nothing in your life just now; but about one month from now it will. Then it might hit you both on comfort and in the pocketbook.

Why not fill the bin now? Let us serve you with a real coal—

Jeddo Highland

A. D. RUNYON COMPANY

MILLINGTON, N. J. PHONES 18 AND 19

CHARLES HERRMANN

Practical Plumbing, Tinning and Heating

Standard and Crane's Co. Plumbing Fixtures and Supplies

Chestnut St. Stirling, N. J.
Phone Millington 81

Phone Millington 230

Fresh Vegetables
At the Lowest Prices Always!

FARMERS MARKET

Home of Baldwin and McIntosh Apples
George Neumann, Prop.
Valley Road Stirling, N. J.

MILLINGTON SERVICE STATION & GENERAL STORE

BANQUET HALL FOR ALL OCCASIONS

Phone 225 Millington

THE

Aristocrat

ICE CREAM PAR EXCELLENCE
CHARLES KEY, MILLINGTON, N. J.

HOME MADE BAKING AND REFRESHMENTS

The Valley Road

ALBERT RICHTER

Painting and Decorating

Dealers in

Paints, Oil and Glass

DOMESTIC AND IMPORTANT WALL PAPERS

Phone 34-R Stirling, N. J.

Oldest Importers of Oriental Rugs in New Jersey
Est. 1893 Formerly 17 Years in Plainfield

ANANSON'S

Armenian Native Rug Weavers

Oriental Rugs and Carpets

Repairing, Cleaning, Stretching By Experts
Rugs Washed By Hand
Rugs Called For and Delivered—Packed and Stored For the Season

Home Office, Stirling, N. J. Tel. 146 Millington

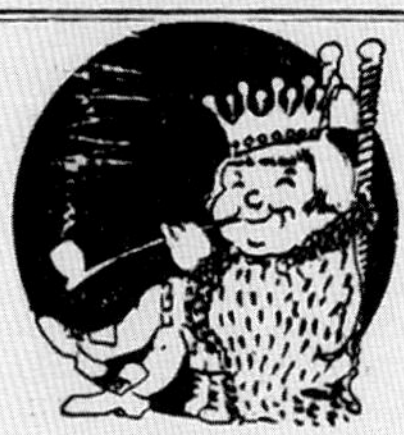

Old King Cole Would Have Been a Jollier Soul, with

Our Choice Coffee and Teas, Fancy Butter and Eggs

Henry Pape's Mayonnaise Approved by McCann the Food Specialist

ALBERT BERGHOEFER

Millington, New Jersey

PAGE 12

CASTLE BROS., Inc.

Plumbing, Heating and Metal Work

Telephone 139R Millington

A sampling of local businesses in the township, from the *Valley Messenger* newspaper, 1931. (Irma Mikulyak.)

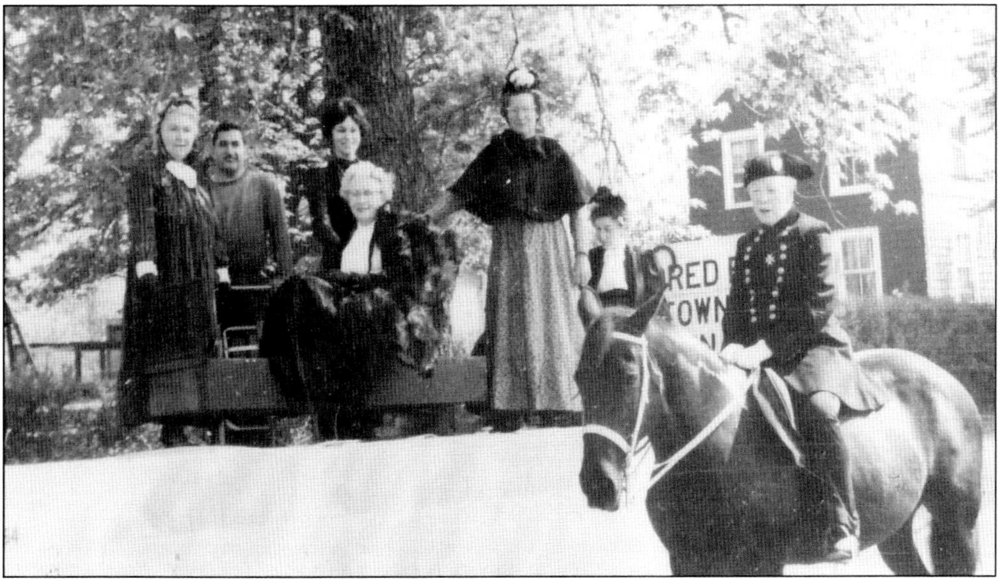

The charter members of the Long Hill Township Historical Society in 1964. These residents enjoying the Long Hill Township Tercentennial Celebration are, from left to right, Mrs. Margaret Rist, Mr. Ben Merrill, Inge Rist Lincoln, Gwendlyn Thomas, Mrs. Esther Cornish, and Mrs. Martha Mertz (on the horse). Gwendlyn Thomas was appointed as the first president. (Inge Rist Lincoln.)

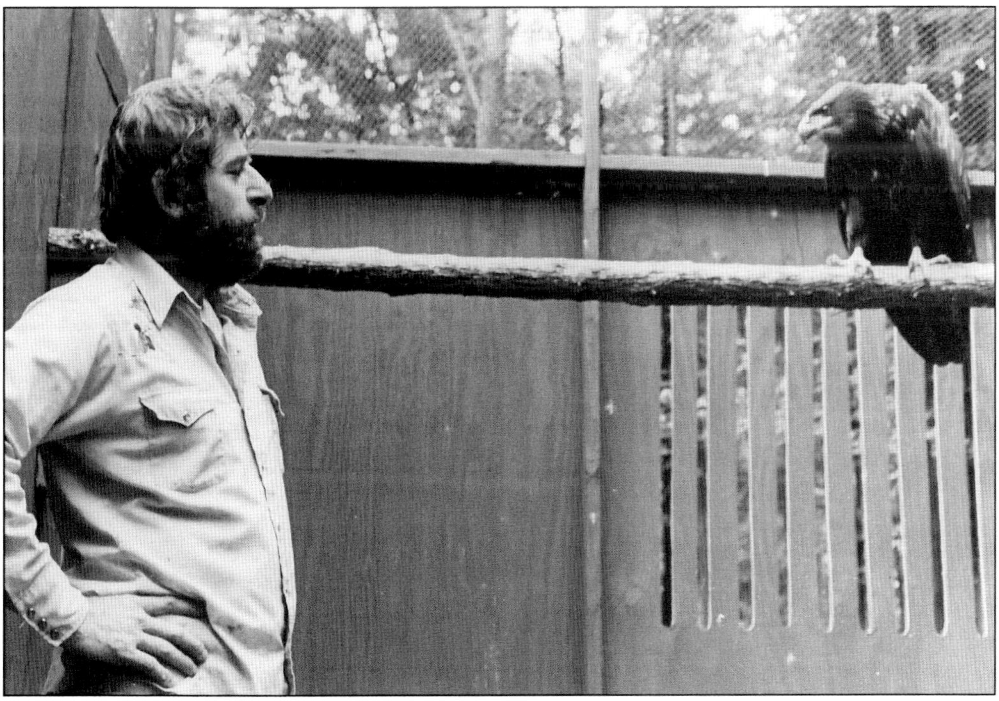

Leonard J. Soucy Jr., D. Sc., with one of his birds of prey, a golden eagle, c. 1968. Leonard is president of the "Raptor Trust" at 1390 White Bridge Road in Millington. He and his wife, Diane, founded the 15-acre "Bird Hospital." This sanctuary for birds of prey is known worldwide and is open to the public to be studied and enjoyed. (Emma and Archibald Stiles.)

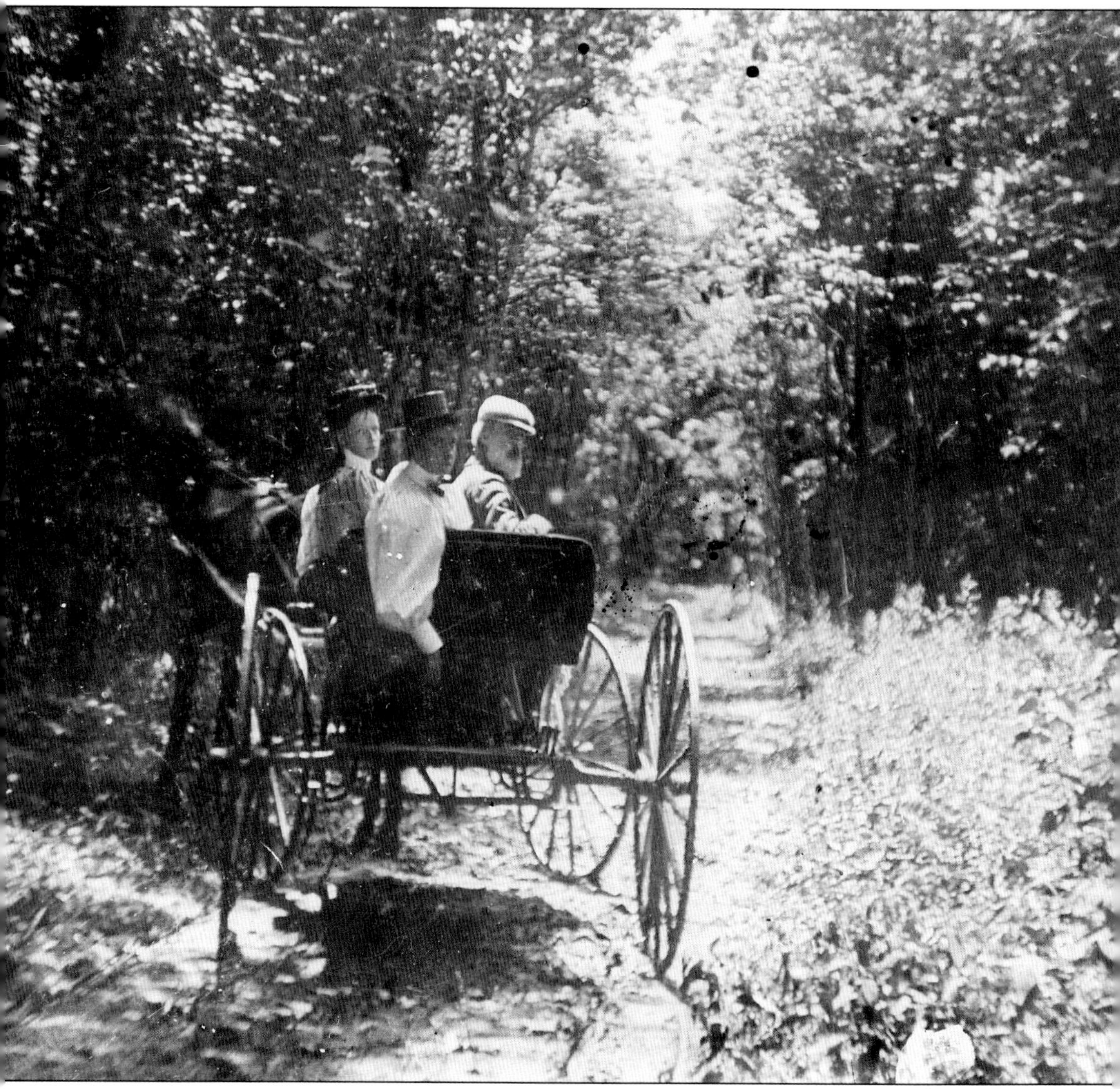

Dr. Munson, Julia Bean, and Mary Bean, former residents of Millington, out for a leisurely buggy ride along a shaded path. (Long Hill Township Historical Society.)